RENDEZVOUS
WITH
THE TRUTH

WITH EYES TO SEE
AND EARS TO HEAR

EVELYNE FELTZ
WITH CONTRIBUTIONS FROM HOMER ADAMS

Publishing Coordinator – Sharon Kizziah-Holmes
Cover Design – Jaycee DeLorenzo

INDIE
PUB
PRESS

an imprint of A & S Publishing
Paperback Press, LLC
Springfield, Missouri

ISBN -13: 978-1-960499-62-2

DEDICATION

For my readers, may my story be a source of inspiration, encouragement, and hope.

TABLE OF CONTENTS

ACKNOWLEDGMENTS

Homer Adams – to whom I am grateful for his significant and compelling contribution to the later part of my biography. He expressed in his own words his perspective on the same events leading up to our encounter, how our lives and our stories became entangled and emerged at a timely part of our spiritual journey, and the road we decided to travel together.

ABOUT EVELYNE FELTZ

Evelyne Feltz was born in Paris, France in 1949. Her father was from Alsace Lorraine on the French German border and her mother from the Charentes Maritimes in the Southwest of France. Her generation is part of the "Baby Boomers," a few short years after the end of World War II. Her heritage is officially French, but she is also half German from her father's side since Alsace Lorraine was under German occupation at various times throughout history.

From early childhood, her parents migrated to different countries, exposing her to various cultures and heritages at an early age. She assimilated other values, customs, beliefs, and languages being part of minority groups within a majority community. She grew up in North Africa, mainly in Tunisia and Morocco. As a young woman, she moved to the South Pacific and lived in the French territories of Tahiti and New Caledonia.

She was educated in French speaking schools at a time when the French culture still held strong footholds in North Africa. She spent time in religious boarding institutions without receiving any faith-based education or foundation herself. It proved to be challenging because she was excluded, at her parents' request, from all attendance to religious related gatherings and functions.

She traveled the world extensively as an adult and acquired a broad understanding of cross-cultural differences. She felt more like a citizen of the world rather than being attached to a specific country for many of her years.

Establishing roots and experiencing a sense of belonging came much later.

She was on a quest for Truth, meaning, and purpose. It was not until the age of 69 years old, when she made life altering and transformative choices.

What is Truth? Where is Truth? What would I do once I find it? Can I ever find inner peace, harmony, and happiness?

ABOUT HOMER ADAMS

Homer A. Adams Jr. was born in Tucson, Arizona in 1948 as one of the first in a generation of "Baby Boomers." He came into the world during the early part of post WWII during the height of celebration of the war's end and beginning of a new era for reconstruction and prosperity in America.

He grew up in humble beginnings in a small town along the Atchafalaya River far away from city life and more complex systems and temptations. He was provided with three squares a day, a roof overhead, and clothes to wear. He was allowed to participate in extracurricular activities, as much as the family budget allowed under tight and restricted access to frivolous activities. For the most part, he remained protected from exposure to much of the glamour of life.

He became a Christian at the early age of nearly 13. The conversion to Christianity was not without its obstacles and dramas. However, the Bible teaches if you bring the children up in the traditions and love of God, they will return to those principles time and again during the course of their life. So can be said of his journey.

The account of his life as portrayed in the narrative attempts to share some of the experiences he had at significant forks in the road as he became aware, matured, and found a path foundational to growth. The element of time and the tick tock of the clock would always add an urgency to every decision or situation. While his contribution to Evelyne's biography represents only a small part of his life, it confirms his overall belief system and reveals in a powerful way the presence of God and His nature. This came at a timely part of his own spiritual journey.

His own biography, "The Learning – The Road to Wisdom," provides a look into the inner self of thoughts, feelings, and motivations in a story searching for Truth.

PREFACE

Time is the measured equalizer in our lives. It cannot be fully defined by the scientific world but is demonstrated through the many scales of its passing: day and night, the ticking or hands moving on a time piece, history, or a mirror through which we observe the progression of the aging process.

The writing of my biography is a dialogue encompassing the passage of time through my life. It has equalized the highs and lows experienced in ways leaving me in wonder of the beauty of nature, filled with gratefulness, thankfulness, and reverence for God the Father, His son Jesus Christ, Who came to save Mankind, and for the Holy Spirit, with Whom I consult on a daily basis, without Whom I could not fulfill my walk in Christ for the Glory of the Kingdom of God.

I reverently respect time because it points in one direction. The fate we all must face at some point in our earthly life. I realize in my new-found Christian Walk in Faith, the greatest tragedy handed down through time since the fall of Adam and Eve, is the loss of Innocence. It appears to me now Innocence was sacrificed when Adam and Eve ate from the Tree of the Knowledge of Good and Evil in the Garden. Innocence allowed us to walk in the presence of God.

I hope to finish the remainder of my life worthy to approach the face of God in the end on some fine morning, saved and sanctified by Christ through Whom all blessings flow.

My biography is not a lonely cry in the wilderness. There have been many others to be sure. Rather it is a story of being born into this world without being given adequate direction or training in anything spiritual or a foundation in Christianity. I was left to find my own way. The story is a depiction of misdirection taking me nowhere and leaving me utterly unsatisfied in my quest for Truth. In the end, I found my way to Christ though an incredible conversion and growth, arriving at a place of understanding and peace within myself.

To this end, this theme will find its way into the dialogue of the profound life changing experience I longed for. Later in the text, we will introduce dialogues written from the pen of Homer Adams, whom I fortunately met and later married (in the eyes of God). He became my mentor, consular, and companion in our ascension to spiritual form.

He will express in his own words the events leading up to our encounter, his state of being and how - through the passage of time - we became entangled on the road we decided to travel together. Much of the later part of the biography is two independent perspectives on the same events, orientation about our observations, feelings, emotions, actions, and ultimately decisions made.

BOOK ONE

Evelyne Feltz

everyone else to the hospital first. My mother was left on the side of the road as the last one to be taken to the hospital because she was in such bad shape they thought she was not going to survive. With broken bones from the waist down, she ended up spending months laying on a wooden plank until she healed. Surviving and eventually walking again, this terrible accident affected her hips and legs resulting in lifelong suffering.

Forced to reckon with numerous life tragedies, her character became stronger and more resilient. I admired her in many ways. She was a warrior and a survivor. No obstacles ever stopped her when she set her mind on doing something.

I do not know how my parents met or how long they dated before getting married. Based on the wedding picture I still have today; they both were handsome. My father was tall and good-looking. The first years of their marriage were spent in Paris where I was born.

Mother and Father's wedding picture

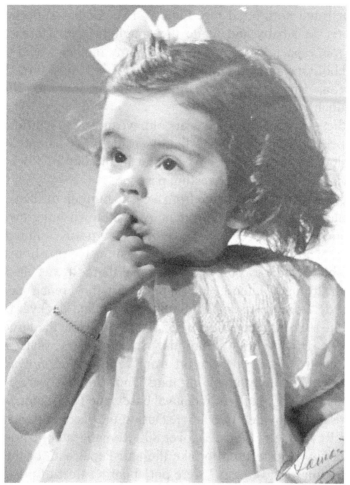

Evelyne as a toddler

I have no specific memories of this period of my life with three exceptions, which left a profound impression on me. These three memories took place in the room where I was sleeping. One of them, if real, was never validated. It involved looking at a stuffed predator type of bird directly placed on the wall in front of my crib. It was scary and frightened me. I asked my mother, but she did not know what I was talking about. The second memory was in the dark of the night. As an outside light filtered in the barely cracked door, I could see tiny fairies like people walking in and out of the room through the sliver of light from the ajar door. They were non-threatening and the feeling of lightness and brightness they brought to the room intrigued and comforted me. Finally, I remember suffering from tracheitis as a baby and while the coughing spells threatened to choke me, especially while lying down, my mother would pick me up and hold me straight until it subsided. This I know directly from her because she awoke many times during the night to relieve me and probably saved my life.

At the age of maybe three years old, we moved to a different part of France where my mother's family resided. My parents rented a house located at the corner of a street in the city of Rochefort, a historical town with an interesting past.

Rochefort derives its name from a castle built on the banks of the Charente to resist Norman invaders. A small township grew around the castle in the 11th century. The modern town was built in the 17th century when Jean-Baptiste Colbert, minister to Louis XIV, established a military port and an arsenal there. It was chosen as a place of "refuge, defense, and supply" for the French navy. The arsenal de Rochefort served as a naval base and dockyard until it closed in 1926. In September 1757, Rochefort was the target of an ambitious British raid during the Seven Year's War. Another infrastructure of early Rochefort from 1766 was its *bagne* a high security penal colony involving hard labor. *Bagnes* were common fixtures in military harbors and naval bases, such as Toulon or Brest, because they provided free labor. During the Jacobin period of the French Revolution (1790-95), over 800 Roman Catholic priests and other clergy who refused to take the anti-Papal oath of the "Civil Constitution of the Clergy" were put aboard a fleet of prison ships in Rochefort harbor where most died due to inhumane conditions. Rochefort is a notable example of the 17th century *ville nouvelle* which means its design resulted from a political decree. The reason for building Rochefort was because royal power could hardly depend on the rebellious nearby town of La Rochelle, a protestant stronghold, Cardinal Richelieu besieged a few decades earlier. Well into the 20th century, Rochefort remained primarily a garrison town. The tourist industry, which had long existed due to the town's spa, gained emphasis in the 1990s.

I share this history because it is unknown to most and worth noting.

My most enduring memories from the years we spent in Rochefort are centered around my connection with my mother's side of the family. These years provided me with the opportunity to bond with my maternal grandmother whom to these days has left me with warm, fuzzy feelings. She was kind, caring, hardworking, compassionate, and believed in God and Jesus Christ as her Savior. I dearly hold onto her small French prayer book and rosary. They are treasured possessions of mine.

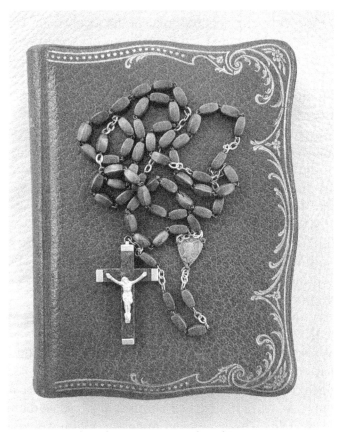

Grandma's Prayer Book and Rosary

Each summer, my cousins and I would spend summer school break, which lasted about three months, at her modest country house built right alongside the main road on the outskirts of a tiny village. It was common in most of Europe to have houses built right next to roads with no buffer such as a front yard. This is prevalent with old or historic houses. One can explain the reasoning behind it since there were no cars when the homes were first built. Noise or traffic were not an issue. It was also more practical living. This type of setting no longer makes sense in our modern world.

The summers at grandma's entertained me because every day was a new adventure. We had bikes, allowing my cousins and I to explore nearby villages, ride through the forest, or even run errands.

Grandma raised chicken, rabbits, and ducks. She had a vegetable and fruit garden as well as a flower garden. She was self-sufficient except for purchasing country bread at the local baker. Huge loaves of bread he would cut and sell by weight. She would send us to get milk from a nearby dairy farm by carrying copper milk cans back and forth. She exchanged some of her veggies for milk. Bartending was common in villages. Once a week, a vendor in a display truck would come by, both a meat vendor and a fish vendor. She would occasionally buy from them but was frugal by necessity. Most of the food we ate was raised right on her little piece of land. I did not like it when she killed a chicken, a rabbit, or a duck for dinner. I watched her slice their throat and let the blood run into a container, which she later used to make a *sanglette* cooked in a pan with garlic, onions, and parsley. Nothing was ever wasted. She made her own butter and cheese. She was an incredible cook. Once a year, she would buy half a pig and used every part to make all kinds of sausages and salted meats. Everything was either smoked or canned for conservation.

There was no plumbing in her house. We hauled the water from her well, filling containers called *brocs* many times a day. My cousins and I got a bath in a big bucket once a week, outside in the summer, but in the kitchen called *souillarde* near the coal stove in the winter. The water was not changed in the winter because it took a long time to warm it on the cast-iron coal stove, so the first one to bathe was lucky. The others had to contend with soiled water. She did have electricity in some rooms, but I remember candles too. We used a pot chamber at night and the outhouse during daytime. It was a wooden structure at a distance behind the house with two holes and newspapers for wiping. The privy was not private. Many a times we would be two of us sitting next to each other. I preferred it when my grandma would stay with me. It was dark in there with the door closed and I feared critters or falling in the hole. Grandma's presence made me feel safer.

She had an attic filled with all sorts of paraphernalia, a dark and scary place. The bedroom where my cousins and I slept was upstairs requiring one to go through the attic to access it. I remember many scares as my cousin Luc would disguise himself, covered with a black hooded cape, and wait in the dark to jump at me when I walked by. Frightened is a weak word to describe how it made me feel but he thought it was remarkably humorous. Also, in the bedroom I remember an old portrait of a past family member, all dressed in black with black hair and dark eyes, which seemed to follow me as I moved throughout the room. Another place where Luc loved to scare me was the *chay*, a long dark corridor used as a stockroom filled with barrels on each side. They kept tools, supplies, and stored food there. He would hide behind a barrel and jump at me screaming when I walked by. He absolutely loved terrifying me, always following the scare with laughter, enjoyed at my expense.

More adventures … we played in the fields with other kids and imagined stories where we would become queens and kings for a day, picked wildflowers to make crowns, and adorned ourselves.

Christmas time was special at my grandmother's house as the entire family reunited for the holidays. A lot of wonderful cooking and fireside stories went on. We had a real Christmas tree and on Christmas Eve, after us kids were in bed, my father would purposely make a lot of noise in the attic portraying Santa delivering our gifts. The excitement and anticipation were wonderful, but we knew we had to wait until the morning to see what Santa brought us. It certainly had nothing to do with the gifting opulence of today. Indeed, we were lucky to get anything at all. My mom as a child just got an orange considered a rare and exotic delicacy then.

An important character and a significant personage in the life of my grandmother was a man we called Uncle Joseph. The story of Uncle Joseph, looking back at the role he played in our family, deserves to be told as I remember from my observations. When my grandma was abandoned by my grandfather whom I have never met, she was left to fend for herself raising three daughters. She went through many hardships with a broken heart. I do not know how long after she struggled on her own and under what circumstances, but I do know a man from the local community took to heart my grandmother's situation. He might have been a family friend, but he was someone she knew. I was told he offered his help to her and committed to supporting her and her daughters in any way he could.

I suspect he loved her. I remember how devoted she was to him. He lived in my grandma's house where he had his own quarters. He was a coal merchant by trade and drove an old dirty truck full of coal nuggets in the pickup bed. Coal was an important commodity, and everyone used it for cooking and heating stoves, and many other uses. Laundry was done once a week, and it was a laborious process. Women heated water in a boiler on a coal fire. Laundry was soaked overnight, and the next day entailed a grueling process involving many steps all done by hand and a washing bat. The laundry was then hung to dry on clothes lines outside and if the weather was inclement inside.

Uncle Joseph spent most of his time on the road delivering coal to people in nearby towns and villages. He was busy and seldom at the house. We, luckily, spent time with him when he was home and I remember some of the stories he told us kids because he felt we were spoiled, and wanted us to understand how his growing up drastically differed from ours. Staying with me all these years is a story about himself as a young boy working in the fields for a "master," as he referred to him. He worked from dawn to sunset and his pay was room and board. When it was mealtime at the master's table who sat at the end of a long wooden table, each boy called a *commis* was only allowed to eat when the master opened his knife and had to stop eating when he closed his knife and immediately go back to work. If you had not shown up in time because you did not finish your assigned job, you just missed out on your breakfast, lunch, or dinner and would have to be swifter next time around. Also, because I had a very good appetite and ate a lot, he would "joke" about how it would be cheaper to have a picture of me to look at rather than having to feed me. Uncle Joseph was never clean, and his big, twisted *moustache* was always catching food. The loud slurping sounds he made while eating soup still bring a smile.

But he was a man of his word, dedicated to my grandmother and her family. He chose to spend the rest of his life supporting her and in return she was totally committed to him. When he got older and sick, she took care of him until the end. After he died, and they emptied his room, they found a small fortune in gold coins buried in his mattress. He never trusted banks.

Family reunions were important and while we lived in Rochefort, we spent the weekends at Grandma's. This included my extended family, aunt Liliane and her husband, my cousins, Gabrielle, and Luc, who was still my mom's undisputed favorite.

I will never forget how happy my grandma was to have all of us reunited. Meals were the focus of time spent together. Grandma prepared elaborate meals using the fireplace or the coal stove to make delicious local specialties. *La pote de Mojettes Charentaise,* one of my favorites, a stew made of local white beans (called *mojettes*), homemade broth, local meat specialties, a variety of vegetables, *bouquet garni* (Provence herbs tied together), slowly simmering all day in a black cast iron pot hanging on a hook above the woodfire pit in the chimney. Fireplaces called *cheminees* were the focus of a room, used both for cooking and warmth.

Sunday brunch could be a three to four hours affair. It was a time for family sharing and connection. I enjoyed it thoroughly while it lasted. It gave me a sense of having roots and stability which were lacking in my life for many years to come.

I warmly remember my aunt Liliane, who was kind to me. She had poor health. She raised my cousins by herself after her husband died from a doctor's mistake being given a wrong medication. He was a war veteran. I also remember my aunt Marianne, my mom's other sister whose story was controversial in the family. It is said during German occupation, she "dated" German soldiers and was punished by the French for it. It was dealt with by public shaming for women who were found guilty. They would get their head shaved to be recognized by everyone and were forced to walk the village streets in procession while they were shown contempt by the crowds. She met an American soldier during French liberation, married him, and left the country to move to the United States in Los Angeles, California. We will speak again about my aunt Marianne who played a role in my life much later.

Talking about war, my Uncle Joseph and my grandma explained to us how during World War II their village was occupied by the German military. During German military occupation, it was common for German soldiers to come to your house and collect food supplies or other goods. Everyone was under the obligation to cooperate to avoid retaliation. In my grandmother's case, it was eggs, vegetables, or whatever she had available when they stopped by. The soldiers who came to her house were friendly and polite, and at times would sit by the fireplace for company, chatting about their lives back in Germany. They missed their families and had similar lives and were just people trying to survive. They did not mistreat most of the villagers. They were following orders and both occupants and occupiers coexisted by complying with orders from above. Unfortunately, it did not happen so peacefully everywhere. But my grandmother never complained about German occupation. She simply shared stories from her past fascinating me.

Returning to my life with my parents in Rochefort, there remain a few more memories. Some not so good because my parents constantly fought, and nothing was hidden or spared from me. I knew too much and witnessed some of their angry bouts which would have been best kept secret. On a good note, I remember how much I enjoyed visiting my aunt Liliane who was touched by my disarray. She always comforted me and gave me the affection I desperately needed.

While attending school, I made friends and sat next to a gypsy girl who had lice. By proximity, I became infested too. My parents scolded me and demanded I never approach her again. The lice were prevalent and a nightmare to get rid of. As a result, my hair was cut very short. The solution used burned my scalp and I stayed away from the gypsy girl.

I loved the Autumn season. To this day, I still smell the sweetness of the fresh cool air and how beautiful the huge leaves from the *platane* tree, plane tree in English, were. They flew all over in the wind and carpeted the streets. Their colors were a palette of yellows, reds, oranges, and every nuance in between. I loved to pick the prettiest ones.

Once while vacationing at my grandmother's, as I walked down the street, I stepped on top of an old rusty gully grate. My right leg went right through, and a rusty nail pierced my knee. My grandma took me to the local village doctor who gave her a disinfecting solution. The next day, I was running a high fever. By the time my parents arrived for the weekend, I had a life-threatening infection. The fever made me delusional, and I was in a great deal of pain. My parents took me to the nearest hospital about one hour away. I was immediately given tetanus shots in the belly which left me screaming. The doctor told my parents I may not make it because I should have been brought to the hospital sooner. It took me a long time to recover. I am grateful to have been blessed with a strong and healthy constitution.

My parents both worked, my father as an engineer draftsman at the *Chantier Naval de la Rochelle,* involved in the creation and design of ships, boat building and manufacturing. Mother started a business selling real estate. She got involved with a crook, who used her skills and had the funds to start the business but was dishonest and used my mother's enthusiasm and eagerness. She had a taste for entrepreneurship needing stimulation and challenges. Staying home was not for her. She eventually got tired and bored and sought a more exciting future. She decided to seek opportunities overseas and open new horizons for us.

Her desire to explore the world and create new life experiences was about to begin a new chapter for her family. She knew my father's profession could open doors. In the after-war boom, having a trade was highly sought after and apparently my father could use his expertise as a draftsman anywhere. She subscribed to specialized magazines known to advertise overseas career opportunities such as *Le Chasseur Français* which is still in publication today. She contacted every possible company advertising for my dad's profession and sent his resume and letters of introduction to a diversity of employers in Africa who could use the skills of an engineer/draftsman. Africa was the continent of choice because of the many ties with France and the French language was spoken on most of the African continent. The research created a tremendous amount of work for her in addition to her daily responsibilities. It took months of effort, but she responded to every offer and evaluated it with my dad's input. He went along for the ride because he knew there was absolutely nothing, he could do to change her mind. He loved her and was going to follow her to any corner of the world. Some job opportunities were tempting but not good enough for various reasons. The incentives included in the relocation package influenced their decision. Then one day, an irresistible offer came in.

TUNISIA

The position offered to my father was in the south of Tunisia, right on the border of the Sahara Desert, near the Oasis of Tozeur, Sousse in the Gafsa Governorate, in a village called Metlaoui. At the time, it was a phosphate mining town.

He was offered a job in his capacity at the *Compagnie des phosphates de Gafsa*. The agreement required him to leave first and spend six months there on his own as a test drive. My mother and I would join later. He reluctantly agreed with the promise no longer than 6 months would pass before his family would come or he would quit his job. The following months were spent getting ready for the upcoming permanent move. My mother had a business to let go of and of course all the many arrangements required for a move overseas needed to take place. My father wrote many letters and seemed anxious. He did not care about the remote location and the extremely arid climate of this part of the world.

All went fast and the next thing I know is the memorable journey my mother, me, and our cat Kitchou took to reunite with my dad. Our destination was Tunis, the capital where my father would be waiting for us. Our little car, a *Citroen Deux Chevaux*, Citroen 2CV in English, was loaded with the possessions mother decided we could not part with. We drove to the city of Marseille where we caught the ferry to Tunis the next day. The car had to be loaded on the ferry the night before with early morning departure. We spent the night in a nearby hotel. A cab drove us to the embarkation point the next morning. The cab driver insisted the cat who was in his crate must be tied on the roof rack of his vehicle and not inside the cabin. Mother argued, but he would not budge despite her insistence. Kitty was probably scared because he meowed all the way and kept on protesting until we reached our destination. He made us noticeable on the ferry. It was uncommon then to travel with your pet. We spent two days on the deck in primitive and stressful conditions. The Mediterranean was not calm, and the ferry was just riding the waves. We were all seasick including the kitty who was on a leash because we couldn't just leave him in his tiny crate. We spent much of our time sitting on a bench next to the ship rail because we had to lean over to throw up and clean up the cat's messes. It was not a pleasure trip.

Finally, exhausted, filthy, and dehydrated, we arrived at the port of Tunis. I recall my dad walking to the end of the pier to watch the ferry slowly enter the harbor. He waved at us as he ran to greet us. Finally, our turn came to get off the ferry, go through customs and onshore where we met my dad who had a huge smile on his face. It was one of the few times when I remember seeing him excited and truly happy.

We still had to drive to Metlaoui where a house reserved for the company's employees, one of the perks, waited for us.

We spent a few days in Tunis. This was my first encounter with North Africa. I was about 7 years old and too tired to really have an impression. I first reacted to the newness of it all with apprehension having just left familiar surroundings, a way of life ... and everything and everyone I knew. I already missed my grandma and my aunt Liliane. The cat was still distraught and beside himself. I spent a lot of time with him, maybe consoling him and finding refuge with him since I pretty much felt the same way he did. My parents' life together resumed, which I don't care to remember. I was exposed too young and too soon to matters not concerning a child.

While in Tunis, we visited the famous site of Carthage, today in a residential suburb. Carthage, capital of the Carthaginian Empire, was one of the most important trading hubs of the Ancient Mediterranean and one of the most affluent cities of the antique world. Developed from a Phoenician colony into the capital of the Punic empire, it dominated large parts of the Southwest Mediterranean during the first millennium BC. The Carthaginian Empire was in a constant state of struggle with the Roman Republic, which led to the Punic Wars. The Carthaginian general Hannibal was regarded as one of the greatest military minds in history. The third Punic War destroyed the city and nearly all the Carthaginian empire fell into Roman hands from then on. It was re-developed a century later as Roman Carthage, which became the major city of the Roman Empire in the province of Africa.

It took an entire day to drive to Metlaoui, my new home to be for a while. I was in a state of shock as everything was unfamiliar. The intense desert heat also affected me.

There are two ways to look at this particular time of my growing years, but as a child, I did not know the difference. I reacted and responded to my surroundings and situations with anxiety and apprehension rather than excitement. Today, I am grateful for the many opportunities throughout my life to be exposed to different cultures, philosophies, belief systems, sceneries, and wonderful ethnic foods as depicted in my story. These experiences greatly contributed to my understanding of people and the world at large. It helped me be more receptive, unprejudiced, and tolerant. A real mind-opener.

Metloui was a phosphate mining town owned and ruled by a French company. Historically, Tunisia was a protectorate of France like much of the African continent. To this day, the French language is still the language of choice in many African countries. Metlaoui history goes back to prehistorical times, Megaliths can be found in the surrounding areas. Roman ruins have been excavated since I left.

Phosphate is available throughout North Africa, Morocco, and Algeria. This part of the African continent had been flooded. The phosphate rich deposits are believed to have formed from marine sediments along with the skeletons and waste products of creatures living in the seas. I still have the prehistorical shark tooth my father set into a decorative clear acrylic block.

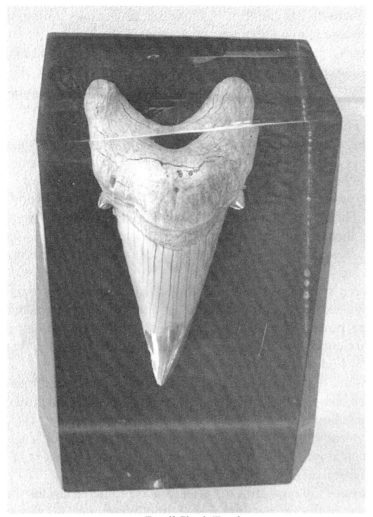

Fossil Shark Tooth.

The heat was unbearable and air conditioning did not exist. My parents cooled off the house by spraying the outside walls with cold water in the evening. Screened windows stayed open at night. Screens were important not only because of all the insects but critters like huge scorpions.

I was on the onset of a series of life adventures, experiences, eye openers, and lessons learned the hard way as will be displayed in the unfolding of my story. Today, looking back at all these years, I realize God, Whom I did not know then, had a grand plan for me with many twists and turns leading me, in His own timing, to find and choose Him on my own and awaken to the Truth.

Tunisia in the 1960s, especially in small villages, did not have supermarkets or even food stores as we know them today. We had a company food pantry featuring a restaurant, called the *mess*. The products were imported from France and reserved exclusively to the local French community.

The only other option was open-air markets. Local Tunisian farmers displayed their products in the town square, in the heat and dust either laying them on tables, wicker baskets, or directly on the dusty ground. Huge pieces of meat hung on hooks covered with flies. They used balance scales with weights. The meat was cut to order then folded inside a piece of newspaper. No pork for sale because we were in a Muslim country. It was either lamb, mutton, goat, horse meat or live chickens.

Spice markets offered a colorful and tempting assortment of various exotic spices displayed in attractive artistic handmade pottery bowls. They also sold delicious freshly picked dates, figs, and apricots from the nearby Oasis of Tozeur. Vegetables were not easy to find. The arid climate of the Sahara explains why.

I went to a private French school reserved for the children of the French company staff. I have no memories related to the time spent in this school.

Typically, the mining towns were French owned, self-sufficient, self-contained, and offered a variety of free services for the exclusive benefit of the local expatriates.

Most of my memories from Tunisia are centered around the trips we took in the surrounding areas while living there for a couple of years. I distinctly remember once as my father was driving our little Citroen, getting caught in a *Sirocco*, a tornado in the US, a hot Mediterranean wind coming from the Sahara reaching hurricane speeds. As we saw it coming in our direction, we got off the dirt road. My father turned the car around with the back facing the blowing hot sand. I understood it was safer this way. Still, we could not prevent the sand from invading the cabin and the car from being pushed away by the force of the wind. No visibility at all. It did not last long, but we were scared while it lasted, not knowing our fate and how much protection the car provided. When it was over, we found our way back onto the dirt road by looking for road signs, otherwise we could have been lost in the desert. It is difficult to imagine a time with no cell phones, no technology allowing for instant contact in times of distress.

Another time, a huge *naja*, known more as a cobra snake was laying on the road. I was mesmerized as my father stopped the car to observe the beast as it took its time crossing the road. Huge black scorpions were also common occurrences. My mom almost got stung once by going to turn the water off outside at the spigot in the dark. My father, who fortunately was nearby, told her to look first with a flashlight before she put her hand out in the dark. Sure enough, Mister Scorpion was there probably trying to get some water as well.

Our Persian cat Kitchou, who spent a lot of time outside the house especially at night when it cooled off, must have had a few encounters with various critters but was either lucky or smart enough to stay out of the way of the harmful kind. He would occasionally bring one of his victims inside the house to play with as cats like to do, no doubt showing off his talent.

I cannot forget the time when I got a tape warm, called *tenia* in French, most likely by eating undercooked meat. My appetite was ferocious because I was feeding an unwelcome host which proved to be several meters long when a purge got it out of my body. The head remained unfortunately and after a few months, it grew back and my grandmother whom I was visiting at the time is the one who had the awful task of helping me get rid of the beast by literally pulling it out of my body. Unforgettable in a disgusting way. Thank You, Grandma. This was unpleasant for you too, especially measuring it after the fact. At last, after a couple of years of relentless eating, my appetite went back to normal as well as my body weight.

Bordered by Algeria to the west and southwest, Libya to the southeast, and the Mediterranean Sea to the north and east, Tunisia offers a fascinating history going back to antiquity. The country was inhabited by the Berber, Phoenicians, and Romans, all of whom left their imprint. Tunisia hosts several World Heritage Sites. Also, a getaway to the Sahara Desert with unbelievable sightseeing possibilities.

The area where we lived had some interesting sites nearby. Worth noting is the *Gorge de Selja*. At the beginning of the 20th century, a railway line was built from the harbor of Sfax to the mining town of Metlaoui where we lived. The mining company decided to extend the line to the Redeyef plateau. The railway line was laid in the gorge crossing the mountain range. Many tunnels and bridges were built. For the next century, the line was used for phosphate transportation and more recently for tourism. The *Gorges de Thelja* have been set aside as a natural reserve. A natural valley with deep ravines in the chain of the *djebels* of the Saharan Atlas. Punic vestiges exist in the form of forts built on top of mountains. Inside the gorge of *Selja* are Roman ruins as well as defensive walls. The valley extends through several kilometers along the sinuous Thelja and offers a landscape of unique tourist attraction in Tunisia, with its famous Red Lizard train journey from Metlaoui with renovated train cars from the phosphate mining era. The sightseeing train did not exist at the time I lived there because tourism was not emphasized. The line existed for the exclusive transportation of phosphate. The site is also known for the Golden Eagle Aquila as well as a gorgeous red lizard with a complicated name.

The Oasis of Nefta, Tozeur, Tamerza, Mides, and Douz are a must see for anyone visiting Tunisia. Sidi Bouhlel Canyon has become known for its stunning beauty. Some sites are easy to access while others are in remote locations and make it a challenge to get to. The only form of transportation is still either a donkey or a camel. Tozeur was nearby for us, and we visited it several times. It was the first time I saw an Oasis in the middle of the desert, and I was awe struck by its amazing beauty. Here in the middle of nowhere but dry, hot, and rugged desert, lays a paradise of lush green and shady gardens, forests of palm and fig trees, roman ruins, a river fed by artesian wells running through its center, a vibrant *souk* and the city's old town.

God Almighty has created stunning and special scenery for our sole pleasure. Here out of nowhere but arid, waterless, rugged, harsh, and unfriendly territory lays what the garden of Eden might have resembled.

The oasis of Tozeur has a long history as an important historical site. Many caravans passed through this oasis when making their way through the Sahara Desert. The city is located northwest of *Chott el Djerid* another remarkable Tunisian site. The *palmeraie* one of the most prominent features contains around 400,000 date palms, but there are also areas laden with fruit trees shaded by the palms, including orchards of figs, apricots, pomegranates, and banana trees. Lush green and shady areas provide a sharp contrast to all the surrounding barren land.

The *medina* (old town) is also one of the town's main points of interest with traditional desert style houses displaying beautiful decorative brick facades of intricate patterns. The geometric brick designs are similar to the age-old design motifs found on many Berber carpets. Some of the houses have upper floors extending across the street to join with houses on the other side, forming covered-bridge passages providing inhabitants with shelter from the harsh sun. The colorful *souk* displaying an array of unique items is certainly worth seeing. I remember camel rides being available. I did not like camels too much, they intimidated me with their huge size and disgusted me with their overall odor. They have a repulsive rancid smell; their hinder parts are crusted with urine as they use their concentrated pee to cool themselves down. Their poll gland secretion in mating season is offensive as is their foul-smelling breath. They also make a grunting noise, from deep growling and gargling. They always sound like they are complaining or grumbling. In short, I was frightened by them.

I did not know but a long time after we had left Tunisia, the Tozeur and surrounding areas were selected as a filming location where a few episodes of *Star War*, *Indiana Jones and the Raiders of the Lost Ark*, *The English Patient*, *The Little Prince*, and a few other famed movies were shot. I am not surprised. The scenery naturally lends itself to a prime exotic film setting.

Stretching to the east and south of Tozeur lays Chott el Dejerid the Sahara's largest salt pan.

Another sightseeing trip from Tozeur is a journey to the three upland oases of Chekiba, Tamerza, and Mides. You will drive through the stunning hill country of Djebel en Negueb (an offshoot of the Atlas Mountains). Roman ruins can be seen from all locations.

About nine kilometers north of Tozeur is the oasis of El Hamma du Djerid offering the enjoyment of stunning hot springs and an endless horizon filled with date trees. The hot springs have been used for medicinal purposes since the Roman period.

We also had the opportunity to visit the impressive site of the Roman amphitheater El Jem, one of the largest Coliseum ever built in North Africa. Designed to seat a whopping crowd of 35,000 people, it is one of the most accomplished examples of Roman architecture, almost equal to that of the Coliseum of Rome.

Tunisia may be a predominantly Muslim country, but it is also a progressive nation where other religions and cultures are widely respected. Family and hospitality are important to Tunisian cultural values.

Historically, many nations left their mark on Tunisia. Phoenicians, Roman, Byzantine, and Islamic empires. After the fall of the Roman Empire, Tunisia fell into the hands of the Vandals, then the Byzantines, and finally the Arabs. Following the Muslim conquest of the Maghreb, most Berber tribes eventually converted to Islam.

In the 16th century Tunisia became a pirate stronghold, then expulsed by the Ottoman Turks who brought stability to the area until the 19th century. France invaded and made the territory a French protectorate during the early 1880s. Tunisia was a fully independent republic in 1956. The country has known a tumultuous history under various rulers through the passage of time.

The Tunisian people were tolerant of us and always showed warm hospitality making us feel welcome despite the political unrest. European, Middle Eastern, and African influences are all part of their national identity. I remember them as being curious and open-minded.

Their food is mainly a blend of Mediterranean and native Berber cuisine influenced by Italians, Andalusians, French, and Arabs. Tunisian food is quite spicy. A popular ingredient is *harissa* a mix of ground chili peppers, garlic, and caraway. They use cumin, coriander and paprika. Also known for their olive oil. The main dish is couscous served in a bowl with meat and vegetables. My favorite was their *tajine* which is different from the Algerian or Moroccan *tajine*. Theirs was more like a quiche without a crust, made of eggs, cheese, meat and various vegetable fillings, and baked like a cake. The seafood was outstanding, served as *poisson complet*, the entire fish either fire-grilled or sauteed. We had seafood mostly when travelling on the coast.

I truly enjoy remembering all this as these are the memories worth focusing on. I am grateful for the numerous opportunities I had to visit some of the most remote and unique sites on our planet.

So, Thank You, Mother, for your insatiable curiosity and drive to discover and want more in life. Without your initial desire to explore the world, none of this would have happened. Thank You, Dad, for going along with the program and including me into early discoveries I cherish to this day.

Some time went by in this arid, hot to a fault, exceedingly dry, rugged, uncomfortable, unwelcoming but stunning part of Tunisia. A place of extremes rightly so. A must see for its unique and incredible sites. But living there was a bit primitive and basic without material comfort, culture, or entertainment, just the bare necessities. It got the best of my parents including me. The most grueling part was the intense heat and dryness. We were not handling this climate well health wise and always seemed to be sickly. I suffered from an annoying and painful recurring cystitis. It was hard on us physically and mentally. As usual, my mom was the first to decide it was time to look for a different scenario.

With the benefit of the practice acquired previously and her unfailing determination, this time with the entire cooperation of my dad, they both started to look for a better set of circumstances.

MOROCCO

Touissit, near Oujda, in the Jerada Province of the Oriental Region of Morocco by the Algerian border was our next destination. My father had landed a job there. There is nothing remarkable about Touissit. It was and still is a mining village with few inhabitants. Semi-arid climate by the Atlas Mountains, the landscape reminds me of parts of New Mexico. It is exploited for deposits of lead-zinc among other minerals. We lived there less than two years.

Schooling in the village was not fun and highly stressful to me. It was a small school with primarily Moroccan students and mostly boys. The class was taught in French, but the other students spoke Arabic with French as their second language. These boys were mean to me. I was a girl in a predominantly Muslim country, a foreigner. a minority, and girls were considered inferior. About 9 years old and already tall for my age, I was relegated to the back of the classroom so I would not block the teacher's and blackboard view from other students. Being born with a lazy eye, I wore glasses and had difficulty reading from a distance due to myopia. These kids picked on me, called me names, laughing and pointing their fingers. For example, they played with my last name and from Feltz, it became *fesse* which means "behind" as in my butt. I made no friends there and felt self-conscious because of my height and isolation from others. Bullies are real. They made me a target and an object of derision. I dreaded going to school, did poorly and disappointed my parents. I received no sympathy at home when I complained about my school condition. I felt a keen sense of loneliness and separation. I was shy, had no self-esteem, or confidence. Negative reinforcement was all I knew. Curiously, but not surprisingly, I remember comments from others stating I always looked sad and unhappy. My only companion who accepted me as I was, was our cat Kitchou, who always followed us. I felt out of place everywhere I went. I did not belong, there was such a huge void in me, and I could not understand why.

Healthwise the cystitis with painful urination continued and made me even more miserable. I thought I was being punished for not meeting others' expectations and kept it to myself for years. I kept it low key probably because I was also ashamed of which part of my body the culprit affected me. Years later as a young adult, I found out I had a birth malformation, my urethra was partially blocked and needed a little surgery to open it. I will never completely grasp why I suffered so many years feeling shameful and keeping this a secret.

We lived next to the Algerian border, on the Atlas plateau notorious for its high winds. There was a lot of discord between the Algerian guerillas, *fedayeen*, on one side of the mountain and their Moroccan counterpart on the other side, where we lived. At night, we could hear the fighting going on as they shot at each other. It became a form of entertainment for us to step outside. The sky would light up and it was quite a show looking in the distance over the mountain top. It was our fireworks and replaced movie time or TV watching which we did not have anyway. I don't know how safe we really were. What a relief when my parents had enough and were thinking about moving again.

It was my first encounter with Morocco.

A new job hunt started and eventually my dad found another position in a different part of Morocco. Another mining town by the name of Khouribga.

Evelyne, about 9 years old with her cat Kitchou

KHOURIBGA

Khouribga in the Berber language is the capital of the
Khouribga Province in the Beni Mellal-Khenifra region of
Morocco in the center of the country, about 120km (75
miles) from Casablanca, 154km (95 miles) from the capital Rabat
and more than 200km (124 miles) from the famous city of
Marrakesh. This medium-sized town was far more civilized than any
of the other places we had been to. It was more urbane, organized,
and cultured. It offered amenities more reminiscent of what we had
known in France. The city was founded in 1923 by the authorities
of the French protectorate when they discovered phosphate in the
region. Morocco was the biggest exporter in the world with the
largest international reserve. The phosphate mines in the Ouled
Abdoun Basin are a notable reservoir of fossils, especially the
Mosasaurus, extinct group of aquatic squamate reptiles which
roamed the ocean eons ago. Besides phosphate exploitation, this
area is known for vertebrate fossils, with deposits ranging from the
Late Cretaceous to the Eocene epoch. These secular time frames are
under scrutiny and contested today. The theory of evolution is also
on shaky grounds as new scientific and archeological evidence of a
much younger earth is emerging but under a great deal of resistance
and denial from the current establishment. But this is another story.
A story only time and acceptance of the Truth can reveal from a
Biblical perspective.

We settled in Khouribga and moved into a spacious home with a
big yard. A tall brick wall surrounded the property ensuring privacy,
a common occurrence in North Africa. Housing was again provided
by the company my dad worked for, OCP which stands for *Office
Cherifien des Phostates*. It seemed like living in luxury compared to

our previous experiences. We had a maid and a gardener, habitual in Africa then. Privileges still left from recent colonization. You did not have to be wealthy to afford these perks. So, I lived the "high life."

My mom was working for the French Consul and my dad for the OCP.

Schooling there left me with pleasant memories. I have a fond remembrance of my teachers. For the first time, I made a couple of good friends who stayed in touch for numerous years even though life took us in different directions. I was doing well in school and my strong points were writing, spelling, dictation, history, geography, and language learning. Science and math were not my preference, but I did ok all things considered. History was my strength. I developed a passion for Greek Mythology. I knew the names of all their gods and deities and what they represented. I also read books about French history, not the official one taught in school but the behind-the-scenes stories. *La petite histoire*, as we say in French. I knew the names of all the influential women, in most cases famous mistresses of the Kings of Europe who "worked" relentlessly behind the scenes provoking scandals and were involved in the royal decisions and decrees. I read many times over the saga of Maurice Druon who wrote the series of *Les Rois Maudits* translated in English as "The Accursed Kings." Very edifying to learn the truth of who they really were, a history banned from the classroom due to the revelation of their evil ways. Reading was a passion for me and still is today, just not the same kind of reading anymore. My choices today are far more spiritual and nonsecular.

My parents also began a social life, making friends, enjoying themselves, organizing fun gatherings and social events. The consulate and my dad's company provided entertainment such as dinners and dancing nights where the kids could participate. The dancing was exciting to me. I enjoyed learning how to dance and was blessed to have a friend of my parents taking me on the dance floor to teach me various steps. My favorites were the *Pasodoble* and *Cha Cha* ballroom dancing style. He taught me a little tango and waltz too. For some reason, I remember his last name was Catalano. This is probably one of my most cherished memories. We also had various artists coming to town and I remember having the honor of meeting Charles Aznavour. He gave a concert one night and a few other teens and I somehow got a picture with him. I also remember seeing a concert with Salvatore Adamo whose songs I absolutely loved. *Tombe la neige* was on top of the charts and I cried every time hearing it. Lost and impossible loves. My girlfriends and I went crazy and ran after his car after the concert screaming like so many did for Elvis Presley. Most songs expressed sadness, but I was a sad child/teen and identified with a feeling of loneliness and separation while listening.

My parents' model was not an inspiration in my search for Love, or in their attitude towards me. I can't remember much demonstration of affection. I never seemed to do anything right and felt like a burden at times. My mother always made it clear she stayed with my father because of me, not by choice. It was clearly a sacrifice on her part, and I was the cause of it.

I never lacked anything materially. My mother had found this great clothing store downtown Casablanca held by a Jewish lady, a dress maker and designer who made custom dresses for us. Beautiful and original dresses, I was proud to wear them. My girlfriends always commented on how they would have liked to have the same.

I was already an avid book reader as mentioned before and had a taste for impossible loves it seems with far and away charming princes. I could get lost in my dream world and certainly had a thirst for true and exclusive love. One book, I still own today because it still holds a fascination, is *La Nuit des Temps*, in English "The Iced People," by Rene Barjavel, a French author known as a precursor of modern science fiction. A science fiction thriller and incredible love story taking place through space and time. Still a must read and relevant today as following short summary displays:

"When a French expedition in Antarctica reveals hidden deep under the ice the ruins of a 900,000-year-old civilization, scientists from all over the world flock to the site to help explore and understand. They find people in suspended animation. The scientists decide to wake up the man, Coban, who could personally deliver the knowledge they sought to cure all the problems of the world and beyond. And then they wake Elea who reveals what her civilization was like, her lost world, her lost man Paikan. She hints to an incredibly advanced knowledge her still dormant companion possesses. A story for mankind and possible future scenarios."

I have a vivid recollection of the wonderful local foods prepared

31

by our Moroccan "maid." My, oh my! How could I forget the *couscous* (national dish served with a variety of meats and vegetables), *tajines* (stews of spiced meat and vegetables slowly cooked in a conical shape clay pot, either beef, lamb, chicken), *harira* (Moroccan lentil soup usually served as a starter), *zalouk* (a common side dish made with eggplants, tomatoes, garlic, olive oil and spices typically served with crusty bread), *briouats* (deep fried filo pastry filled with almonds), *bastilla* (chicken or pigeon stuffed flaky pie), steamed sheep head (not my favorite, whole head steamed for hours with cumin, salt and chili including cheek meat and tongue), *spicy sardines* (stuffed and cooked with a spicy chermoula sauce, then deep fried), *brochettes* (lamb or beef served with a side of cucumber and tomatoes salad) and so much more. We also experienced eating *mechoui* (whole sheep or lamb spit-roasted on a barbecue served with saffron rice and various spices) under a Berber tent prepared by the locals. Not to forget, the Moroccan mint tea, ceremonially prepared and served as a tradition. Moroccan food is still today one of my all-time favorites.

A true engagement of the senses. Eating with your hands is expected as well as burping after your meal if you are a guest at a Moroccan house. Usually, Moroccans eat from the same large communal plate placed in the center of the table. Typically, dining was done at a low table whilst sitting on the floor or a cushion we call *pouf.* Everyone digs in with their right hand using just the thumb and first two fingers straight from the dish. If we were not eating enough, they insisted we do, or they would think we did not like the food and get offended. Water bowls were provided to rinse your fingers.

Hospitality in Morocco is a way of life and is one of the most notable aspects of Moroccan culture. I remember the friendliness, warmth, generosity, and kindness of the locals. When invited in a Moroccan home, we were treated like royalty. Hospitality is rooted in the belief guests are a gift from God and should be treated as such. They wanted to share their vibrant cultural traditions. They were also interested in getting to know us. I remember how important family was to them and it was common for multiple generations to live under the same roof. They traditionally honored and respected the elder members of their communities by making sure they were always taken care of. Roots and traditions are still deeply implanted within their culture.

Historically, their cultural heritage has many similarities with Tunisia. It is a blend of a religious and ethnic tradition encompassing Berber, Arab, African, and Jewish descent.

One of their most remarkable cultural traditions is the equestrian *Fantasia,* also known as *Lab Al Baroud* (Arabic for "gunpowder game"), a stylized reenactment of a wartime calvary charge, present in many North African countries including Algeria, Libya, Mali, Mauritania, Niger, Tunisia and of course Morocco where it is called *Tbourida.* I had the privilege of being a spectator at one of the most exciting equestrian performances. *Fantasia* is a traditional folklore inspired from historical wartime attacks of Berber and desert knights. It usually takes place during cultural or religious festivals or can be the entertainment of choice at a lavish wedding.

It consists of an odd number of horse riders, all wearing colorful traditional clothes, who charge along a straight track at the same speed to form a line and then at the end of the charge fire into the sky using old muskets. The difficulty of the performance lies in synchronizing the movement of the horses during acceleration of the charge, and especially in firing the guns simultaneously so that one single shot is heard. Arabian horses, all well-bred and well-groomed stallions of Barb bloodlines, are complete muscle. The horses are adorned with beautiful saddles, clothes, and fringes matching the riders' outfits. No ordinary horse is allowed to participate.

The entire performance reflects the strong relationship between man and horse as is perceived in Islam. While originally a male-only demonstration, in more recent years women have been allowed to compete and ride in Fantasia festivals, with all-female troops often beating the men! Women accompanied the race making high-pitched tongue trills called ululation, a long, wavering, vocal sound accompanied by a rapid back and forth movement of the tongue.

Fantasias are all about color, culture, action, adrenaline, and excitement.

Morocco has always been one of my overall favorite countries except for the South Pacific. I revisited it many years later and found it had lost some of its charm. Globalization is the culprit. All countries are becoming uniform to some degree. Same hotel chains for example. Uniformization is the new worldwide standard it seems. Original authenticity has been suppressed and replaced by international standardization. Despite all the changes, Morocco was and still is an enchanting country with a rich, diverse history, landscapes, and vibrant culture.

You will find epic mountain ranges, ancient cities, sweeping deserts, 1,200 miles of coastline running along the Atlantic Ocean all the way to the Mediterranean Sea. I was extremely privileged to explore this unique country when it was not a beaten path. My parents wanted to explore the world and took me along for the ride. We had a DS Citroen, considered a comfortable car on the road; we also had a small *caravan* ancestor of an RV I suppose. For some trips, we would stay in local hotels. For others, we would favor the *caravan*, especially when we spent weekends at the beach on a regular basis.

We explored the country from North to South and East to West. Writing about those trips would deserve its own book. But here are some of the highlights.

I remember most travels to the South, especially The Ksar Ait Ben Haddou, near Ouarzazate, an old Berber village made of adobe houses built on a hillside. One of the most beautiful places you will have the chance to see. More than 40 movies have taken place in or around the area. *Gladiator* is the most known of all. Driving through the Dades valley canyon's winding roads is an amazing experience. Essaouira on the Moroccan Atlantic Coast is known for being the third largest sardine fishing port of the country. Little did I know part of the *Games of Thrones* series was filmed there. Historically, Essaouira was on the route of the Trans-Saharan Gold-Salt trade route. Caravans brought goods from sub-Saharan Africa to Timbuktu forming a huge trading network stretched across the Sahara and linked wealthy empires of West Africa and the Mediterranean region.

The unforgettable and unique Marrakech everyone is familiar with or at least heard of is a former imperial city, home to mosques, palaces, and gardens. The Medina is a densely packed, walled medieval city dating to the Berber empire. Thriving Souk (marketplace) known for its custom-made rugs, textiles, pottery, jewelry, and snake charmers.

You must bargain when purchasing anything there. If not, you will lose the interest and respect of the merchant. Bargaining is an art and a cultural tradition as long as it does not harm one of the parties to the transaction. It is a part of the Moroccan and Islamic culture. Moroccans anticipate bargaining when they are in the souks especially. Everything is negotiable. Merchants love and expect you to play the game. Never appear too eager, don't give up, the first price is never the final offer, know when to walk away, do not fall for theatrics and know your currency exchange.

The symbol of the city, and visible for miles, is the Moorish minaret of 12th-century Koutoubia Mosque. I still remember the smell of roses cultivated in all gardens and how breathing was intoxicating at times. Marrakech is known as "The Pink City" in Western Morocco, for its city walls and ramparts of beaten pink clay, built by the North African Empire's conquerors in the 12th century.

Numerous Kasbahs, ancient fortresses, old villages can be seen when driving through the countryside. The Atlas Mountains and the Tichka Pass cannot be missed. The Draa Valley known as the "date basket" with its agricultural terraces. Tinghir and the Todra Gorge. Mergouza entrance to the Sahara Desert with nearby sand dunes. The list goes on for the South.

Fez, one of the imperial cities which is also the name from a hat worn by Moroccan men, is the historical and spiritual capital of Morocco. Fez is known for its Medina, listed as a World Heritage Site and home to the world's oldest university. An ancient walled city often compared to the walled city of Jerusalem.

Meknes is also an imperial city mostly known for two nearby locations. The ancient city of Moulay Idriss and the Roman ruins of Volubilis, a partly excavated Berber-Roman city. Mauritanian capital, founded in the 3rd century B.C., became an important outpost of the Roman Empire. Covering an area of 42 hectares (equivalent to 103.784 acres), it is of outstanding value demonstrating urban development and Romanization. Graced with many remarkable vestiges, Volubilis produced a substantial amount of artistic material, including mosaics, marble, and bronze statuary. Much remains to be unearthed but is representative of the creative spirit of the human beings who lived there over the ages.

Agadir on the shore of the Atlantic. I specifically remember the name because the city of Agadir was destroyed by an earthquake in 1960 when I was living in Morocco. I was about 12 years old. At the time, I lived several hundred miles away, but I recall awakening in my bed at night because the ground was moving, the bed swayed, and the whole room shook. I was scared. The deep rumbling sounds coming from under the ground catapulted me into a panic mode. It stopped and started again several times due to aftershocks. I remember being alone that evening, intensifying my panic. We were told the next day of the gravity of this event. Within a period of a few seconds and over an area of only a few square miles, the bulk of the city was destroyed and over a third of its citizens killed.

Casablanca was interesting but more of a fast-paced bustling metropolis. Morocco's business powerhouse and industrial center with a modern swagger is unseen in other parts of the country. I always wondered why the classic movie "Casablanca" starring Humphrey Bogart and Ingrid Bergman received this name. Maybe because it sounds exotic. Casablanca as a city especially in modern ages is not representative of an exploration of the universal themes of love and sacrifice the movie story portrays. Casablanca did not leave me with fond memories and soon I will explain why, just personal circumstances having nothing to do with the city itself.

Rabat, the capital where the King resides since Morocco is still a semi-constitutional monarchy, was ruled by King Hassan II who succeeded his father Mohammed V, the central figure in the independence movement of Morocco who helped forge national unity around the throne. Rabat, another imperial city, is worth visiting. Located on the North Atlantic coast, it was plagued by Pirates attacks through much of its history. Noted for the "Tour Hassan," (Hassan Tower) and Mausoleum of Mohammed V. The Kasbah des Oudaias, or fortified city wall, offers a picturesque view of the North Atlantic. Bab Oudaia or 17th century Andalusian gardens are to be noted too. The Medina is great for local shopping. The Chellah is the site of an ancient Roman settlement and an intriguing archeological attraction but not as impressive as Volubilis.

Tangier in Northern Morocco at the Western entrance of the Strait of Gibraltar is worth noting because it used to be the summer site of the Moroccan royal residence. Strategic gateway between Africa and Europe since Phoenician times. Also visited for its whitewashed hillside medina, home to the Dar el Makhzen, a palace of the sultans, now a museum of Moroccan artifacts. We went through Tangier many times over when traveling to France crossing

Spain all the way to visit my grandma in the Southwest of France.

Spain is another captivating country. We would stop and take time visiting Seville, Granada, Valencia, Madrid, Alicante, and Barcelona.

Seville in Andalucía is known for its flamenco dance and architectural designs. Occupied by the Moors, Muslims, for centuries like most of Spain. They left a profound influence still reflected in the unique and stunning architecture.

Granada is so amazing with its Alhambra, show-stopping hilltop fortress and palace complex. One of the most famous monuments of Islamic architecture and one of the best-preserved palaces of the historic Islamic world. Flamenco dance and concerts festivals take place in the lush gardens of the Alhambra in the Summer, one of Southern Spain most beloved cultural tradition. My parents took me to a flamenco dance performance one evening. My senses were overwhelmed. The stage set up was grandiose and the profusion of lights mesmerizing. The smell of flowers in the gardens was fragrant, soft, delicate, and sweet. And then the dancing, the artists, the music, the ambiance. How fiery, proud, expressive, and graceful. An explosion of sensations between the sounds, the castanets, the clapping, the costumes, the rhythm of the music and the incredible performances. An experience I did not forget. Granada is a great example of medieval architecture dating to the Moorish occupation. I am still amazed I can remember my evening at the Alhambra so vividly.

Barcelona, the city, was like walking through an art museum. Don't miss the Sagrada Familia and Park Guell, Antoni Gaudi's modernist masterpiece. I still remember visiting a museum with El Greco's paintings and how his style of elongated bodies struck me as odd and unnatural, almost frightening but I was impressionable then.

Once while crossing Spain with my dear aunt Liliane, my mother, and my cousins, we had a car break down on a country road in the middle of nowhere near the Mediterranean coast. We waited a long time for help and got rescued by a nearby farmer who hauled us back to his village. We stayed there a couple of days while the car was being repaired. We took advantage of the idle time by exploring the surroundings. It was common for the villagers to use donkeys as a means of transportation and ride them loaded with big sacks. We found ourselves riding donkeys, my first time. Somehow, I ended up with a stubborn and not so friendly donkey who did not appreciate my lack of skills and quickly picked up on how inexperienced I was. He decided to make fun of me and certainly did as I struggled pitifully to stay on his back. He took off running, stopping abruptly and, of course, I flew right over his head landing on the ground a few feet in front of him. My only consolation is the beach as I was fortunate to land on the sand easing the impact. While I was hurt, my pride and ego were bruised even more.

I was showered with experiences which come along once in a lifetime. Thank you, Mom, and Dad, for exposing me to discoveries and adventures few get to know. At an early age, I had already been exposed to unique cultures, sceneries, and people. Thinking back, I would not trade my situation even though the downside was also real.

At some point, my parents decided it was time to send me to a boarding school in Casablanca. Not just any boarding school. I do not understand their choice since they were not believers but nevertheless, they picked a religious organization, *L'Institut Carmel Saint-Dominique*. The institution still exists, a community of Dominican Sisters of the Immaculate Conception consecrated to Christ in the Dominican charism whose mission is living the Word of God through teaching, evangelization, and health care.

The *Institut Carmel Saint-Dominique* in Casablanca had a solid reputation for offering higher quality academics than local public schools. An all-girls private school known for its rigorous curriculum also included religious instruction and prayer time. They accepted girls who did not have any religious background or education as well as those who did. My parents requested I be exempt from all religious activities and not influenced in any way. This resulted in times of intense isolation after the regular teaching schedule. They believed I was too young to decide for myself. The education I received there was excellent. The order was strict, and my unhappiness continued. I felt lonely and excluded. Why was I living in a Catholic organization, yet nobody cared to teach me anything about the Bible or Christ. My time to become a believer had not come. God had other plans for me.

One day, one of the Dominican nuns/sisters came to me and told me something had happened to my parents, and I needed to go home.

The unfolding of events or where and with whom I stayed is unclear in my memory. My parents had a big fight. A physical confrontation of enough magnitude had resulted in my mom being hurt, beaten up by my dad, and ending up in the hospital. My father too ended up in the hospital. In her case, she was physically hurt. In his case, he had fallen into deep depression and suffered a nervous breakdown requiring medical attention. My presence was a formality for a couple of days as I witnessed the seriousness of the situation.

I was sent back to boarding school because neither one could care for me. Left in the dark, mostly uninformed for a while and it was probably best. Eventually, my parents separated. I was around 14 years old.

My mother moved to Casablanca and filed for divorce. She never wanted to associate with my father in any form or shape again and was adamant about it. She had a restraining order. He could not legally see her. He was desperate and tried many times to contact her. There was no going back for her. She was told his mental health was fragile and he could commit suicide. Mutual friends proposed a meeting between my parents. They would accompany her so she would not be alone with him. She refused.

In the meantime, she had pulled me out of the convent, and I moved with her and the cat into a small house in Casablanca. Still going to school during the day but would stay with my mother at night. I think she felt safer by having me around.

She decided to send me to visit my father instead of going herself to see if my presence would calm him down and solve her issue of not wanting to confront him. I was put on a bus to go spend a few days with my father. I was apprehensive and worried to say the least and my feelings were justified.

A memory I tried to forget but the negative impact of the visit I had with my father who was then mentally unstable, stayed with me for many years. I never really had any closeness with my dad. For the most part, he left my mother in charge of my rearing. I was placed in a situation with a father who was torn up emotionally and unwilling to accept the prospect of a divorce. This was not a position for a child/teen to be confronted to, causing me more emotional and mental distress.

One evening at the dinner table my dad, who kept rambling about my mother unable to talk about anything else, started to look at me in a strange way and I began to feel uncomfortable. He called me by my mother's first name a few times. I reminded him I was his daughter, but he was seeing her, not me. The expression in his eyes scared me. I sensed danger and remembered how violent he had been with her; I feared his reactions. I knew instinctively I had to protect myself while alone in the house with him. Something took over in me and my gut told me to be as low key as possible and find ways to appease him. Even though I did not know God then, I realize now He sent an Angel to me or inspired me enough to find the right words to control the situation. Later that night, I locked myself up in my room and stayed up. I could hear him pacing through the house and standing by my door. I hid in a closet. Finally, at some point likely out of exhaustion, he went into his room and closed his door. The next morning, at sunrise, I got my things together and quietly left, assuming he had fallen asleep. I walked to a friend's house and told them what had happened and refused to go back to my father. They understood. He needed medical care, and it was not appropriate for me to be with him in his distressed condition. I was sent back to my mother. I did not see him for several years after this unsettling episode.

Mother soon found work in a well-known travel agency in Casablanca. The owner and her quickly developed into more than working collaboration, but also became friends and eventually lovers. It proved to be the right relationship for her with a good man. He treated me well and kindly. He fell in love with my mom and reciprocally. It turned out to be a solid and successful relationship. Eventually, they got married. It lasted only a few years. They were happy and traveled the world together. He was diabetic and during a trip to the Canary Islands, he ran out of his medication resulting in his death.

But what happened to me? I worked in his travel agency too, as a helper early on when I was not in school. The two of them would go on business trips and leave me behind. The employees were not sympathetic toward me. I was the daughter of the new woman in the owner's life who had become their boss too in a relatively short time. They did not make my life easy.

Also, I realized my mom did not appreciate her new man paying attention to me. She interpreted it in the wrong way. His behavior with me had always been honorable. He wanted me to feel accepted and welcomed.

This was also the time when I had my first boyfriend. First love, or so I thought. One day, I escaped with my new sweetheart whose name was Logan. We decided to stay together and hide at his parents' house who were out of town. When I returned to my mom's place, she told me I was not to see the boy ever again. And if I did, I would face dire consequences.

Of course, I escaped once more. When I returned, she kept her word and sent me to another Catholic Convent in the city of Biarritz, France to pursue my education. It was the same organization where I had been in Casablanca, also run by Dominican Sisters. She had the local police in Casablanca watch me at the airport to make sure I would board the plane to prevent any possible run away on my part.

I was on the onset of a few years of testing in an unknown environment and for the most part left to myself.

REFLECTIONS

My early years were not easy psychologically and emotionally even though I never lacked anything materially. I chose to not put a strong emphasis on the negative impact it had on me because today, I fully understand my parents did the best they knew how, with the tools available to them given their own life experiences and choices. They had to overcome their own unhealed traumas. Every generation has different priorities and resources. It is also a known fact; behaviors repeat across generations until someone breaks the cycle. Overall, my upbringing was a significant part of what forged me into who I have become today. Later in life clearing negative patterns became part of my focus, setting me on a path of renewal and conversion.

The lack of affection, guidance, direction, Christian values, the feeling of being unwanted and a burden to my parents, created difficulties establishing closeness, trust, and intimacy with others throughout my life. Continuous feelings of emotional isolation, insecurity, lack of self-esteem and anxiety resulted in preventing me from creating deep meaningful relationships as an adult. An impaired sense of self and the feeling of never being good enough caused stress navigating boundaries, often choosing toxic friends and partners.

I developed extreme sensitivity and empathy for others as a positive consequence. I believe I was chosen to break the generational cycle in my family. I learned throughout the years to become self-aware of my traits/behavior and destructive patterns. I took accountability in doing my part to bring about positive transformation.

BACK TO FRANCE

Biarritz is an exceptional destination in the heart of the Basque country in the Bay of Biscay adjacent to the Pyrenees mountains near Spain. Once a small fishing village, known for whaling. Consequently, the town's coat of arms features the image of a whale below a rowing boat manned by five sailors wearing berets. Biarritz was made fashionable after 1854 by Napoleon III and his Spanish empress, Eugenie. Visited by Queen Victoria, Edward VII, and Alfonso XIII of Spain, Biarritz began to call itself "the queen of resorts and the resort of kings." Today it is known as the surfing capital of the world, luxurious seaside tourist destination and gateway to the majestic Pyrenees mountains. Another beautiful and unique city with a historic heritage.

This is the town where my mother chose to send me. Just a different location of the same Catholic boarding institution where I was in Casablanca. The goal was to pursue my studies working towards getting a *Baccalaureat* colloquially known as the *BAC*. It is the final exam all French students must pass to graduate from high school. An extensive, national examination taken at the end of the *lycee,* upon completion of the 11th and 12th grade. The French *BAC* is widely accepted for entrance into higher education institutions. Its graduates gain admittance to some of the best universities in North America and worldwide.

The name of the school today is the *Immaculate Conception* Private College and still exists. This period of my life and time spent there remains vague. I was in a state of depression and spent a lot of time alone. I was not participating in religious activities per my mother's request. In France, prior to 1974, the majority age was 21 years old so I could not exercise my right to participate even if I had wanted to.

My only surviving memory in this establishment is a time during a weeklong holiday when a nun/sister invited me to join them on a trip to Lourdes. They took pity on me since I never went anywhere as opposed to most of their other students who visited their families on weekends or vacations. I was about to embark on an unforgettable life lesson.

I not only never forgot these significant few days but unconsciously what I experienced in Lourdes became a precursor to forging and leading me in my spiritual pursuit.

Lourdes in France is a town known as the most famous healing shrine in the world. Each year the French shrine of Lourdes draws millions of visitors from the entire planet. It is known for its healing waters and miracles. A major Catholic pilgrimage site. Pilgrims from all over the globe visit the Grotto of the Apparitions, where, in 1858, the Virgin Mary is said to have appeared to a young local peasant girl by the name of Bernadette Soubirous, later canonized as St Bernadette. A site of healing and hope. Unfortunately, today, the town center is filled with shops selling religious trinkets and "holy water" from the underground source on the grotto site.

An area like no other I had been to; spiritual energy breathes through this village at the foothills of the Pyrenees mountains. To date, there have been 70 confirmed miracles in Lourdes.

I witnessed maybe thousands of people, accompanied by someone, either in wheelchairs or lying on a gurney. Crying, praying, supplication, wailing tore through the air as long lines were patiently waiting for their turn to reach the Sanctuary of Our Lady of Lourdes, the shrine where the Pilgrims can drink the healing waters of the original spring discovered by Bernadette and blessed by the Virgin Mary.

I had shivers even though I was not yet a believer. I could not help but feel deeply touched by a sense of sacredness and holiness as I stood in the shrine. It felt like a supernatural presence filled with compassion upon the sorrows and sicknesses of all pilgrims was hovering in the air and it was almost palpable. So much hope and faith displayed in front of me. It brought spontaneous tears to my eyes. Such a special moment in time and space. The memory lingered in my subconscious for years to come as a seed was planted.

I also accompanied the Catholic Sisters to hospitals filled with people enduring incurable illnesses. Some were in bed, some in wheelchairs, and some on gurneys, everywhere including the hallways. Empathy filled me with powerful feelings of hopelessness. I was put to work, anything, just holding hands, saying kind words, comforting others in any way I could. Including helping someone with bedpan assistance or giving them water or something to eat. I remember a bedridden overweight woman whom I helped with a bedpan and how challenging it was to roll her on her side, place and center the bedpan under her, give her privacy for a moment and then reverse her back sideways and finally wipe her. This was a humbling experience I am sure for her and even more so for me, with my lack of experience and a feeling of embarrassment I could not help.

A new window of perspective was opening right in front of my eyes as I was facing a new form of misery and suffering, I had not been exposed too before. It certainly left me with many existential questions. What I was confronted with was not about me and my own emotional lacks. I was exposed to suffering such as physical illnesses and incurable diseases accompanied by despair intermingled with hope and faith for a possible miracle.

After a few days as a witness and active participant, it was time to return. We took the train back to Biarritz and life as I knew it in the boarding school resumed after this memorable experience. Marked by the events of the last week, a revelation was making its way into my psyche and my heart. I had been focusing on me and my own needs all these years. My tunnel vision was expanding. For the first time, I felt an awareness and a new consciousness emerging. There was a lot more to life than I thought, and the world did not just revolve around me.

I was a teenager then, distressed, impressionable, and vulnerable. What I had just gone through and witnessed in Lourdes washed a powerful wave of empathy and compassion through me, leaving me speechless. I realized I could feel intensely for others and understood for the first time my problems were insignificant compared to the hardship and agony I had observed.

WORKING ON CRUISE SHIPS

Then an unexpected and exciting summer opportunity arose. It was summer school break and in France summer vacation lasts a couple of months and always includes July and August. I had two and a half months off school and did not know where I would spend the time. My mom, through her new relationship with Leo, now her husband, who was a well-known travel agent, came up with the idea of getting me some work experience on a cruise ship. Leo had numerous contacts in the business and found a position as an assistant to the Cruise Director for a company called Transtour. They offered cruises in the Mediterranean and the Atlantic. I was assigned to two routes alternatively on a medium size cruise ship, probably about 500 passengers from diverse European countries. Cruising started in the 1960s and was nothing compared to the mega cruise ships of today. Many cruise ships doubled as cargo transportation then. It turned out to be a grand adventure for me. I am still grateful to my mom for the opportunity.

One ship's itinerary was from Marseille, France to Yalta and Odessa in Ukraine including multiple stopovers on the way. The most notable ports of call were, maybe not in the correct order, Malta, Naples, and Athens. Then the Turkish straits, the Dardanelles and the Bosphorus both international passages connecting the Aegean and Mediterranean seas to the Black Sea. They are on the opposite ends of the Sea of Marmara. The Bosphorus Straight runs through Istanbul, making it a city located on two continents Europe and Asia. Finally cruising the Black Sea all the way to Yalta and Odessa in Ukraine and back.

The second itinerary had for destination the North Pole called the

Land of the Midnight Sun in Norway. We embarked in Le Havre, France and headed straight north along the Atlantic Coast to the North Sea going through the Channel Islands, by Denmark, and then into the Norwegian Sea. We visited phenomenal fjords, Oslo, Trondheim, and Bergen are highlights.

Each cruise took about 12 days, alternating three times in a row. Even though my responsibilities were demanding and stressful at times, these experiences were a wonderful opportunity. I will expand on some of the highlights.

Prior to settling on the ship for the next few months, I met with the Cruise Director for training. I remember a nice and experienced lady who prepared me for the task. My functions were as her assistant, to help her make sure things ran smoothly. She was in charge and delegated to me the less exciting tasks. For example, I oversaw counting passengers when we stopped at ports of call for the day. I had to make sure everyone who had boarded the excursion bus made it back to the ship. As fringe benefits, I accompanied them on all the tours as I walked alongside the local tour guides. I had a free pass to the marvels we discovered and first "seat" while surveying my group. The excitement of the experience, however, did not overshadow the seriousness of my responsibility to not "lose" anyone.

While on the ship, my tasks included welcoming everyone alongside the cruise director to various functions such as the captain's table dinner, a special evening including a cocktail reception followed by a formal dinner with the presence of the captain and his officers, a greeting gesture to welcome the passengers on cruise opening night. It is an honor, and quite interesting, to be invited to dine at the captain's table especially on more than one occasion as my cruise director and I were solicitated. They spoke Russian and we spoke French, so we used English as a common language which restricted our exchanges since no one spoke fluent English. I remember vodka being the liquor of choice rather than wine and I did not handle it well as it made me nauseated. The other nights were more casual.

Worth mentioning, passengers were either well-disciplined and courteous or undisciplined and unruly. The swimming pool attendance is a good example. Without fail, every morning, disputes arose between different nationalities in particular between the

French and the German. The French would early in the morning "pick" their lounge chairs by the swimming pool before anyone else would show up. When the Germans arrived all the good spots were taken and personal belongings claiming "ownership" were on the lounge chairs already. Disputes and arguments followed. I was supposed to make everybody happy by intervening as moderator suggesting they take turns each day giving everyone the opportunity to enjoy the best spots. This is when I learned some diplomacy skills. When a passenger had a complaint, I was the first one on the scene and if I could not resolve the issue, I called my director for rescue, or a member of the cruise ship staff depending on what the problem was. I was the link between passengers, cruise ship director, and the ship's staff.

This critical position led to strong connections with the staff, including the captain and his crew, mostly Russian. Passionate people with deep, strong feelings. Proud and task oriented. Guarded until they felt they could trust you. Dynamic and life loving. This is the impression I received working on the ship back in the 1960s surrounded by Slavic people.

The sites visited were the highlights of the job. The Acropolis in Athens and its monuments are universal symbols of classical spirit and civilization. They form the greatest architectural and artistic complex bequeathed by Greek antiquity to the world. During the classical Greek era, it was a sacred space devoted to the cult of the city's patron goddess, Athena, as well as other local heroes and deities.

The fortifications and temples in Malta. Famous for its beautiful architecture, scenic cliffs, breathtaking coastline, and dive sites. The island has a long and fascinating cultural heritage reflected in its UNESCO World Heritage Sites, including the ancient city of Valletta, the Megalithic Temples of Malta, and the Hal Saflieni Hypogeum.

Pompeii near Naples is an archeological marvel of preservation after a tragic volcanic event, the eruption of Mount Vesuvius in 79 AD. It was buried under the ash and largely preserved. The excavated city offers a unique snapshot of Roman life. Today Pompeii is one of the most popular tourist attractions in Italy.

Mesmerizing Istanbul, economic, cultural, and historic hub of Turkey. As the ship entered the Bosphorus Strait, we were immersed in the island's heavy water traffic making this city unique. The striking national flag of Turkey, red with its white crescent moon and star, floated proudly at the entrance of the straight. The farther into the strait we were struck by the history of our surroundings. The city served as an imperial capital for almost 1600 years. Roman Byzantine, Latin, late Byzantine, and Ottoman empires succeeded. Istanbul played a key role in the advancement of Christianity. Numerous churches were built across the city. Hagia Sophia Grand Mosque is a major cultural and historical site. It was originally built as a basilica for the Greek Orthodox Christian Church and its function has changed several times over the centuries since. The Blue Mosque whose design is the culmination of two centuries of Ottoman Mosque development. Topkapi Palace where the Sultans of Turkey ruled the Ottoman Empire for five hundred years. The Sultanahmet District reflects cultural influences of the many empires that once ruled here. The Dolmabahce Palace was built in the mid-nineteenth century, in the last period of the Ottoman empire. The Galata Tower has a unique place in Istanbul's history dating back to the fall of Constantinople to the Ottomans.

A visit to Istanbul wouldn't be complete without spending some time at the famed Grand Bazaar, one of the largest and oldest covered markets in the world with 61 covered streets and over 4,000 shops. Each day it is estimated to attract an average of 250,000 to 400,000 visitors. It is often regarded as one of the first shopping malls in the world. Its construction goes back to the 14th century shortly after the Ottoman conquest of Constantinople. It went through some major catastrophes such as the 1894 strong earthquake rocking Istanbul and had to be partially rebuilt. You can find anything there from furniture, gold jewelry, carpets, leather goods to clothing, spices, cafes, and much more.

Once passing through the door of the iconic Grand Bazaar, we were transported into another world. A world of exotism, vibrant colors, and pungent aromas floating in the air from all the spice markets. A historical and mysterious place. I remember lamps for sale hanging from the ceiling of the stalls, glowing like a constellation, vividly colored spice shops displayed alongside jewel-like lokum (Turkish delight), eye-catching handmade Turkish rugs with unique weaving patterns. Locals and visitors are expected to haggle as bargaining is a cultural tradition in most Muslim countries.

It is easy to get lost in this maze and it stressed me because I had to keep track of every person in my group while following our guide. It was not a time to be distracted because of my responsibility of keeping count. But I do remember a funny anecdote as we passed merchants of carpets and rugs. One vendor made a comment to me as I walked by. He was inviting me to go inside his shop because he said he wanted to show me a magical carpet and I might be interested in "flying on it with him". He was using the myth of the flying carpet. Legend has it the Queen of Sheba gifted King Solomon a green and gold flying carpet studded with precious jewels, as a token of her love. It is said a flying carpet was woven on an ordinary broom, but its dyes held spectacular powers. Regardless of his intentions, I took his remarks as a funny way to give me a compliment.

Yalta and Odessa both historic cities in Ukraine were also the Tzars summer residences outside of St Petersburg. Yalta is remembered for its 1945 Yalta Conference where treaties were made impacting Europe. The Americans and the British generally agreed future governments of the Eastern European nations bordering the Soviet Union should be "friendly" to the Soviet regime while the Soviets pledged to allow free elections in all territories liberated from Nazi Germany.

The Norway cruise was spectacular with its grandiose fjords. The history of the Vikings can be explored in several museums, not only in Oslo, but throughout Norway. I thought the Norwegian people were handsome, blue eyes, blond, and tall figures. I recall them bathing in the fjords in the nude, a common occurrence in Europe.

After this exciting cruise ship summer interlude and first hands-on educative experience, it was the end of school break and time for me to return to the Dominican sisters boarding school in Biarritz with a heavy heart to continue my formal education in this private religious establishment. Returning to such dull existence after the excitements of the summer was more than I could bear emotionally and psychologically, but it was my mother's will. I did not have a choice still considered a minor until 21 years old per French law. I resumed a boring life in a sterile environment where I made no friends and have no recollection of any warmth nor welcome. Not belonging to the "nunnery team," consisting of the Catholic staff or "sisters" and other pupils or "boarders," I was regarded as an outsider assuming I was being looked upon as an atheist. Most other girls who studied there were Catholics and had little interaction with me. This was a time when I read to occupy my time when not in class or doing homework. I was still on the curriculum taught for preparation of the French *Baccalaureat*.

The next summer school break came around and a new experience awaited me. This time, I was sent to England for a couple of months as an *Au Pair* with a British family. I ended up near a pretty seaside town, probably Brighton in the county of East Sussex. The family I stayed with was on a horse barn property and offered horseback riding. The couple had twin boys around 3 years old. I had limited interaction with the family. They had me working most of the time. I don't even remember having meals with them, I was eating in the kitchen by myself. They were not interested in getting to know me, they just wanted somebody to help with housework and babysitting the boys. I realized later my poor experience was simply because I had a misconception of what an *Au Pair* is. It had never been explained to me I was expected to be a maid servant and caretaker of the children. If I had been told I was going to be a nanny for a couple of months, it would have changed my expectations.

I nearly got badly kicked by a horse in a field on their property. It really was my fault. I knew nothing about horses and had never been exposed to them. One day, on a break, I had the bad idea to walk among the horses. I carelessly walked too close behind one of them making him nervous. He responded by kicking his back legs. I was just slightly beyond kicking distance. An Angel must have protected me.

Tired, upset, and feeling exploited, I decided to explain to my mom what was happening. I simply asked, "Please, remove me from this family who treats me so unfairly." Her response to my plea was straight forward and simple, "I want you to stay there for the time agreed, be patient, and make the best of it." A couple of weeks later, I reiterated my request but to no avail. When my ordeal ended, I returned to France.

A pleasant surprise awaited me. Instead of returning to boarding school where I was not doing well not only personally but academically, mother had made arrangements propelling me in a new direction. She felt instead of pursuing an academic education, what I really needed was learning a trade with practical and realistic applications. In her mind, what would really help me was to get secretarial training, thus following her steps, learning skills allowing me to find a job in the real world anywhere. I ended up in Paris enrolled in a secretarial school by the name of Pigier still in existence today. She had also planned for room and board in a Catholic, girls only, guest house or *pension* as we call it in France. I stayed there for a year until I received a *Diplome de Secretaire*, secretarial diploma. I have positive memories of this time. I would go to school during the day using the *metro,* Parisian subway, and get back to my boarding establishment in the evening and do homework after dinner. I met other *pensionaires,* guest mates, while living there, who went to different schools. I became good friends with a couple of them. When not at school and in our free time, we visited Paris, walked a lot, and had great fun. This newfound freedom was wonderful. Our only obligation was to be back at our guest house by a certain time in the evenings before curfew. We did not want to find closed doors. If we followed regulations, we did fine.

Shockingly, after a year of enjoying my new situation in Paris, my dad contacted me to explain he was coming to France for a visit and would like us to reconnect. I was nervous because the memory of our last encounter still lingered on my mind. Supposedly, he was doing well, had healed, and really would love to see me. The divorce had taken place and he felt ready to start life over.

I was about 19 years old and had not seen him for several years, so I agreed to meet with him. We had a positive reunion. He showed no signs of depression and spoke only about the future. Obviously, he was ready and eager to move on with his life. He had reconnected with my mother's side of the family, and they invited both of us to go visit. The thought of seeing my aunt Liliane and grandma was heartwarming. The decision was easy to make. My contact with my father was constructive and made me feel good. I was looking forward to getting to know him better. The timing was perfect. I was done with my secretarial training.

We spent some time visiting my grandma, my aunt Liliane, and others. They were happy to see us, reconnect, catch up, and so were we. My mom's family was fond of my dad and had always been from the beginning when they first met him. He was also fond of them because of their kindness towards him. He had no connection with his own blood so in a way my mom's family became his.

This is the time when I had the privilege to discover who my father was. We shared many open-hearted conversations. I truly felt the birth of a real connection with him. He was positive, happy, no longer haunted by mother. He had realized he could not only survive but thrive on his own and focused on looking forward to a new life. The past was over.

He shared with me what he had in mind for the future, "our future" if I decided to be part of it and accompany him. He had left Morocco for good and was ready to relocate. He had done some research as to where he could begin a new life, as far away from the past as possible. He spoke about moving to the South Pacific and had Tahiti in mind as a destination. He never had trouble finding work before so he felt confident it would be easy once over there. He knew of people who had made the move from North Africa to the South Pacific, more specifically New Caledonia. But his heart was set to go to Tahiti first.

His news transported me with hope for a new life too. My own situation had dramatically improved after a positive and constructive year in Paris. I was doing better psychologically and emotionally. A new horizon and a new window needed to open in my life and my dad presented me with the perfect opportunity and the timing could not have been better. He had the solution for both of us. The decision to go with him was the easiest one I had ever made. I was onboard with his plans. The idea of moving to Tahiti sounded like a dream come true. Mother was fine with my plans to join my father in his new endeavors and wished me well.

TRIP TO TAHITI

O f all the places he could have picked, he chose a mythical island in the South Pacific. Not only did I have the opportunity to discover my father and get an unbiased understanding of who he was as a human being, but the circumstances in which this new chapter of our lives took place were like a fairy tale.

In May of 1969, the year and month of my 20th birthday, the two of us embarked on the *Tahitien*, owned by the *Messageries Maritimes*, to cruise around the world, 22,000 kilometers (13,671 miles) to the legendary Tahiti Islands in the South Pacific. The trip aboard the ship took almost two months with numerous exciting ports of call stops along the way.

The *Messageries Maritimes*, a France-based company, was famous in shipping circles, especially on the Europe-Asia trade lanes. Two sisterships, the *Tahitien* and the *Caledonien*, sailed for two decades between 1952 and 1972 on regular routes between Marseille to Asia and the South Pacific. Both were beautifully designed passenger-cargo liners. The two liners accommodated 373 passengers: first class, tourist class, third class, and steerage. We traveled in tourist class. These ships were among the last of the real working cargo-passenger liners, plying their trade until long sea journeys were displaced by mass jet passenger travel.

I transitioned from being isolated in a convent to one year of studies in Paris, then sailing on a cruise ship to the South Pacific, Tahiti of all places. Life onboard felt like such freedom. Not only did we visit more beautiful places, but we met new people sharing a common purpose with us, building a new life in a faraway land filled with opportunities lacking back home in France. The increasingly violent attacks on Gaullism and Communism, the decline in French geopolitical power, and the end of postwar economic growth had led to unprecedented unease about the nation's collective future. Many people in France were struggling to make a living and concerned with the forthcoming uncertainties. French colonies in the South Pacific were thriving and offered work opportunities, especially the island of New Caledonia. France held three territories in the South Pacific: New Caledonia, Wallis and Futuna, and French Polynesia, accounting for about one third of the Pacific Islands combined, represented an exclusive economic zone.

Tahiti had a healthy economy due largely to tourism, the pearl industry, and, to a certain extent, the military nuclear testing bases and their associated activities. The presence of the *Centre d'Experimentation du Pacifique (CEP)* for over 25 years had generated a somewhat artificial economy which had brought with it high incomes and a consumerist mentality.

New Caledonia's economy was driven by one main sector, first and foremost the mining industry, a major source of nickel with roughly 10% of the world's supply, also magnesium, iron, cobalt, chromium, and manganese. The mining industry was booming in the 1970's and offered numerous career opportunities.

Most Americans I met when thinking of the South Pacific visualize Australia and New Zealand and often overlook the role France played in the region. France's territories have historically been isolated by a linguistic barrier and their unique trading relationship with Europe. France also limited opportunities to engage with the independent states of the Pacific by focusing exclusively on its own territories.

I truly enjoyed the carefree lifestyle aboard the ship, this time around I was not part of the staff but a passenger. The ports of call were Pointe-a-Pitre in Guadeloupe, Fort-de-France in Martinique, Curaçao, Cristobal and Balboa in Panama, Taiohae in the Marquesas Islands and Tahiti.

My relationship with my father had a chance to develop without interference or drama. At night, the perfectly clear unobstructed night sky on the vast ocean inspired him to share with me one of his favorite hobbies, astronomy. We would go to the top deck near the chimney late in the evening and he would point at celestial objects, stars, planets, constellations, and give me their names. I was in awe at the mesmerizing firmament in full display above us. I still cherish these unforgettable moments with him.

He was an avid reader of philosophy and psychology and would suggest books for me to read. He favored Carl Jung and Sigmund Freud for psychology and Pierre Teilhard de Chardin, Rene Descartes, Jean-Jacques Rousseau and Voltaire in philosophy. He was fascinated by the study of the human psyche. He loved classical music, and this certainly contributed to my personal taste for it.

On one of the dancing nights onboard the ship, I met a dashing young man by the name of Federico who showed interest and curiosity about me. He invited me to dance with him quite often. He would spend time with me at the swimming pool daily. We talked while having a drink together. He accompanied me while on excursions for the day at the various ports of call. We had fun together. I was attracted to him, and we began a casual relationship based on mutual physical attraction. He was on his way to New Caledonia from Nice in France and had a cousin over there waiting for him. Electrician by trade, he had already been guaranteed business by his cousin who had many connections.

I was also spending quality time with my dad mostly through open minded talks and sharing thoughts and memories. We were more focused on the future because the past brought sadness to both of us. We connected with other passengers and spent some time socializing. Some of these connections proved to be useful later. My dad also met a woman onboard the ship he seemed to like.

Of all the ports of call, I recall the one in Martinique where we climbed on top of the volcano *Mount Pelee* (bold mountain in French), still active today. Its last major eruption in 1902, destroyed the port of Saint-Pierre, killing approximately 30,000 people. It is considered the most active volcano in the Caribbean. The challenging hike took about four hours and included steep and rocky terrain. With an elevation gain of about 600 meters, it offered a breathtaking panoramic view of the island.

I vividly remember going through the Panama Canal on our stop in Panama City. Its construction costed over 25,000 lives and is considered one of the man-made wonders of the world, as well as one of the largest and most difficult engineering feat ever undertaken. The heat, jungles, swamps, and all the creatures striving in them are notorious. The scenery was unbelievable. With binoculars, we could watch wildlife because the ship was close to each embankment. We observed various types of monkeys moving through the trees in small groups and exotic bird species.

The narrow canal took a lot of skill and experience for the captain to maneuver. The Panama Canal locks are a lock system lifting ships up to 85 feet to the main elevation of the canal and down again. There are twelve locks in total.

It is amazing to think the Panama Canal is about 50 miles long from shoreline to shoreline. Prior to its existence, the only way to get from the Atlantic to the Pacific for ships traveling between the East and West coasts of the American continent, was to sail all the way around dangerous Cape Horn at the southern tip of South America. A voyage of some 8,000 nautical miles longer than going through the Panama Canal.

Panama in the early 1960s, underwent a political conflict over the control of the Panama Canal Zone. Numerous riots took place, and the oligarchy was under fire. There was public resentment over United States policies and presence and Panama charged the US with aggression, severed relations and appealed to the United Nations. Multiple negotiations took place, and in 1969, the very year we visited, a failed coup was attempted, a provisional president was designated, and a New Panama Movement was formed.

We visited the historic district of Panama City, *Casco Viejo*, featuring cobblestone streets and colonial-era structures such as the neoclassical Palacio Presidencial and vibrant plazas boasting restaurants, cafes, and bars. The number of bars was staggering. The atmosphere was heavy, murky, dense, and unfriendly. The streets overflowed with people dancing and drinking. Sailors were everywhere barely standing up from drunkenness looking for trouble and adventure. It appeared quickly as our group was walking around, we were not welcome. The looks we received were a giveaway. The comments shouted at us revealed the hostility surrounding us. For the most part, we did not understand what they were saying because they spoke slang words in Spanish. But we could tell there was anger, resentment, and contempt.

The gestures and body language were revealing and crude. They just did not want us there. Those of us taking pictures aggravated the situation and someone in our group got their camera snatched away angrily. My father kept a close watch on me, herding me to the protection of the center of our group. The way men were looking at me while making suggestive gestures and remarks was unsettling. We accepted the fact it was in everyone's best interest to turn around quickly. I was relieved when we returned to the ship.

Within a couple of days of leaving the Panama Canal as we were sailing through the Pacific Ocean, on May 2, 1969, about 600 miles west of Balboa port, at 5:10 am while we were still sleeping in our cabin, fire erupted in the engine room. To avoid panic among passengers, instead of blasting the ship horn, we were individually told to gather immediately on the main deck by the swimming pool. The captain explained what was taking place in the engine room as black smoke billowed out of the chimney in deep contrast against the blue sky. He asked us to keep calm while the crew frantically kept the situation under control. Water needed to be quickly carried to the engine room and he requested the male passengers to form a bucket brigade to help speed things up. He told us an SOS had been broadcast for help. He also said we needed to wear a life jacket in case it became necessary to step on the lifeboats.

Most people kept calm and offered help. Women who had young children panicked. At first, I got scared, but excitement took over after a while. A chain formed quickly to fill water buckets with pool water handed down from one person to the next all the way to the engine room to put the fire out.

La chaîne des seaux puisant l'eau de la piscine

Forming a chain to bring buckets of water from the swimming pool to the
engine room to extinguish the fire.

Several hours passed before the fire was under control. The ship, no longer thrusted by the engines, had stalled and was now drifting, lost at sea. The captain informed us the SOS had resulted in a rescue ship being sent, but it would take some time to arrive, and he could not be specific. We were at the mercy of the elements floating around without direction not knowing where the current and wind pushed us. Many of us became seasick, including me. We could not return to our cabins because they had flooded. Our belongings were brought onto the deck at some point much later.

It turned out we were not rescued for several days. We drifted 96 miles to the east. We remained on the main deck during the day and at night slept in the first-class dining room. For fun, men were fishing and tossed their catches into the pool, including a few small sharks.

Tarpaulins were installed to provide us with protection from the sun. The tropical heat was brutal with 100% humidity and unbearable without shade. Fortunately, the evenings cooled off. No water in the toilets until we were able to have buckets filled with sea water which helped tremendously. Food consisted of snacks, dried fruits, canned goods and non-perishable items. Personal hygiene was kept to a bare minimum. Buckets of fresh water were made available to us, and we were told to use it sparingly.

The young people, including me, found the situation exciting and thought we were living a once in a lifetime adventure. Mothers were worried about their babies and toddlers. My father and many others in his age group felt this was epic too. We were in the making of storytelling for the future. A few elderly people were concerned and anxious about the outcome. We knew we were going to be rescued, it was a matter of waiting patiently. Life onboard was a campsite of 420 people.

This was a time when Federico, and I spent many hours getting to know each other better. We would sit in the lounge area and share information about who we were and what we liked. His decision to move to New Caledonia had been prompted by a cousin who lived there with his family, had a successful business and loved the relaxed and carefree lifestyle of the island. He had strongly encouraged him to make the move, promising an easy career where he could use his skills as an electrician. Federico was going to stay with his cousin at first until he figured things out and settled. He was enthusiastic speaking about it. He looked forward to the lifestyle his cousin was raving about. Very active, he loved water sports, snorkeling, diving, and fishing. His cousin owned a small yacht and spent time exploring the lagoon. He literally could not wait to get there. Knowing my father and I were going to Tahiti, he suggested we remain in touch and for me to go and visit him.

One night, we endured a severe tropical cyclone, deafening thunder with high winds, lightning, and violent rain. The ocean stormed with crashing waves battering the ship relentlessly. The lightning emblazoned the sky flashing surreal light all around us. The ship began spinning on itself like a dog after its tail. The children and most women were screaming in fear. The situation seemed out of control. Everyone was seasick. It was one of the most frightening moments I have ever known. The staff kept us in the dining room behind closed doors and tried to calm us to no avail.

We were holding on to each other and the believers prayed. A state of general panic reigned. After what seemed like hours of nightmarish uncertainty for our fate, the storm stopped. I am sure everyone who was on the ship and is still alive today must remember the disquieting horrors of that night.

I turned 20 years old on May 6 amidst the chaos of these events. An unusual birthday in an unexpected setting. The ship staff made the situation tolerable and even enjoyable by serving some much-needed wine and provided music for the occasion to our delight. This is not a birthday I will ever forget.

On May 9, we were rescued by the *Marquisien,* a sistership, and hauled back to Balboa to be transported by airplane to our destination.

TAHITI

As we arrived at Faa'a Airport in Papeete, capital of Tahiti, located on the main island, a nice surprise waited for us upon disembarking from the airplane, a traditional Polynesian welcome ceremony. Tahitian music, *Vahines,* pretty girls dancing the hula dressed in grass skirts graciously handed each passenger a Tahitian flower necklace. The *tiare* flower is delicate and gives out an intoxicating fragrance reminiscent of gardenia. Unlike any scent, sweet and warm but also light and relaxing. It is the national flower of Tahiti and the emblem of the Polynesian islands. The *tiare* whose scientific name is *gardenia taitensis is* the favorite daily adornment of the Tahitians, both men (*tane*) and women (*vahine*) who wear it the same way fashionably placed behind one's ear. It is fun to know on some islands, wearing the flower on the left ear means "looking" and right means "taken." On other islands, left matching the wedding band means "married" and right means "single."

We were transported for the first night to a free of charge beautiful hotel somewhere in Papeete which included dinner and breakfast. Federico and I spent our last evening together. The next morning, we said goodbye since his journey was taking him to New Caledonia. We both felt sad about the separation, and we promised each other we would remain in touch.

The following day, my father found us temporary accommodation. Before looking for work, he decided we deserved a little vacation to recover from our grueling adventure at sea.

It so happened the nearby island of Moorea had one of the most exciting Club Med resorts of the time. Club Med was owned by a French travel and tourism operator headquartered in Paris specializing in all-inclusive holidays. They had multiple luxury getaways throughout the word from ski resorts to beach resorts. They are typically located on the most beautiful sites of our planet. Their Moorea Island resort had the reputation of being one of their most exciting locations. We spent a week in total indulgence in a Tahitian *Fare*, traditionally built from local wood with a distinctive roof covered with pandanus leaves and palm tree branches. Each day offered a multitude of options and endless entertainment. For the first time ever, I snorkeled in a South Sea lagoon. Almost indescribable, the color of the water scintillates with the brightest shades of blue, from cyan to turquoise, passing through emerald to dark sapphire. The delightful illusion is created by the interplay of light, water, and the brilliant white sand carpeting the depths of the lagoon. We enjoyed a sunset dinner cruise. Endless buffets were available all day until late into the night. Dancing on the beach at night was popular. We had a blast in this unique setting of endless fun.

After a week in this tropical paradise, we went back to Papeete where reality set in.

We found a weekly furnished rental and started to explore the possibilities for work. Tahiti was a tourist paradise and the economy derived from it to a large extent. The French military nuclear testing bases and their associated activities were prominent. The pearl industry and most remarkably the exquisite black pearls grown in French Polynesia are the only ones allowed to be called Tahitian pearls.

Regarding my dad's profession, the opportunities for work were just not there. It seemed a drafting engineer did not have his place in this tropical paradise.

Besides, it rapidly became clear it was costly to live there. Everything was expensive and even if we had found work, it was very likely we could not afford the lifestyle. Paradise has its price. My dad could see his savings depleting rapidly after a couple of months.

In the meantime, we remained in touch with people from the ship who had continued their journey to New Caledonia and encouraged us to join them. Federico and I had kept in touch. He already had found work. He described the island in positive terms. The promising picture his cousin had painted for him had come true. The friends my dad had made on the ship reinforced the facts. Everyone had found work within the first month of their arrival. Federico and I really wanted to see each other again. The woman my dad had met on the ship and liked had also moved there. New Caledonia was proving to be the place for us to continue our journey.

In the 1960s, New Caledonia enjoyed strong economic growth. It was the "Golden Years." I already mentioned it was driven by the mining industry, nickel exploitation mostly. With my dad's experience in the mining industry from Tunisia and Morocco, it seemed like he would be in a good position to find work matching his experience.

It was not long before we flew to Noumea, the capital of New Caledonia.

Another chapter was about to open for both of us.

NEW CALEDONIA

Unlike Tahiti, the most legendary and romanticized paradisiacal group of islands sought after in the world, New Caledonia when I have referred to it in the United States throughout my life, always brought questions from my interlocutors. Where is it? What is over there? Why would you choose to live there?

Aircalin at Île Des Pins, Nouvelle Calédonie

This is why… a paradise tucked away to the end of the world.

These questions for the most part came from Americans. Only US war veterans would know about New Calcdonia. Why?

Because, during World War II, New Caledonia played an important role during the Pacific War. The island had a strategic position in the South Pacific. The political situation in New Caledonia was tense when the war broke out in the Pacific. Operation FS was the imperial Japanese plan to invade and occupy Fiji, Samoa, and New Caledonia. A garrison of 16,800 US troops, built around 51 Brigade and 70 Coast Artillery Regiment, organized into Task Force 6814 arrived on the island on March 12, 1942. They were joined by 67 Fighter Squadron. New Caledonia was defended primarily to prevent its occupation by the Japanese, but it proved to be of strategic value as a support base for the Guadalcanal campaign.

The American base of New Caledonia explains why US veterans were familiar with the island.

New Caledonia today is still a French Territory comprising dozens of islands. It is known for its palm-lined beaches and marine-life-rich lagoon, which, at 24,000-sq-km (9266,4518 square miles), is among the world's largest. A massive barrier reef surrounds the main island, *Grande Terre*. It is a major scuba-diving destination. The New Caledonia barrier reef is the longest continuous barrier reef in the world and has been classified as a UNESCO World Heritage Site since 2008. It is in the Southwest Pacific Ocean, south of Vanuatu, about 750 miles east of Australia and north of New Zealand about 1,480 miles.

The archipelago, part of the Melanesia subregion, includes the main island Grande Terre, the Loyalty Islands, the Chesterfields Islands, the Belep Archipelago, the Isle of Pines, and numerous remote islets.

We call it *Le Caillou*, the Pebble. The people of European descent are called the *Caldoches*. The natives are of Melanesian ethnicity. Numerous people from Southeast Asia, former French colonies such as Vietnam, Cambodia, and Laos have also emigrated over there.

New Caledonia for the most part has remained a "tourist" secret to the joy of its inhabitants. Its natural beauty and resources are largely unknown to the rest of the world.

I still feel nostalgia when I think of this paradise, I had the privilege to live on.

It is in part due to the memories of my personal life, but also when I think of New Caledonia, it represents to me a marvel of nature tucked far away at the end of the world.

God has blessed us with such a beautiful planet. Many wonderful sites could have been the original paradise created for Adam and Eve. To me, New Caledonia is one of them, at least while I lived there. Things might have changed nowadays, but still the people living there now feel secluded, privileged, and are highly protective of their beloved *Caillou*, an affectionate term to which they refer to their remote island.

British explorer James Cook was the first European to sight New Caledonia, on September 4, 1774. During his second voyage, he named it New Caledonia, as the Northeast of the island reminded him of Scotland. The first missionaries arrived in the 1840s. The crew of the American ship *Cutter* was killed and eaten by the Pouma native Kanak Clan as the story goes. Cannibalism was widespread throughout New Caledonia. As the tale says, "If warriors eat their enemies, they will gain their strength."

Formal possession of New Caledonia by the French, under orders from Emperor Napoleon III, took place in 1853.

New Caledonia became a penal colony in 1864. France sent about 22,000 criminals and political prisoners. After they were granted amnesty in 1880, some settled on the island and became the foundation, the original stock of the French population. Their descendants still live on the island today.

In 1864, nickel was discovered and prompted the establishment of the *Societe Le Nickel* in 1876. The same company where my dad found work in 1970.

To work the mines, the French imported laborers from neighboring islands, as well as, from Japan, the Dutch East Indies, and French Indochina. The French government attempted to encourage European immigration, without much success. A hundred years later, it was the opposite and restrictions had to be imposed on European voluntary immigration. The influx of people moving from France was uncontrollable. The island had grown in reputation for its quality of life and freedom from French politics.

The indigenous population, the Kanak people, were excluded from the French economy and from mining work, and ultimately confined in reservations. This confinement sparked violent reactions and numerous guerrillas started a Kanak rebellion.

Europeans brought new diseases such as smallpox and measles, which caused the deaths of many natives. The Kanak population declined from around 60,000 in 1878 to 27,100 in 1921.

As mentioned above, New Caledonia became an important Allied base in 1942. It was the main South Pacific Fleet base of the United States Navy. The very fleet which fought off the Japanese Navy in the Battle of the Coral Sea.

In 1946, New Caledonia became an overseas territory. By 1953, French citizenship had been granted to all New Caledonians, regardless of ethnicity.

Numerous conflicts went on between the French Government and the Kanak independence movement provoking violence and disorder. It started while I was still living there in 1976. Division still goes on today and new agreements seem to always be in the making.

At the time we arrived in New Caledonia in the early 1970s, the economy was booming and because of the opportunities there was an influx of people coming from France.

My dad rapidly found work with the *Societe du Nickel*. He also started dating and was really enjoying his life. Two of the women he dated had a positive impact on my own life. He eventually married one of them. Her name was Arunny, and we became close. Our relationship lasted for the remainder of her life.

I entered the work force myself and landed a variety of assignments with local businesses through a temporary placement agency. I eventually found a full-time position and became the administrative assistant of the director of the *Credit Foncier et Immobilier de la Nouvelle Caledonie*, a bank specialized in loans for businesses and real estate. My year studying in Paris resulting in my secretarial diploma was paying off. Thank You, Mother, your reasoning offered practical and tangible results.

My relationship with Federico, whom of course I had reconnected with, took a serious turn. We rapidly moved in together, became engaged in a few short months, and got married. I was expecting my first child. In a way, the decision we made to tie the knot was really because of my pregnancy and was encouraged by the people around us as the right thing to do. Our story could be construed as a teen drama between two people who barely knew each other. It was infatuation for me. I was immature, insecure, naive, and starved for love and attention. I am not sure what feelings Federico really had for me but getting married was obviously something he felt compelled to do due to circumstances.

Federico was dynamic, full of enthusiasm, and highly energetic, you could even say to the point of being hyper. I was always impressed by his variety of interests and drive to succeed. He did well in his trade as an electrician and eventually partnered with a friend who was a plumber and the two of them formed a thriving service company with more customers than they could handle.

He loved the great outdoors and was athletic. Daring and without fear, he preferred slightly dangerous and exciting sports. He would go spearfishing and deep dive with just a mask, fins, snorkel, and a speargun. Learning how to hold his breath for a long time and never intimidated by the impressive sea creatures he would encounter, it was common for him to grab a huge turtle, manta ray, or even a small shark, ride their back, and swim away holding on to them under the water for as long as he could. Scuba diving was one of his favorite sports. It allowed him to explore the grand barrier coral reef and at times bring back impressive fish from the deep. We never lacked seafood and it was our main source of protein. Huge lobsters were on the menu all the time. He was not afraid to pick up coral snakes either. He had fun throwing them at me while running after me on the beach. I was terrified and he knew it, having a great time as I would scream in terror.

He learned to pilot small airplanes and took me along, occasionally. He became confident flipping the plane over and letting it free drop for a while until I would beg him to stop. Flying over the reef and lagoon offered spectacular views.

He was an exciting guy to say the least. Our relationship was shallow and based on the superficial and physical, but I did not realize it then. My own observation of my parents' life together had not offered me a model or a substantial example of what to expect in my marriage.

Our life together lasted a few short years. We made friends with several couples, we all worked hard, and played hard. We maximized the lifestyle the islands offered.

Most weekends, we would go boating, fishing, snorkeling, sailing with our friends and would spend the weekends on one of the numerous deserted islets. We enjoyed a private island for just our little group and would sleep on the boat at night. Having parties on the beach in the evening, cooking, drinking, dancing, listening to good old music from the 70s era around a bonfire and storytelling, created a grand time in a utopian South Sea setting.

The pregnancy with my first child was precarious and I almost had a miscarriage a couple of times. The doctor's advice was to stay put and constantly lay down to prevent a premature birth. Giving birth to my first daughter was an ordeal and left me weak for several months. She was a beautiful angel, and we named her Laetitia. At the age of approximately 11 months, she suddenly passed away.

On a fatal day, I dropped her off at her childcare as usual in the morning on my way to work. By noon time, Federico called me and told me to come home immediately. He said we had to rush to the hospital. His words, "The little one is dead." I did not connect with what he said at first. He had to repeat a few times. Whose "little one" was he talking about. When he said her name, Laetitia, I realized he was talking about our daughter. We rushed to the hospital, and taken to a room where Laetitia, whom I did not recognize at first because she had lost all colors, was laying on a slab … white as a sheet with her eyes closed. She was gone.

Why, why, why … we asked. We were told she experienced "crib death." She simply stopped breathing in her sleep. There was never another explanation given. The people who watched her at the childcare where it happened said she was sleeping and when they went to check on her, they immediately realized something was wrong, and they called the ambulance. Nobody knew when she stopped breathing. They tried reanimation to no avail. To this day, the details of her passing are still a complete mystery to me.

What followed is not something I can easily describe. I went into a state of shock and disbelief. Truly, I did not let myself grieve. I felt so alone and empty. A total state of separation and isolation. Nowhere to go. The people surrounding me physically removed me from the situation. At the funeral, I was taken away before the end of the ceremony and did not attend to most of it. Our daughter's death became a subject we never discussed. It was taboo and buried with her.

My own dad made a devastating comment not realizing the magnitude of the impact it had on me. He suggested, had I raised my daughter at home myself instead of working and leaving her in a daycare she most likely would still be with us. Guilt added to my sense of loss. Subconsciously, I shut down and suppressed all emotions. I was not letting myself feel anything. The pain was unbearable, so I buried it deep inside and pretended everything was fine.

I know Laetitia was an Angel. She belonged in God's realm. I believe today she was a messenger of God. I was not ready. If anything, it probably reinforced the belief God was not merciful.

I have never let myself heal completely over the abrupt loss and sudden death of my first daughter.

This was approximately the time when my mother reconnected and resurfaced in my life. She had been informed about the passing of Laetitia and asked if she could come and visit us all the way to

New Caledonia from Morocco.

She also had suffered a terrible loss. Her second husband, the travel agent I had met who got me the cruise position, had died after they had been married just a few short months. She took it very hard.

We were all going through trying times and experiencing various stages of mourning, loss, and grief.

Mother was still a travel agent. Her late husband had bequeathed his travel agency to her. He did not have any family members he could or wanted to leave it to.

She came to visit with us, and I do not recall her visit to be a positive one. She and Federico did not get along to say the least. It was the first time she had met him. It turns out neither of my parents made a positive connection with Federico. They did not care for his "peacock style attitude" towards them. He could be abrupt with his choice of words at times when addressing certain people whom he had made a "judgment" about rapidly without attempting to know them.

But my mother and I had reconnected, and, in a way, I was happy about it. Her strength of character was still evident. We decided to remain in touch, and she invited us to come and pay her a visit in Morocco in the near future.

Federico and I decided to take a much-needed vacation and probably felt getting away would allow us to "heal" our deep wounds. A two-fold trip was decided upon. France and Morocco.

Our marriage was rocky. Nobody's fault. We were not a good match for each other. We had different opinions and outlooks on most subjects. The passing of our first daughter did not improve our relationship either, we were just growing further apart.

We flew half the planet around since New Caledonia and France are on the opposite side of the world.

We landed in Nice, France, where Federico's family lived. It was my first time meeting his parents, sister, and other members of his family. I felt welcome and started a close relationship with his mom. She reminded me of my grandma. A woman fully dedicated to her family, an incredible hostess and by far the best cook I had ever met. Italian home cooking was her specialty. She had a big heart and was kind to me.

Federico's parents originated from Italy.

To my dismay, I witnessed when the family reunited and shared a big meal together, this "other" woman was invited as part of the clan and held a place of honor at the table. No one present seemed to have any issues with it. I was told she was the "mistress."

Federico's dad was the patriarch type and ruled over the family. In part due to his cultural background, he boasted infidelity as normal and widely accepted in his world. His wife was essentially the respected mother of his children and in charge of all domestic tasks and mistresses were tolerated, even well accepted. The wife had to come to terms with it. It was a common occurrence in the Italian culture.

This explained and helped me understand certain traits of my own husband's behavior. I already knew this was not something I could or would accept in my own house. I had not been raised in this patriarchal culture and it was against what I believed to be acceptable in a marriage.

Morocco was a great trip, we stayed in Marrakech in a five-star hotel. My mother, being a travel agent, had perks and connections. We were spoiled on the trip and catered to like royalty. The only negative was Federico's sarcastic attitude towards my mother. He was not used to strong independent women. What I had witnessed in his family confirmed women did not really have a voice as far as he was concerned.

We found our way back to New Caledonia eventually.

I was expecting a baby again. This time, the pregnancy went well. I gave birth to another beautiful girl we named Sophie.

Sophie's birth did not improve our relationship. One of my fears had come true and Federico was not the faithful type. I had known this for a long time even prior to meeting his parents but chose to pretend it was not real. Eventually, we separated and filed for divorce. Our daughter was about two years old and in my custody.

At some point, I realized living in New Caledonia did not feel right anymore. A small town where everybody knew everyone. Small town mentality. Scrutinizing others and judging them seemed to be a favorite pass time. There was nowhere to hide my pain as I fought through hardships.

I had a car accident driving alone one night. The old car tumbled over a small bridge with no ramps on either side. The car fell into a creek below which fortunately for me was practically dry at the time. Sophie was not with me that night. I had lost consciousness and was found hours later by someone who noticed the car in the creek. I had flown through the shattered windshield and landed on a pile of rocks. I was taken to the local hospital still unconscious. A bad concussion from a direct blow to the head, double whiplash, and some broken ribs required quite a bit of recovery time in the hospital. Sophie stayed with a close friend. I recovered and decided to leave the territory of New Caledonia.

Meanwhile my mom had sold her travel agency in Morocco. Colonialism was fading away and the Moroccan government was forcing foreign business owners to take in a Moroccan partner and split their interests 50/50 or more. It was called *Moroccanization*. In 1973, the government required Moroccan majority ownership in many firms and established state financing for this program. Mother said no and preferred to sell at a loss undoubtedly. She had known this was coming for a long time and had prepared for it through a slow transition.

She bought a travel agency in Nice, France. The owners were aging and wanted to retire. She kept a couple of the former employees and moved her living quarters right above the agency where a small apartment was included in the deal.

She knew about my divorce situation, my car accident, and all my troubles. She could relate to my precarious position knowing Federico, whom she did not like anyway.

She suggested Sophie and I move back to France and offered a temporary situation staying with her. I accepted the offer.

Sophie's grandparents from her father's side lived in Nice as well and were eager for us to be there.

Federico's mom dreamed of being a grandmother to Sophie and was thrilled at the idea of having her nearby.

We made the move back to France, where I ended up working for my mother and sharing her little apartment.

During most weekends, we visited with Sophie's grandparents.

What could have been an opportunity for recovery, both physically and emotionally, was fraught with discord. Sophie became a weapon for Federico, who never forgave me for my decision to leave him. He chose to fight for Sophie's custody, opening a case on the grounds I was unfit to be a mother and did not have a stable life to offer our daughter. Forced to fight this battle long distance, the lawyers made the process unnecessarily ugly. Not only did I not have the financial means to fight back, but stress played havoc in my life. I acknowledge not being emotionally available, stable, or of any support to anyone including my daughter. I made mistakes. I paid a high price at every level but in the end, I got custody anyway.

My mom's assistance was invaluable during this time, but I did not see it. She did not spare me her justified opinions or console me. Displays of affection were not her personality. She told me the truth as she saw it. I both hated and much later in life appreciated this aspect of my mother. She was and had always been strong and resilient. It was her nature, and she had proven it many times over during her life. I displayed weakness and she did not accept it. Her actions towards me were one of tangible and material help, not giving in to my emotional distress. She wanted me to be strong and not feel sorry for myself. Looking back, I am grateful because she rescued me. She did her best for me within the scope of her perception, and own view of the reality of my situation.

Her travel agency in Nice was not doing well, and it became a struggle to keep it afloat. She was tired of working hard for little results and decided to sell. Then she relocated to Paris where she purchased two apartments with a view, both overlooking the popular Park Monsouris in the 14th district of Paris.

This beautiful public park was created under Napoleon III, inspired by parks in London. It is one of the largest green spaces in Paris. It comprises of a lake frequently visited by a variety of water birds, beautiful statues, remarkable species of rare exotic trees, a restaurant, walking paths with inviting benches, and beautifully matured landscaping.

She decided to live in one apartment and rent the other as a source of income. Smart decision. It worked out well for her.

Paris also became my next step. I moved there and started working for a temp agency with weekly or daily assignments throughout the city. I took the subway every morning and evening. I rented a small studio not far from where my mother lived. Sophie was going to preschool. I dropped her off in the morning and picked her up at night. It was hard for both of us. My morale was going from bad to worse. My mom got involved with Sophie and would pick her up from preschool for me. They spent time together. Mother was still transitioning from Nice to Paris.

Sophie and I took a pleasant interlude to go visit with my grandma whom I had not seen in several years and had never met Sophie. The two of us travelled by train. Our last leg of the trip took us near my grandma's village. A tiny terminus about two miles away from where she lived. She walked to pick us up. When we met with her, it was a joyful reunion and warmed my heart. Grandma did not have any means of transportation and she thoughtfully brought a wheel barrel in which to put our suitcases. This was so unique and touching. I am so glad I had a camera with me to catch this moment. I still have the pictures and they deserve to be shown. This was the last time I saw my grandmother before life events would take me away again. The few days spent with her are precious memories.

Grandma pushing a wheel barrel loaded with our luggage. So precious!!!

Grandma, Sophie, and me. Wonderful and heartwarming memory

We returned to Paris and resumed our stressful life.

We would occasionally take the train and spend weekends with Sophie's grandparents in Nice. They offered to keep her for a while and told me her dad had asked them to intervene. Everyone felt it would be in Sophie's best interest if she remained with them for a while until I became stable in my own life and was able to spend more time with my daughter instead of leaving her in a daycare. After a few trips, I could see their attitude towards me changing and the pressure was on. My situation was challenging, unstable and I did not feel welcome anymore. I was becoming the enemy because of my resistance cooperating with them. They had the blessings of Sophie's father and persisted. In the end, I gave in and ended up leaving Sophie in their care with the understanding it would be temporarily. I am not proud of my actions then, and I have no excuses for leaving my daughter behind even in the care of her grandparents. The series of events following are not clear in my mind, but it is certain I did not fight hard enough to keep Sophie with me.

Federico had visitation rights, she eventually returned to New Caledonia suppositively for a couple of months before she would come back to France and to me as per our custodial agreements. He never sent her back. Apparently, he had someone stable in his life in a serious relationship. Her father and life partner decided to keep her. Federico took me back to court and reopened the case claiming Sophie's custody for a second time. The new battle he engaged in against me lasted a few years. In the meantime, I did not see her, and we lost all contact.

I was a wreck. I did not have a clear vision for my life. I was reacting and feeling sorry for myself. The sense of void and emptiness was at an all-time high. The accumulation of recent hardships took a toll on me. A combination of emotional, mental, physical, and psychological distress I could no longer bear. In dire need of nurturing, acceptance, compassion, and probably even sympathy, I underwent a form of deep depression where life no longer had any appeal or meaning. I did not have a support system. No friends nearby. My mom helped me to the best of her ability when needed but did not show much empathy. I don't know how long I remained in this shape. I kept on working and became involved in an abusive relationship to top it off.

Then one day, alone in my apartment, I decided the best solution was to end my misery. I swallowed a lot of pills. I did not know if I had enough of them to put an end to my life as I was no expert in how to commit suicide. I had no idea of the "dos and don'ts," and certainly had not studied the subject. Interestingly, after taking the pills, I walked to my mother's place, about 45 minutes away. Survival instinct is real. By the time I got there, and she opened the door, I had started feeling the effects. She immediately knew something was wrong and after realizing what I had done, she took me to the bathroom and forced me to throw up. I don't remember what happened next, but it was a long night for both of us. She said I slept for 24 hours straight. She was not happy with me and for just cause. So, in the end, I was rescued by my mother again.

I still wonder today if my objective had not been a desperate attempt to get her attention, the kind of attention I was starving for. She truly was a key and powerful figure in my life, and I had always been deeply longing for her acceptance, her nurturing and the expression of her love. Practical help was her style, and I was not seeing it.

Regardless of my relationship with my mother, I personally made bad choices and inevitably paid the consequences. This was a time in my life where it was much easier to feel and act like a victim. I reacted as if I did not have any control over what happened to me. I saw no future and blamed others for my circumstances. The price was also paid by Sophie who lacked stability. I take part of the blame and accountability for my errors and lack of awareness.

Time went by. I truly do not have a clear memory of the following years. Then one day my mother, who always liked changes and new opportunities, came up with a fantastic idea.

Her sister, my aunt Marianne, had moved to California many years before. She had married an American soldier after the war, and he took her back to the US.

Mother said, "Let's go visit Marianne in Los Angeles." The trip was planned. Marianne was delighted to welcome us to her home. She had divorced and remarried. Her second husband was a charming Russian who had emigrated to the US and used to be a Cossack dancer back in his younger days while he lived in Ukraine.

CALIFORNIA

I was shocked at the size of the city of Los Angeles. Mesmerized by the complexity of the freeways and the incessant traffic. My aunt lived in an apartment complex with a swimming pool in the Laurel Canyon area. Her husband was pleasant with a great sense of humor. He loved to tell stories about his life before America, especially being part of a troupe of professional Cossack Dancers performing all over the world including the United States.

They had a big comfortable American car and took us on various excursions and short trips to visit not only the surrounding areas but beautiful parts of California. I loved every minute of it. I enjoyed their company. They were retired, active, and took advantage of all the area had to offer. Fun was on the horizon again and I was regaining a taste for life. The weather was outstanding. Sunshine every day. They introduced us to a few of their friends. Life was good. I was getting along with them. Practicing my English each day especially with my new "uncle" who did not speak French, and I certainly could not have a conversation in Russian. He had a big heart. We truly liked each other. He loved to joke with me at my funny and broken British English. I think he enjoyed practicing conversation with me for my exclusive benefit.

I was not looking forward to returning to France whatsoever. But after all, we were there just for a visit.

It turned out my mom and aunt clashed again, even though they were now adults and had not seen each other since they were teens. They were both highly opinionated and strong-minded individuals. When they disagreed, instead of finding ground for consensus, they just kept on arguing in a futile attempt to prove each other wrong.

My aunt Marianne had similarities of character with her sister.

She had a mind of her own too. Overweight to the point of obesity, she had health issues. She was an outstanding cook and especially loved to make desserts. Her famous cheesecake was to die for and just one bite probably had 1000 calories in it. It was huge and she would serve us generous portions and would not take it lightly if we left any on our plates.

The apartment was not spacious and with the four of us, it got crowded at times. Especially with the two sisters in competition with each other.

To my consternation, one day, mother decided to shorten the trip and announced abruptly we were going to leave sooner than planned.

I loved it there. The idea of returning to France just did not appeal to me and I resisted.

I knew without the shadow of a doubt returning to France was not what I was called to do. Every fiber of my being screamed, "NO" A wave of stress submerged me when I imagined returning to the doom and gloom of my daily grind. I knew subconsciously our trip to California was not a coincidence. I belonged where I was, and I had to find a way to make it come true.

Divine providence was with me. God's plan was unfolding.

(Jeremiah 29:11 *NIV*)

"For I know the plans I have for you," declares the LORD, "plans to prosper you and not to harm you, plans to give you hope and a future."

Our Creator knew what life scenarios, circumstances, and experiences I needed to bring me to Him in acknowledgement, recognition, and ultimately repentance. We think everything we do is what we want to do, while also being a part of God's plan. A mystery too big for us to fully grasp.

After mother's decision was made clear, aunt Marianne and her husband both sat down the next morning as we were having coffee and made a suggestion to my mom. What I heard came to me as a wonderful surprise.

I immediately understood they meant every word they said. They came across clearly with a choice of phrases speaking to my heart.

They proposed I stay with them indefinitely. It was just the two of them they said, away from family. Having me around would brighten their life and make it more enjoyable. They had time, they were eager, and already making all sorts of plans for me. The thought of my presence in their lives gave them a whole new outlook, excitement, and purpose. Hope was building up within me and I could not help but show my joy. Mother did not see any reason to resist our enthusiasm. I was an adult and could make my own decisions. She thought it was a great idea and a unique opportunity for me to start over in a new country and in a part of the US the whole world envied. California was looked upon as the land of opportunity, freedom, and beauty, especially from overseas.

She left, and to my delight I stayed.

Life was taking a positive turn as well as my state of mind. I experienced lightness and happiness. A huge weight was lifted off my shoulders. I began looking forward to each day. Gratefulness and thankfulness filled me. A feeling of joy emerged. My long-term depression melted. A constructive, optimistic, and enthusiastic outlook was arising.

A lot happened in the following months. I made new connections. New acquaintances. New friends.

I quickly realized my aunt Marianne had something in mind. She enjoyed being a matchmaker and set off to get me into a romantic situation. She belonged to several ladies' clubs, and they all had connections. Soon enough, the word spread. A French niece from Paris, France had arrived on the scene and was available. She took me to various functions with her and my social life went into overdrive.

I was being "shown off," on "display," and to be truthful, I liked it. My aunt was proud of me and emphasized a side of me I had not really experienced before. I realized I was attractive and received a lot of attention, in deep contrast with the previous tragic episodes endured before. The attention I received was overwhelming and, yes, got to my head to a degree. After all, I lived in California where social life can be superficial and emphasizes physical appearance and glamour over more substantial qualities. Conversations don't go deep when the focus is on the outer façade. Not much under the veneer.

I explored a side of me I was not familiar with. Always starved for attention, now I bloomed. The prevailing problem was the unending void lingering behind the immediate fun. Flattering, yes, but not the right kind of attention and one-dimensional.

Then, I met my second husband to be, Karl. Originally from Sweden, his family had emigrated to the States for a couple of generations. We really hit it off and liked each other. Good hearted and kind, he was a salesman in the computer business. He was not the kind of guy my aunt would have picked for me. She preferred a lawyer she had introduced me to and was disappointed when Karl and I decided to be serious about each other. Status mattered to my aunt, who became angry, feeling I had let her down.

After a few months, another reality set in. It so happened my legal status in the country would not allow me to stay. I needed a green card to legally remain. Karl and I most likely would have dated longer given the opportunity, but under the circumstances he asked me to marry him. I accepted. His brother and wife, who lived in Los Angeles, approved, and welcomed me in the family.

The wedding date was set. My mother came back for the occasion. My aunt and her husband also attended. After the wedding, we set off for Palm Springs in a huge motorhome, owned by his brother who loaned it to us for our honeymoon.

Then, we moved into a little house with a small swimming pool. Karl resumed working, and as for me, well, I started to look for work. Again, the solution was at first a temp agency, Kelly Girls. They sent me all over the place on various short assignments. I was driving Karl's suburban, a huge car and remember how scared I was at first driving this enormous automobile on the freeway. I got lost many times. When he could, he would drive me and pick me up.

I recall once being sent as a replacement receptionist to the Actors Guild office on Wilshire Blvd. A prestigious office. I mention it because one day Sydney Poitier walked in, and I was the first person he spoke to. It was my first encounter with a famous American actor, and I was thrilled.

Our life was hectic and busy.

This is when, still in court fighting for Sophie's custody for the second time but having won visitation rights, she came for a long visit during her school vacation. I was excited at the prospect of reconnecting with her, but at the same time apprehensive. We had been a few years apart without any connection and I knew her father had a serious relationship with a woman who was involved in raising Sophie. Her name was Nathalie.

It was an awkward time. I had remarried and was now living in the USA. My daughter was about 7 years old. Karl and I picked her up at the Los Angeles airport for a visit that was going to last a couple of months.

Seeing Sophie again was joyful for me. I dreamed of reconnecting with her as her mother. We both were nervous, which caused tension at times. She spoke a lot about Nathalie and how much she loved her. She did not respond to me the way I had hoped. She behaved like she was visiting a family member, possibly a friend even. My attempts to connect as a mother to daughter were not fruitful. She kept her distance. It was an emotional rollercoaster for me. I was not sure how to react and behave. We were on shaky ground, with no roots or foundation established between us. I felt like an outsider. She referred to her mom and dad back in New Caledonia. When she said "mom" she was speaking of Nathalie. So, I concentrated on making sure she had a good time and a fun vacation. She did not want anything beyond.

Overall, she enjoyed her vacation with us. We had a beagle named Curly and she was having fun throwing him in the pool. Karl and I did our best to entertain her and make her feel right at home. She did not speak English, so I was her voice. She absolutely loved fast food and particularly Wendy's hamburgers.

By the time she left, we had established a friendly report. She had fun, but she also clearly showed how happy she was to go back to New Caledonia. She missed her life over there.

A few months later, to my immense surprise, I was granted custody once again. I was stunned and overwhelmed with excitement. Here was my long-expected opportunity to be able to get Sophie in my territory with no outside interference. My life was stable. I was ready and could care for her while at the same time, we would be building a long overdue mother and daughter team. I started to dream and organize our new life together in California.

My time had come to be a mother. I was getting prepared for our return home with Sophie not as a guest but as a full fledge member of our household. I had the full support of Karl who did not have any children of his own. I am grateful to him as he truly did everything in his power to facilitate my reunion with my daughter.

Shortly thereafter, we were on our way to New Caledonia to pick her up. I was also looking forward to going back to my beloved island for other reasons.

I had not seen my dad in several years and he had remarried with a wonderful woman originally from Cambodia. Arunny, whom I had met and bonded with prior to my departure from the island a few years back.

This was such a special time in my life. Going back to New Caledonia was so meaningful to me, an island I missed then and still miss now. Seeing my dad again and getting better acquainted with Arunny filled me with joy.

In truth, the excitement was mixed with a big dose of anxiety. The big question mark was Sophie's reaction to her moving with me and Karl and starting a new life in California with the two of us, away from her "family" and familiar island life. While on vacation with us, her behavior had indicated she was in a visiting mode but anxious to return home.

The bulk of my anxiety was about Federico. How was he going to react? He had shown such animosity, antagonism, and carried on relentless attacks against my character throughout the years of battle for divorce and custody. I was terribly apprehensive and the idea of seeing him froze me to the core. I could not somehow prepare myself for the encounter. I knew it was not going to be easy to face him. Little did I know it would be even worse than I thought.

After a long flight with a stopover in the Fiji's islands, we got to the Tontouta airport in New Caledonia where my dad waited for us. He was happy to see me and meet Karl. I was the interpreter. Neither Arunny nor my dad spoke any English.

They both had followed the tragic years of my legal battles with Federico and did not seem positive and encouraging regarding the outcome. They did not want to see him themselves. The relationship between them was nonexistent.

The next day, I made provisions to pick up Sophie and discuss how we were going to make the transition. I was not planning on abruptly taking her away from familiar surroundings because I realized how traumatic it could be for a young girl. I understood a few days were necessary to prepare her to make the transition as smooth as possible.

I needed to be sensitive to Sophie and her emotional needs. I knew too well how the lack of sensitivity and empathy from my parents made me feel at the same age. I instinctively sensed how paramount it was to reverse behavior with Sophie. I was myself emotionally fragile and apprehensive. I followed my instincts and did what I believed was best for both of us given the circumstances.

I had the court order in my favor, therefore all the right and justification to be there. But Federico made it clear right away, I was not welcome, and he resented the legal outcome. He had no intention of cooperating, but we finally agreed, in the next few days, to give Sophie some time to adapt to the transition. I could pick her up in the morning and bring her back at a set time in the afternoon.

This is when I met Nathalie, his new wife to be then, for the first time. I must admit in contrast with Federico's behavior, she was polite, and even showed kindness and some compassion towards me.

So, the next morning, I picked my daughter up to spend the day together.

She stated again both her and Nathalie had a close relationship and referred to her as "my mom," which set the tone. Sophie was about eight years old, and Nathalie was expecting a child herself. The year this all happened must have been between 1980 or 1981. Sophie's half-sister Isabelle was born in 1981.

The coming of her half-sister may also have influenced and reinforced Sophie's decision to remain in New Caledonia. She became close to Isabelle and still is today.

As the days went by, I sensed no desire from Sophie to leave her "nest." In her mind, we were just visiting, and she never showed any inclination to come back with me to California. Rather, she adopted a behavior much like her father toward me. Distancing herself, the connection between us was becoming more tense every day.

When I spoke about the plans we had for her in California, she showed no interest whatsoever.

She did not try to connect with her grandfather, my dad, either. She became hostile toward all of us.

We were at a turning point, a major crossroad, and the outcome would impact our relationship for years to come. Possibly even our lifetime.

I reminded her we were leaving in the next couple of days and let her know she was loved and at the brink of starting an exciting life in a new country and made it as attractive, reassuring, and safe as I could.

Her reply was decisive and without any ambiguity. She restated I was not her mother; she had a mother already and her name was Nathalie. She wanted to stay with her and her father. She told me to return where I came from, and she was not going with us. - End of Story -

I was shocked. In a way, it was like I was losing my second daughter who did not recognize me as her mother. The choice was made, and life consequences would follow for us both.

With stabbing pain in my heart, we dropped her off at her father's house.

Uncontrolled emotional reactions followed for a while on my part, and I let it all out. Crying, sobbing, shaking while I was awakening to the reality my relationship with my second daughter had utterly failed.

I had to make my own choices. I could force her to go with me since I had the legal right to do so but how would such a decision affect her already fragile and vulnerable mind-heart coherency. More damage most likely would follow. I remembered when my own mother forced me into an airplane to leave Morocco on my way to a Catholic boarding school in France. I felt devastated.

A lot of hard thinking began. A wee small voice spoke to me.

From her perspective, I was not really her mother and obviously someone else had taken my role. Someone whom she had formed a bond with and who now had become her "mother." Part of me understood. She was a child and I had not been present in her life when she needed me the most.

It became manifest she belonged where she wanted to be. I could not find it in my heart to force her to follow us.

That evening, and with the guidance and opinion of my dad, his wife, and Karl who had been witnesses all along, we discussed the situation in detail. Their opinion was definite. Let her stay with her father and new "mother." My dad said, "You are young. You are starting a new life with Karl. You can still have other children. Let her go."

Letting her go indeed seemed the wisest decision I could make.

I turned the page and chose visitation rights with the hope time would work in our favor.

After seeing Sophie one more time the next morning, it was clear and without the shadow of a doubt her attitude from the day before had not changed a bit. I told her I would not force her to follow me. She could stay with her dad and new mom. She did not hide how much relief she felt. We said goodbye.

I went back to court while I was still there and signed papers stating I was giving up my custodial rights. I kept visitation rights once a year during school vacation.

I sensed this was the right decision for the highest good of all. Time eventually would be on my side.

A couple of days later, Karl, who had been supportive all along and I returned to California.

On our last evening at my father's house, his wife Arunny went out of her way cooking a great meal. I specifically remember it was *Osso Bucco*. I don't know why this detail stayed with me. But it was an outstanding meal. She really tried to help comfort me. I was not doing well with raw emotions unraveling. I could not hold back my pain and tears. I knew the episode I had gone through would take me a long time to overcome emotionally. The long road to healing started again. I struggled with the idea of having made the right decision. Arunny knew it too and she demonstrated how much she understood and cared. Everyone witnessed my anguish and reassured me. Under the circumstances, I had done the right thing.

The next day, my dad drove us back to the airport. I still picture him waving at me for as long as he was able to see me through the windows before boarding the plane. This image remains vivid in my mind. It was the last time I saw him alive.

BACK TO CALIFORNIA

arl and I settled back into our routines. I did not feel like myself. All the excitement I had built up, the preparations I had made, the plans I had forged … the hope of becoming a mother to my daughter. All of it had collapsed like a house of cards.

Lost in my own turmoil, I was just trying to put the pieces back together and keep my sanity. Broken hearted and on the edge of depression again, the feeling of guilt was overwhelming, and I came to believe I was just not fit to be a mother.

This was also the time when my relationship with Karl began to suffer. I had my problems, and he had his own. I appreciated many of the qualities he had demonstrated but also overlooked a couple of undesirable addictions.

There were signs I chose to ignore when Karl and I started to cohabit. This type of behavior was occasional and certainly did not impact our lives together, but once we returned from New Caledonia, these tendencies became more and more frequent. His habits were not something I could easily live with and included a problem with alcohol and marijuana. I confronted him, but he was not inclined in the least to acknowledge the issues.

So, the inevitable began, we started drifting away.

We both really cared about each other. But I could not understand nor accept his drinking and smoking "pot" choices. Every time I would talk about it, he pushed me away and ignored my requests. Eventually, I gave up asking him to deal with the situation. Life continued and time went by.

Then one day, I received a telegram from New Caledonia informing me my father was in the hospital. He had advanced stage cancer of the liver and pancreas. The doctors gave him a few weeks to live. He was in his late 50s. When I spoke to Arunny on the phone, she was highly pessimistic. He had no symptoms when I saw him a few months before while in New Caledonia. The illness had developed quickly. She explained he was a shadow of himself and in a few short weeks had become barely recognizable. I immediately decided to fly to New Caledonia. When my father knew about my plan, he refused to let me come. He wanted me to remember him the way he was when I last saw him. His words were kind towards me, but he was firm. Arunny was the only person he would agree to see. She explained not only had his physical appearance drastically changed, but his mental and emotional state were unbearable. He was not himself anymore. She also felt it best for me not to be there.

She kept in touch almost every day and related the progression of his condition. She told me he became delusional. His last words described what he was seeing in the other realm… visions of the Sphinx waiting for him on the other side of the veil.

The Sphinx is a symbolic mythical creature. According to mythological stories, the Greek Sphinx was known for her riddle and death penalties as a result for wrong answers and the Egyptian Sphinx was considered more compassionate and sympathetic by the Egyptians. Both Sphinx were used to guard entrances of temples.

I do not know why he had these types of vision.

He passed away within a matter of days after refusing to see me.

After his death, I started having nightmares. I would wake up in the middle of the night, distinctly feeling a dark presence between the bed and the wall. I was terrified. Karl did not know what to do. So, I stayed up and kept the lights on all the time. Being in the dark was intolerable. I felt under attack.

It lasted for days, maybe weeks. I could not deal with this sense of panic on my own. We decided to find help and seek counseling with a psychologist. It took a while and a lot of digging into memories and family matters before it was suggested I confront my fear instead of letting it get the best of me. I found the courage to speak directly to the "entity" trying to get my attention. It took a while before I was able to calm down. I asked for help from above. The answer came little by little as I felt guided. Possibly, my dad was not at peace and was trying to reach out. Eventually all the anxiety and anguish vanished when I made peace with him and let him go through acceptance and forgiveness. Asking him to let go of this earth and continue his journey.

An angel must have intervened.

ON MY OWN IN CALIFORNIA

It became clear to me I could not continue my relationship with Karl. His habits impacted my life negatively. On some evenings after we settled home from work and always on the weekends, he would start drinking and smoking until he passed out on the sofa and spent the night there with the television on. In the morning, I was confronted with a mess to clean up including broken bottles. When under the influence, his behavior changed. He could be incoherent, confused, rude, and display anger targeted at me.

I was not pleasant to be around, in all sincerity. I had a relapse of the old days of gloom and doom. I was slowly emerging from dark moments, seeing a psychologist regularly, had lots of ups and downs, and still fighting depression, rejection, and loss. I was taking antidepressants.

Being around me was challenging to say the least as I did not have much to give.

So, the blame is as much mine as it is Karl's habits. We were not helping nor supporting each other. We did more damage to one another than good.

We divorced by mutual agreement.

I found an apartment to share with a roommate who was an acquaintance of a friend. She was raising two young girls. I found out quickly my standards of cleanliness and lifestyle choices were different from hers and not compatible. It would have to do for the time being.

I was still working temporary secretarial or receptionist job assignments and was tired of it. I aspired to a stable full-time position where I could use my French language skills. I started looking and interviewing.

Fortunately for me I was living in a huge international city with an ethnically and culturally diverse population and a sprawling metropolitan area. My various short term work experiences had helped me acquire diverse skills, gain experience and exposure in different settings, and enabled me to improve my resume. I understood better the American workplace and had become comfortable networking. I knew a few people ready to give me good references. Even though my training was administrative, I was attracted to sales. Quite a few international corporations either had an office or were headquartered in Los Angeles. Back then, we still used classifieds in the newspapers. I contacted every company I thought would be suitable and constantly called and mailed out resumes to no avail for a while.

Finally, a French based company, known for its fine reproduction of high-end antique furniture made in Alsace Lorraine, was opening a showroom in Los Angeles and looking for a French speaking Showroom Manager.

I was interviewed several times by different people within the organization who had flown from France for the occasion. Multiple candidates applied, but I was selected in the end after a couple of weeks of anxious anticipation. This was my first full time position in management. I was so excited, not only by the job description, but the exceptional location. They opened their showroom in the Pacific Design Center in West Hollywood on Melrose Ave. The PDC became known as the Blue Whale because of its large size relative to surrounding buildings and its brilliant blue glass cladding. Known nationally and internationally as the world's most prestigious home to over 70 plus showrooms, the PDC represents over 2,200 leading manufacturers dedicated to the very best in residential and business interior furnishings, artwork, educational opportunities, and resource information.

I felt proud to have landed what I thought of as an eminent position for my real first full-time job in the USA. I looked at it as a career and was ready to accomplish whatever it took to make it a success. Training was provided in France before the official opening. The company flew me to their headquarters and taught me everything I needed to know in about two weeks of onsite training. When I returned, I felt ready to conquer the world selling their antique reproduction pieces to architects and interior designers. The showrooms were open to design trade professionals only and required admission first.

My personal life again took a bright turn. As I had when I moved to California from France, I went through a revival and comeback. Hope for the future resurfaced. Landing this full-time position in management had done wonders for my spirits and self-confidence. I felt uplifted with a sense of purpose. Excitement and a drive for achievement built up.

During this period, I met Liam, who owned the receiving and shipping facilities for the Pacific Design Center. Everything going in and out of the building went through his facility first.

Liam and I developed at first a business relationship. He stopped by the showroom every day. He had been part of the Pacific Design Center for many years, knew everyone, and proved to be a real help and support for me. He never hesitated to give me his input and provided me with numerous and useful tips. He genuinely wanted to see me succeed in this exciting but highly challenging world of glamour.

Politics played an important role and having the right connections meant everything. Liam never hesitated to give me the benefit of his own experience and truly helped me learn how to navigate this highly competitive and unforgivable environment. Mistakes were costly. Competition was ruthless.

Building the business was not so much the art of selling as it was the art of networking and who you knew. I learned so much. Having Liam in my business life was like having my own trusted adviser, a personal mentor.

Liam and I started to socialize outside of work when I realized he was remarkably knowledgeable about many subjects and enjoyed debates and substantial discussions on a variety of topics. We shared many great conversations for our mutual enrichment.

What made Liam so special was how different he was from most people I had met so far in California. There was nothing superficial about him and this caught my attention.

There was some romantic involvement, but it did not last. Our friendship did and still does. A true lifetime friend even if we do not communicate on a regular basis.

After a couple of years, life took us in different directions.

JULIETTE

Juliette deserves her own chapter.

Someone had highly recommended a spa owned by a French woman trained in France as a cosmetologist. I made an appointment for a facial. As I walked in, I received a warm welcome in French and was introduced to a lady by the name of Juliette. Everyone working there was from France. Of course, we started speaking our native language immediately. I was delighted by the quality of her service but most of all her demeanor was positive, and she showed a sincere and genuine interest beyond my expectations. She was gentle, spoke softly, always smiling with a sparkle in her eyes. I could not help but notice her warm and caring attitude. We found out quickly we both came from the same part of France which gave us something in common to talk about. By the end of my session, we exchanged phone numbers and promised to call each other. A couple of days went by, and we got in touch. We decided to meet somewhere and have coffee. The conversation we had set out the beginning of a friendship lasting as long as Juliette lived.

On our first encounter, we felt an immediate draw to each other. We met often. Each meeting was delightful and brought me a much-needed female friendship with a twist of motherly care as our relationship developed. She was about 20 years older than me and understood quickly I was in dire need of tender loving care.

Juliette was born somewhere in the Southwest of France. She was found on the porch of a church in Bordeaux as a tiny baby bundled up in a blanket. She had been abandoned. It was assumed her birth mother was probably a young woman, unmarried and poor who was forced into this difficult decision. It was not uncommon then for a young pregnant girl to be rejected by society.

Rescued by someone who found her, she was brought to a foster home. She had no identification on her.

Still a baby, she was adopted by a couple who called her Juliette. She described her adoptive mother as someone cold, mean, and bitter. She never received any affection and was frequently told she was nothing but a burden. She did not give me details about the specifics on how she was raised. It was clear these were painful memories she preferred to keep to herself or had buried in her subconscious. She often wondered why this couple adopted her. She never spoke much about the father figure, but he seemed to be more human and caring in her eyes.

As tragic as her early life appeared, she met her future husband at a young age, still a teen. She kept the sharing of her memories focused on her married life and beamed with happiness when reflecting on cherished times of their lives together. The story of her couple, as she told me, was one of perfect communion with each other. Total bliss. Soul mates. They were made for each other. When she described their relationship, she referred to their togetherness, mutual respect, unconditional love, and complete harmony. She spoke on how intertwined they were and enriched each other's lives at a deep soul level. She smiled when mentioning the many laughs, they shared without having to say a word, just a look. Her husband was the only person who knew her, accepted her, and believed in her before anyone else did or when no one else would. Their bond was transcendent, and they felt like one heart and one flesh.

(Genesis 2:24 NASB)

For this reason, a man shall leave his father and his mother, and be joined to his wife; and they shall become one flesh.

They met at a local farmer's market where her adoptive family had a vending booth. The mutual attraction was immediate. The courtship was short when he asked for her hand in marriage. After a few months of engagement, they tied the knot with the blessing of her adoptive parents who were eager to let her go. She was barely 17 years old. He was about 10 years older.

Shortly thereafter, her new husband was offered a career

opportunity in the United States. They relocated to New York where their first child, Adeline, was born.

They moved around within the United States for a few years and had another child, a boy they named Vincent. Then, her husband received a new work assignment overseas and they migrated to Mexico. They eventually relocated to California when the children were about 8 to 10 years old.

Their family unit enjoyed and shared many years of happiness together as their bond kept on getting stronger with time.

Then, at the family dinner table one evening shortly upon returning to the US, her husband experienced a massive heart attack, dying right in front of his wife and young children. He was healthy and there had been no warning signs. His death was sudden, unpredictable and a tragedy. The resulting devastation striking Juliette and her children is not something she could begin to put into words. Her emotions after all these years were still raw remembering the fatal night changing her and her children's lives forever.

She never fully recovered emotionally. Her eyes were filled with tears while telling me so many years later.

She was still young at the time of this misfortune, only in her early thirties. Alone, with two children to raise, she entered the workforce for the first time in her life and struggled through many hardships.

She also survived breast cancer and was in remission at the time we met.

Pain and suffering, regardless of origin, form, and depth, are an intricate and critical part of life, either weakening or strengthening our character. It is interesting to note how siblings or people who have similar traumatic experiences turn out to be quite different individuals. Some choose to remain in darkness, negativity, and become toxic. Others choose to be positive and turn to unconditional love and godly light. They are a joy to be around. Juliette was one of these people. The adversities she encountered, and heart-shattering experiences did not cause bitterness or resentment. She kept her head up and did not become discouraged. The love she felt for her children helped carry her throughout the years. They became her focus and solace. She was resilient and never complained. She had a sweet, giving heart and always reminded herself of her blessings.

Her attitude with me was one filled with love, caring, and attention. I noticed how she would always have a kind word or a smile for everyone on her path. She would never hesitate to help someone less fortunate than her. Her children adored her. The family of her late husband cherished her as she was always present for them in times of need as they got older. Especially her mother-in-law whom she remained close with to the end of her life. Her numerous friends raved about her and always made sure they remained in close contact.

Her vibes and positive energy created a cheerful environment. I loved to be with her and around her.

She had a beautiful home in Northridge, north of Los Angeles with a large swimming pool in her lush backyard. A 5-bedroom home and she rented a couple of rooms to supplement her income. One day, she suggested I move into her house when one of her rooms became available. The decision was easy, and I happily accepted. As an additional bonus, it brought me closer to my work.

Our friendship was a big part of our connection, but Juliette became like a mother to me. She included me in her family circle and treated me as a family member. She even used affectionate names for me such as "*Ma Poulette*," endearingly means "chickee-poo."

Her approach with me was firm but filled with tenderness, gentle guidance, and complete acceptance. She built me up knowing how destructive harsh words could be.

She was the first woman who really understood me, saw my vulnerabilities and naïve side. Yet, she was never judgmental. Straightforward, she would never hesitate to tell me truths about myself as she saw it, but she always cared about my feelings. She was present and engaged.

Like Liam mentored me in my business life, Juliette mentored me in my personal life.

We had tremendous fun and enjoyed all kinds of activities together. We loved to walk on the beach in Santa Monica or funky Venice Beach. Or on weekends take a ride to surrounding beautiful areas such as Santa Barbara. We loved sushi and every week would try a new sushi place since there were many available in our neighborhood. With other good friends and roommates, we would gather and have dancing nights or pool parties. We loved going to the movies, comedy shows, concerts. We were out and about unless we just stayed home relaxing. Juliette had a female Doberman pinscher dog by the name of Betina. She looked threatening especially when someone unknown was at the door, but it was bluff. She was a sweetheart and I recall walking her enjoying the company.

This was a time in my life when I learned what it meant to let go. We laughed so much. Deep belly laughs about silly things. Juliette had a great sense of humor and made French jokes reminding us both of our culture and background. Whenever we tried to translate some of them to our American friends, the meaning got lost in the process, and no one laughed.

We decided to try an experiment. Juliette was an outstanding cook and thought of offering a paid dining experience in her home. Through her connections, she had been asked if she would host and cook refined French cuisine for epicureans in search of a unique sampling of French regional recipes typically not found in a restaurant. Three couples had shown interest and when approached with this idea, found it irresistible. A day and time were set. We determined the cost of the elaborate meal. They agreed. We put together the menu and decided on the type of wine to complement. Juliette was the Chef, and I was the waitress and helper. We started all preparations a few days prior to the event. A lot of care and love went into the concocting of the meal, it had to be perfect and representative of a French renown specialty. We set up the table in the dining room using her finest China, silverware, and crystal glasses as if we were hosting royal guests. On D-Day, we frantically made sure all details were addressed. As the waitress, I dressed up in a nice outfit wearing a white French apron and the cutest matching maid hat. We were already laughing before our guests arrived. We had a glass of wine to relax. They were punctual and dressed up as well. Men wearing a suit and women in a formal dress. We first served an *apero* with *canapes et hors d'oeuvre* (aperitif and appetizers) to the delight of our guests. We had some classical music on. I played my role efficiently and with gusto. I assisted them sitting down and handed each of them a handwritten menu. Shortly thereafter I began to carry the plates prearranged in the kitchen one by one and served the ladies first. I kept a discreet and attentive eye on the progression of the meal, keeping pace with our guests. As I brought plates back to the kitchen, Juliette and I could not help but notice the men's plates were clean, but most women's plates still had a lot of untouched food. Concerned, I asked if everything was as expected. All of them were raving about how delectable the food was. So, the leftovers were not due to a lack of quality. It was simply a demonstration of being picky which can be so common among certain women. That did not go well with us. We could not easily accept this finicky behavior. Not wanting to waste anything, later that evening we ended up eating some of the leftovers and keeping some for the next day. It was an expensive meal and a lot of time had been dedicated to preparing it. To make matters worse, when it was time to pay the bill, we received a small tip which was rather insulting we thought. Juliette had mixed feelings about the whole experience. We just decided to laugh the whole thing off. The effort was not worth the reward. We never did this again.

I felt so good around her. We shared at a deep level. I found my support system.

The combination of mother/friend did wonders for me and my happiness. Juliette was instrumental in my early awakening. Her positive influence stimulated in me a bright and joyful outlook on life. To her a glass was always half full never half empty. She was an optimist and saw the bright side of every situation. The years I spent with her reflect one of the best experiences of my life. I made a huge leap forward connecting to my inner self and cultivating awareness.

When Sophie visited me, Juliette made sure she felt welcome and at home. She took an interest in Sophie's well-being, especially the emotional side. Her influence was a blessing, her intent and goal was to help my daughter and I improve our relationship. She was influential in helping Sophie to look at me in a more positive way. Juliette always wanted the best for those she loved and took to heart facilitating and encouraging a reconciliation between us. I am so grateful to her. She was a once in a lifetime special human being whose presence radiated compassion, empathy, and unconditional love. I know today, God placed her on my path. Her influence on me had a far-reaching and inspiring impact.

She met my mom who came to visit but the two of them did not find common grounds. Nevertheless, Juliette was a gracious hostess and showed her various popular tourist attractions.

There was tension early on because Juliette was clearly supportive and protective of me, unwilling to accept negative comments or criticism. She directly and unabashedly defended me, even with my own mother.

After a few years of serendipity, Juliette eventually sold her beautiful home due to financial stress. We moved into an apartment. She started to travel to England, where her daughter resided.

Our lives took different directions. Eventually, she joined her daughter in England and then moved back to France where she retired. I stayed.

We always kept in touch throughout the years and reunited many times.

****

To add to my sadness of parting with Juliette, this was also about the time I learned the tragic news concerning Arunny, my father's second wife, whom I had been in touch with after my father's passing. She had moved to France where she lived alone in a small apartment. Her children had remained in New Caledonia and her relationship with them was strained and practically nonexistent. She was ill with handicaps. In her solitude and despair, after years of suffering, she decided to put an end to her misery and committed suicide. She was no longer in this world.

TRANSITIONAL YEARS

The next few years are notable, not because of special events or my external circumstances even though they would be considered unusual by most. Disillusioned and disenchanted except for my long interlude with Juliette who was so dear to me. Her companionship and friendship had been pure balm soothing my aching heart and soul as the French expression well conveys, "*Mettre du Baume au Coeur.*" My few years with her had been a ray of sunshine. I felt deep sadness about us parting in different directions.

Left with a distinct impression, a form of awareness unknown at this point, within my existence something took root. A lingering impression and feeling of missing out on a crucial aspect of my purpose on this earth. A profound existential quest emerged. A question I am sure most of us ask ourselves at some point. Who am I? What is my reason for being here? Where am I going?

For the first time, instead of looking outside for answers, I began looking within. I examined my past. Why did I do, not do, or should or could have done to influence the outcomes. Memories of fleeting moments of excitement, various levels of connection with others, times packed with action, ups and downs, doing, experiencing. What did it accomplish for me? Why did I feel such inner turmoil?

I loved discussing the meaning of life with others and enjoyed debates. Reactions on how they perceived their own experiences, and resulting impact would be a factor of comparison with my own.

Expanding my vision did not provide me with the answers I sought. I could not define what I was seeking and felt a longing unwilling to dissipate.

So, in a thirst for knowledge, I turned to books. I needed

validation for my own existence. My quest led me to theology, philosophy, existentialism, psychology, and Eastern religions. The more I read, the more I questioned.

I tried to read the Bible and concentrated on the Old Testament and could not make any sense of so many chocking revelations about the evil nature of man. No one had ever encouraged me or guided me on how to read the Bible so it would make sense. To the contrary, I had been led to believe the Bible was written by fallible humans who lived in an unenlightened era, it was irrelevant today and just a story full of myths and contradictions. So, I gave up.

Eastern philosophies pulled me in because I related to the ideas of compassion, kindness, tolerance, non-attachment, causality, and nature as evidence of natural order.

The search for the true meaning of my life had begun and would never stop until, many years later, it was revealed to me. I was not ready yet for my late life transformation and rebirth.

In the meantime, my situation took a new turn, and I was called to return to France.

My mom had moved to the beautiful city of La Rochelle in the Southwest of France on the Atlantic coast. My grandma was no longer in this world. My mom cared for her in her later years until she placed her in a nursing home. She was now alone. It seemed an appropriate time to join her. She was lonely and open to reconnecting with me.

Our life in Morocco or interlude in Nice and Paris while fighting for Sophie's custody had become a remote memory.

Despite all the ups and downs we went through together there was an unspoken feeling of being drawn to each other. I simply wanted a true mother/daughter relationship. A meaningful encounter of feelings and emotions never experienced. I dreamed of what a relationship with her should be. I had witnessed the outpouring of love of my dear friend Juliette towards her children and hoped for a closeness with my own mom.

I longed to be loved, accepted as I was with all my imperfections. The recognition and approval of my own mother were paramount in my life. I never gave up dreaming we would have a breakthrough one day bonding together.

Only much later in life, by analyzing my relationship with my own daughter did I see my own limitations and imperfections. A parallel helping me realize history repeats itself. Through self-awareness, I discovered how as a child, I neglected the grace needed to accept my mother's behavior without judgment.

It took me many years to accept my expectations would never be met, at least not in the way I wished for. In all fairness, my mom showed her caring through action and practical help. Our love languages were not aligned.

The move to La Rochelle, France brought me back to her and an important historical city.

Back in the sixteen hundreds, La Rochelle sided with the British. Richelieu, Louis the XIII's prime minister, a cardinal famous for his involvement in royal scandals, besieged the town and built a vast sea wall to prevent English ships from freeing their allies. The Siege of La Rochelle lasted fourteen months and ended the rebellion of the Huguenot, a protestant's stronghold. What makes the city unique are its massive 14th century towers at the entrance of the old port and an imposing fortress with crenellated walls. Other points of interest are the *Gothic Porte de la Grosse-Horloge*, the *Renaissance Hotel de Ville*, and the 18th century *Hotel de la Bourse*. The *rue des Merciers* is typical of the old streets lined with 16th century houses, built over arcades, decorated with gargoyles and strange allegorical figures.

It offered me a completely different environment compared to South Pacific Islands or exotic California.

It took a while to adjust to my new surroundings, as well as settling in with my mom.

I used this time as an opportunity to reconnect with a few family members, like my dear aunt Liliane with whom I had fond memories from my childhood. She was struggling with health issues. Again, I was confronted with the fact my mom still did not appreciate her sister nor her choices in life. So, their relationship was strained and uneasy.

I found it difficult to accept the only three family members who found grace in her eyes were my cousin Luc, to whom I owe being born, my dear grandma, and my own daughter with whom she developed a strong personal bond. Even my cousin Luc displeased her at some point in his adult life because of a breach of trust. She had loaned him money and it took him forever to return what he had borrowed. From that point on, she erased him from her existence. She never liked any of my friends either.

Unable to find work locally, I took a business training program offered by the French government. A few months went by, and I was sending my resume to different organizations throughout France. I got hired for a one-year contract by a 5-star casino/hotel in *Beaulieu-Sur-Mer* as an assistant to their public relation director. My knowledge of English was important to them.

I found a tiny one room studio with a sea view available for seasonal rent. The rental agency gave me a deal for one year in *Saint-Jean-Cap-Ferrat*, a luxury resort town on the Mediterranean coast between prestigious *Monaco* and *Nice*. *Saint-Jean-Cap-Ferrat* on the French riviera is known as the "Peninsula of Billionaires," an exclusive seaside community beloved by royalty and tech tycoons. For a play on words, I had hit the jackpot, I had landed a job in one of the most desirable resorts in the world next to Monaco.

My own life held nothing prestigious. My work was demanding and there was no glory in it. My perks were the surroundings I lived in. From my minuscule studio, I could walk stairs down to a tiny private beach and swim in a small private cove. The weekends were filled with endless walks and exploration of the magnificent peninsula overlooking the Mediterranean. Nothing but a stretch of sun swept the rocky peninsula. A place of grand villas and gardens, art, glamour, and beautiful stretches of shaded coastal paths. Bathed in tranquility and splendor, remarkably unspoiled by tourism to protect and preserve a haven for the rich and famous. I took advantage of my time there to visit the breathtaking surrounding coastal areas, as well as the Provence backcountry.

A year went by quickly. My contract was renewed for another year. But other plans were in the making.

In the meantime, my mom had done a lot of thinking and approached me with a couple of ideas. She had not changed. She still had dreams of faraway places.

One of them was to go to Switzerland and check it out for a potential move. Her reasons were a bit morbid. She held a fascination for "dignity in dying" and assisted suicide legal in Switzerland under strict circumstances. She thought by becoming a resident there, she might one day benefit from this law if needed. She was healthy, did not have any terminal disease and her obsession was quite disturbing. She chastised me for being afraid to die whenever I asked her to stop talking about this phobia.

I had an upcoming vacation. In an endless attempt to please her, I accompanied her. It so happened once in Geneva, she quickly found out the financial requirements to become a Swiss resident were well above her means ending any idea of residency in Switzerland. However, it did nothing to end her obsession for euthanasia.

Far more appealing to me, she also envisioned moving to the United States for her retirement. My knowledge of English, experience of living in California, and the fact I had already become an American citizen made the decision easy. I was ready to move back to the US. My memories from my years in California were warm and happy. It was the land of opportunities and very beautiful. Everything about this idea felt overwhelmingly positive.

Evelyne in her forties

TRIP TO THE US WITH MOTHER

The Southeast of the US was the first target but also Nevada. Las Vegas appealed to my mother. We first landed in Atlanta, Georgia, rented a car, and I started driving.

Atlanta was picked as the starting and ending point of our trip for a couple of reasons. The first one was a bit sentimental. Mother's all-time favorite movie, *Gone with the Wind*, held a special place in her imagination. She loved the complexities of the personality and character of Scarlett O'Hara. She admired her, I sensed, because she portrayed a headstrong woman who never gave up. Set in the deep South in the midst of the Civil War, the sweeping historical drama and life on a Southern Plantation captured her attention.

The most important and practical factor was simply the thriving economy Atlanta offered with a stable job market. It was a solid choice for investing in rental properties as a future source of income regardless of where she would settle to live. She also thought it would be a good place for me to relocate since I should have no problem finding work there. Mother had always shown sound judgment in all important life-changing decisions.

We first visited the coast of South Carolina, stopped in Charleston, and loved it. Charleston is the epitome of Southern charm. As one of the oldest cities in the United States, we enjoyed a promenade on The Battery, a landmark defensive seawall, the lovely architecture of old downtown, and Rainbow Row, a row of pastel-colored historic homes.

Most remarkable was Boone Hall Plantation near Charleston. A working antebellum plantation showcasing a majestic avenue of massive live oaks draped in moss leading up to the main house. They were planted in 1743 by Captain Thomas Boone, son of Major John

Boone to whom the land was originally granted. The astonishing oak alley and the main house have appeared in movies like *Gone with the Wind, The Notebook* and *North and South*. Gorgeous gardens exhibit plants and flowers for all seasons featuring antique rose bushes over 100 years old. Well-preserved slave quarters built of brick cabins have stood the test of time. Boone Hall is the only plantation in the area presenting the Gullah culture portrayed by their descendants. A distinctive group of African Americans whose origins lie along the coasts of North Carolina. With their historically isolated locations and strong sense of identity, the Gullah are said to have preserved more of their African cultural heritage than any other group of African Americans.

Boone Hall is still one of the oldest continuously operating farms in the United States. Originally, its first crops were indigo and rice, followed by cotton and pecans from an enormous pecan tree orchard planted in the 19th century. Today, the farm is well known for strawberries and peaches, as well as a variety of other fruits and vegetables.

We thought the food was outstanding and particularly appreciated the She-crab soup and Shrimp and grits. Southern comfort food is indeed comforting and delicious. The creative influence of African American culture on Southern cuisine is undeniable. Soul food has become popular.

Charleston was a great place to visit but not what mother had in mind as a place to live.

We stopped in Savannah on the way to Florida. Another charming Southern escape and great eating place. Picturesque town with manicured parks, horse-drawn carriages, and antebellum architecture galore. Walking was such a pleasure along moss-covered, oak-tree-lined lanes and cobblestone squares.

Then we drove to Florida. Mother was focused on the Sunshine state. Many Europeans are attracted to Florida because it is heavily promoted as a retirement paradise overseas as much as in the US.

Based on her own research, she had her mind set on two areas, one was Palm Beach on the Atlantic Coast, and the other was the Gulf Coast, with a particular interest for Naples.

Palm Beach did not appeal to us. Nice beaches, lots of luxury shopping, restaurants, and golf courses galore. The wealthy town came with tremendous expense. Very little time was spent there.

We continued our journey towards the Gulf Coast. Driving the turnpike made for efficient traveling but did not allow much sightseeing. Fewer exits and less traffic than on regular highways.

We drove through Alligator Alley in the Everglades, a stretch of I-75 spanning 80 miles between Fort Lauderdale and Naples. We came across alligators dozing on the side of the road and sometimes were able to stop and observe the beasts.

Naples and its surroundings were impressive, flanked by miles of pristine beaches featuring fine white "sugar" sand. Again, high-end shopping, restaurants and golf courses seemed to be the draw. Naples is an upscale seaside town with high end real estate well above mom's financial plan.

Keeping her budget in mind, we decided to explore more of the Gulf Coast, driving North toward the Panhandle with New Orleans as our last stop before returning to Atlanta.

Nothing seemed to appeal to her along the way. It was either too crowded, too expensive, or not to her taste. We stopped in Fort Myers, Venice, Sarasota, St. Petersburg, Clearwater and all the way to the Panhandle to Panama City and Pensacola. It looked the same to her and she all together lost interest in the area. She was eager to move on. Her mind was made up. No more time to lose.

Next stop was New Orleans where we spent a few days and took a break from all the driving. Mother knew quickly New Orleans was not going to be her retirement spot. We would have enjoyed our stay there if we had not been so tired.

A true melting pot of cultures, New Orleans offers a wealth of unique heritage and proud traditions. Amazing architecture and great food make the city unique and diverse. There is none other like it in the world.

The city possesses an abundance of historic architecture constructed over a period spanning almost three hundred years. Home to more than twenty National register historic districts, nineteen local Historic districts, and scores of local and national Landmark buildings. The blend of French, Spanish, and Caribbean architectural influences, in conjunction with the demands of the hot and humid climate, has impacted the urban fabric as much as the culture itself. The variety of building styles includes the Creole cottages and Creole townhouses found mainly in the French Quarters. American townhouses in the Central Business and Lower

Garden districts, raised Center-Hall cottages and Double-Gallery houses uptown as well as shotgun houses found all over the city. The term "shotgun" originates from the idea that when standing in the front of the house, you can shoot a bullet clear through every room.

Much of the city is built upon reclaimed swampland and most of it is located below sea level. Historic cemeteries have the particularity of being above ground with towering vaults and twisting labyrinth of stone pathways, eerie sites mirroring the strange history of the city.

What I enjoyed most in New Orleans was the food even though mother was limited in what she could eat because of health concerns so we kept it basic and simple. Spicy was not something she could handle. She had enough and after a couple of days decided it was time to head back to Atlanta. Truthfully, I felt the same way. I was exhausted from driving anyway. Nevertheless, I enjoyed the Crawfish etouffee, the Gulf oysters, Po-boys, the pralines and delicious beignets.

New Orleans would have been enjoyed far more under different circumstances. The focus of the trip was not leisure or vacation. Mom was disappointed. She realized nothing she had seen so far would make her feel "home" in any way. The language barrier was also an issue and she relied on me constantly for interpretation. We were both frustrated. The feeling was one of discouragement. Her expectations had not been met.

We drove back to Atlanta. From there, we turned the car in and flew to Las Vegas for a week. Las Vegas was a shock and a surprise. Neither one had ever seen "Sin City." The first impression was a spectacular and glamorous fairyland. The Disneyland of adults it seemed. We had seen casinos before, but nothing prepared us for the scale, and multitude of splendid, brightly illuminated casino hotels and gambling dens with their clashing, garish architectural styles, and swarms of tourists. The Las Vegas famous strip, heart and soul of the city, home to the most famous hotels and casinos, displays waves of dazzling pulsing lights and scrolling video screens, glitz, and endless attractions. Flamboyance, exuberance, and extravagance characterize Las Vegas well.

We stayed at The Mirage hotel and casino just built and brand new then. We occupied one of their 3000 rooms, somewhere on one of the upper floors with an incredible view of the strip. I must admit we had a blast and we indulged.

We had rented a car and split our time between checking out various neighborhoods for mom's retirement goal and some sightseeing. We tried our luck playing slot machines and could not resist the All-You-Can-Eat buffets Las Vegas is known for. In those days, buffets were reasonable if not free as an incentive to play slot machines. All this has changed in recent years and the perks of the past are gone.

We drove to Red Rock Canyon National Conservation Area and on the way stopped at Summerlin, a master-planned community considered to be a great neighborhood to live in, west of Las Vegas. Mom really liked the setting of Summerlin and so did I. We gathered as much information as we could and looked at their model homes. She was enchanted by what she saw, and the price ranges offered options she could afford. She particularly liked a duplex style home with a golf course view and stunning mountain scenery in the far background. Lots of trails to walk and amenities galore. Other neighborhoods were explored but none appealed to her as much as Summerlin. Excitement was in the air.

We also took a ride to Hoover Dam in the Black Canyon of the Colorado River, an inspiring symbol of American engineering. The trip was complete with a scenic ride covering Lake Mead reservoir and the Valley of Fire. The Valley of Fire preserves a starkly beautiful section of the Mojave Desert and its brilliantly red sandstone formations including cliffs and petrified sand dunes.

A highlight of the trip was a Grand Canyon West Rim exclusive floor landing helicopter tour inclusive of champagne and a light picnic on the canyon floor. There was nothing like the moment when the helicopter crested the rim of the Canyon and the ground dropped out from underneath. Once reassured everything was fine after the pilot purposely took a dive after warning us ahead of time, the views were jaw-dropping. We flew over and into the Grand Canyon. This truly was a once in a lifetime opportunity, and I am grateful to mom for wanting to share this memorable experience with me. The panoramic views of one of the Seven Wonders of the Natural World were unfolding right in front of us and we were in awe. No word is close enough to describe the unimaginable beauty displayed. We descended 4,000 feet to land at the bottom of the West Rim. I could not feel anything but respect and reverence for the awe-inspiring divine creation.

Our next highlight was a popular Las Vegas show at the time, right in the hotel where we stayed. We booked an evening to see the performance of Siegfried and Roy. Legendary magicians and entertainers who changed the face of the Las Vegas strip with their impressive illusions and white tiger-taming acts. An iconic show scaled above and beyond anything anyone had seen in Las Vegas as well as one of the most expensive at the time it was built. There was no regret on our part. The show was mesmerizing.

The end of our stay in Las Vegas had come. It was to remain in our memories as the best quality time mother and I ever spent together. Mom really surpassed herself in generosity. We shared special and cherished moments.

Las Vegas left her with a lasting impression. The time to make the decision to move there had not yet come. Other events were to unfold first in accordance with divine timing.

We flew back to Atlanta.

In the end and for various reasons, we checked out the residential part of North Atlanta. Mom was moving forward with her original plan to launch her American adventure by investing in a couple of rental income properties. Establishing a flow of income for her future was her first goal and the first step before deciding on her own move. I found a local realtor, a wonderful lady whose personality and demeanor were a delight. She and I became friends and still talk to each other to this day. She quickly spotted what my mother had in mind and the deals were made.

We returned to La Rochelle.

LIFE IN ATLANTA

In the meantime, my daughter, Sophie, who still lived in New Caledonia with her father, had been the victim of a traumatic motorbike accident leaving her with serious consequences and a physical handicap. It would be months later before I learned of her condition. The right side of her body was partially paralyzed, and she had spent months in rehabilitation. I wanted to go see her, but I was bluntly told I was not welcome, and she did not want to see me. It took a long time, but she recovered to a degree. She still slightly limps to this day.

After a few months, to my utmost surprise, out of the clear blue sky, her father contacted me. My mother and I had just returned from our trip to the US. He briefly explained Sophie needed a change of environment, and he could no longer manage her. He wanted to send her back to me permanently under my care. She was a teen then, about 14 years old. I received no detailed explanation for the reasons behind this abrupt change of heart. From being treated as an undesirable and unfit mother for many years, all of a sudden, I had become indispensable and important. I was not even asked; I was told it had to be this way for her own sake.

In a matter of a few days, Sophie was flown to France from New Caledonia on the other side of the planet and moved in with her grandmother and me.

This all happened when the plan to relocate to the US was under way. Sophie was now reunited with me, and my plans had become her plans.

I can't emphasize enough how awkward it was for us in the beginning. We were strangers to each other. She had been forced to move in with me, clearly against her will and she made sure to let me know. I suspected unspoken events took place in New Caledonia making her father decide to part with her. I did not know what had transpired for such a decision to be made. She was despondent and unwilling to share with me.

In the end, it did not matter. I was grateful she was back in my life, and ready to do whatever it took to mend our relationship.

Her physical recovery was still in progress. She limped when walking and had a scar on her face.

I felt like I was adopting a rebellious teenager whom I did not know and was hostile towards me.

It took us several weeks to establish a report. She was clearly depressed. Nothing interested her.

We talked about moving to the US together. I presented the situation in a positive way just as I had when she was seven years old, and I went to pick her up in New Caledonia upon getting custody.

The difference this time, she had been rejected by her father and forcefully sent to me against her own will.

We were given an opportunity to start our life together in a new exciting country. Her grandmother emphasized needing a change and a new beginning together. Mother and I were in total agreement. We got Sophie's attention, and after a while, she agreed to the move. We were going to go first, preparing the way for my mother to join later.

I contacted Olivia, my new realtor friend in Atlanta and described the situation. She immediately and generously offered us to stay at her house at first until we got situated. A couple of her kids had moved out and she had several bedrooms available.

I will never forget the day my mother dropped us off at the train station with our belongings on our journey to Atlanta. Olivia waited for us at Hartsfield airport and drove us to her beautiful dream house with seven bedrooms. She and her husband had seven children and most still lived with them. A couple of them were about Sophie's age.

They were such a blessing and without them, we could not have done this.

We were unexpectedly beginning a new chapter of our lives. By the grace of God, we both were welcome into the nicest family we could have asked for, living the American dream. They excitedly introduced us to the American way of life especially Sophie who had not lived in the US before. We had good times and enjoyed cooking and sharing life together.

After a month or so, we found an apartment to move into. I got a car and managed my mother's two rentals, privileged to use the income temporarily until I found work. Thank you, Mother, for this is how you showed how much you cared.

We found a school for Sophie after getting her a green card. She had to learn English and did well quickly practicing with my friend's kids. She had spent time in Australia after her accident in a hospital in Sydney, so she knew some basics.

Like I had done years ago in California, I began working for a temp agency and familiarized myself with Atlanta.

We were busy and overwhelmed. Hopeful and happy, I started to feel like an American and became quite patriotic.

I connected with a French woman who owned a local branch of an international language and cross-cultural training business. She owned a franchise in the heart of the business district of Atlanta providing services to corporations who did business overseas. They needed their staff to be educated in another language and acquire an understanding of cultural differences between countries worldwide.

They hired me part-time to teach business French at their center. I had a lot of fun and fully appreciated this new line of work. I loved meeting new people and enjoyed time spent with my students.

Within a short year, I was offered the position of Vice-President and Director of the Atlanta branch. A good salary plus commission came along with the offer. I felt so grateful and thankful. I was on top of the world and given a great opportunity. Enjoying what I did was an extra bonus.

Sophie and I eventually would move into a house.

My mother's intention had been to buy a home with me as joint tenants. We did. She would occupy the ground floor, me and Sophie the upstairs. She required to have her own kitchenette and we had it built this way since it was a brand-new house under construction.

She was in the process of selling her place in La Rochelle and the plan was for her to move in with us.

It did not work out that way, she came for a visit and when she looked at the floorplan, she expressed dissatisfaction with the layout of her quarters. She declared she would not move in with us after all but only visit.

So, Sophie and I moved into our brand-new home just the two of us. I now had a full-time career and Sophie had started school.

Shortly thereafter, mother announced she had decided to move to Las Vegas. She had fond memories of our stay there. I know her heart had been set for Las Vegas all along anyway.

She came back, I took a few days off and we flew to Las Vegas together where I helped her find a 55 plus retirement community. We still had Summerlin in mind, but she felt a need to compare other available options before making her final decision. Summerlin was the winner by far. She bought a duplex right on the golf course like the model previously seen on our first visit.

I helped her obtain a green card and took care of the administration of her investments and medical insurance, which turned out to be an expensive proposition because she had to buy into Medicare having never worked in the US. I supervised everything and was her voice since she did not speak English and was not motivated to learn it beyond the basics. At her age she thought it was too difficult and did want to make the effort.

I helped her move to Las Vegas, buy a car, and she lived there happily ever after. She loved to gamble and did well at first, until her luck turned. It was not unusual for her to call me and tell me she had won substantial amounts. I know because I took care of her taxes and we had to declare everything.

This Las Vegas honeymoon lasted five years.

In the meantime, I was in a big two-story house with a daughter who needed a lot of attention but was unresponsive to me.

Sophie had met people at school who were successful at recruiting her into their "church." Whatever they convinced her of, once engulfed with their "program," she became even more distant. She would come home to sleep and was gone by dawn.

I asked to meet these people and attended a couple of services on Sunday mornings. I remember feeling uncomfortable. I asked for a private meeting and was prepared with questions. They were not interested in interacting with me. Instead, I was quickly pressured into following my daughter's example for my own good. I was pushed into becoming an active member of the church with all the responsibilities and duties entailed. When I refused, it was insinuated I would perish and lose my daughter forever. I knew then she was captive of a religious sect whose name I do not remember. From that point on, our relationship was strained to the point of no return.

She eventually left the house and got married to someone who abused her. The marriage did not last but maybe a year.

She reached out to reconnect with me after leaving the sect she was involved with. She had decided to divorce and was ready to accept my help. She never spoke much about her experiences. Her sharing with me was minimal. She worked in my office as a receptionist for a while. Then she met a young man whom I liked and moved in with him. He was serious about Sophie.

Meanwhile, the house meant for all three generations to live in together got sold. I bought my own place in my own name for the first time. A nice little condo less than a mile from work in the Buckhead district of Atlanta.

On Sundays, it became a tradition for Sophie and her new boyfriend to come and visit. I cooked dinner for them. For the first time, we had the beginning of a relationship. She even gave me a letter I still have today telling me how much she appreciated me and had realized for the first time I really was on her side. She expressed how grateful she was for my presence, love, and ongoing assistance. This precious recognition from my own daughter touched me deeply.

These were positive and healing times for us.

I was hoping she would settle down and marry her boyfriend, but it was not her choice. They enjoyed activities together such as running and the great outdoors. She just gave me a hint that he did not understand her needs, and I assumed she did not feel enough emotional support.

She eventually found a job with a French company, who utilized her knowledge of French, in their accounting department. Continuing to work with this company for many years has provided great stability in her professional career.

Her personal life had twists and turns, eventually marrying someone she had met who worked for the same company.

I was aggressively building accounts for my employer quite successfully, making a comfortable living. But rewards come with responsibilities and accountability. I worked all the time, including many weekends, entertaining clients was a big part of my role.

I would visit mother in Las Vegas occasionally, and she would also come for a visit.

After about five years of Vegas, she eventually tired of it. Not doing well at the casinos anymore, the constant heat was getting to her, and she still could not manage English well leaving her rather isolated. Also, the cost of Medicare was exorbitant compared to living in France, where her medical care was free.

With all these considerations in mind, she decided to sell everything she owned in the US and returned to France for her last years of retirement.

She was thinking of the South of France, on the Mediterranean coast. So, I assisted her in selling her rental houses in Atlanta and duplex in Las Vegas.

She did not care for the town she first moved to in the South of France. One day, she called me and asked me to contact my friend Juliette on her behalf. Juliette lived in the lovely resort town of Arcachon in the Southwest of France right on the Atlantic coast near Bordeaux. My mom had checked it out, fell in love, and decided it would be her ultimate retirement place.

Arcachon was so popular there was nothing available for sale. When something popped up on the market, it was immediately snatched. Well, mom had the solution. "Can you ask Juliette if I can stay in her apartment while I look to rent until I can find something to invest in?"

Juliette was not enthusiastic at the idea of my mother staying with her even for a short time, remembering their unpleasant encounter in Los Angeles. But out of her good heart and because she loved me, she said yes.

Juliette found her own solution. She left her apartment keys to my mother. Meanwhile, she traveled to visit her daughter in London giving my mom full run of her place.

It worked out well. Mother did find a furnished seasonal rental with a view on the marina after two weeks and moved in. Juliette came back to her apartment and agreed to help my mom when she needed a ride or other assistance. Mom was no longer driving, and Juliette had a car.

About a year later, she bought an apartment with a view on the bay without going through a realtor. She offered the owners more than the asking price. They accepted and the deal was made. This was her last move. She lived there until the end of her life.

As for me, after many years of intense professional commitment, I burned out and contemplated what to do next. I no longer enjoyed living in Atlanta. I aspired to a more natural environment and a simple lifestyle in a rural area surrounded by mountains.

I had a new companion in my life. We had met in an unusual way. I needed repairs done in my home and the Homeowner Association sent this handyman to me. When he ringed my doorbell and I opened the door, I was looking at this good-looking man. Tall, muscular, dark hair, blue eyes, handsome.

He looked back and I could tell he was also pleased to look at me. After completing the work in a couple of visits, we knew we wanted to see each other again and he asked me if he could call me. He did and we dated. I liked him because he was gentle, attentive, caring, and respectful.

He was a believer and would speak to me about God and how important his relationship with Jesus Christ was. It was the first time I had met a Christian man. He had grown up in Louisiana and was close to his mom still living there, a devout Christian woman who raised him to walk in faith. He enjoyed sharing his love for God with me. We became close and lived together. He never pressured me in becoming a Christian and only prayed someday, I would come to see his truth.

Oliver was also tired of Atlanta's fast pace of life and ready for a move to a more rural area. We both felt the same way.

We began doing research. The Western States somewhere along the Rockies sounded good. But where? Oliver and I had been toying with a dream of having dogs. Great Pyrenees to be exact. I don't know why but these big white fluffy canines mesmerized me. I was interested in getting involved in dog shows and could picture myself raising dogs on a little ranch in the mountains. Little did I know what I was getting into.

We decided to take a trip to Colorado. I had a little ranch in the mountains in mind. We had already acquired our first Great Pyrenees, a beautiful male named Katu, inspired by K2 Mountain in Nepal. I had been looking online at different options in my price range and one area in Colorado particularly stood out.

Located in South Central Colorado, north of New Mexico, Westcliffe in Custer County is part of the frontier pathways scenic byway, where jagged peaks, deep canyons, sprawling meadows, and aspen-covered forests thrive. With exceptional stargazing and unobstructed views at an altitude of almost 8,000 feet, Westcliffe and adjoining Silver Cliff are small mountain towns recognized as International Dark-Sky Communities by the International Dark-Sky Association. Westcliffe is a quiet hamlet where cowboys and cattle roam along county roads, still very much a ranching community, located about two hours from Colorado Springs and thirty minutes from Pueblo.

The area is not as popular and pricey as other mountainous parts of the state such as internationally known Vail, Aspen, and a few others.

We drove there from Atlanta and spent a couple of weeks exploring with Katu, our male Great Pyrenees. Custer county in Colorado felt like the old Far West. A picturesque area tucked between the Wet Mountains to the east and the Sangre de Cristo Range to the west.

The Sangre de Cristo range owes its name to its red-tinted, snowy peaks. The colors change from sunrise to sunset. Sangre de Cristo translates into Blood of Christ. It was named by a Spanish explorer who marveled at how, especially at sunrise, the range would turn into a palette of reds. These mountains display a stunning natural phenomenon called an alpenglow often drenching the peaks with luminous reds and pinks shortly before dusk, twilight between complete darkness and sunrise or sunset. Spanning from Poncha Pass near Salida in central Colorado to the peaks southeast of Santa Fe, New Mexico, the Sangre de Cristo Range is to me most arrestingly beautiful and iconic.

Anything with a direct view of the Sangre de Cristo carried a high price. Eventually, I had to go further toward Canon City and ended up finding the perfect pearl near Florence in the Wet Mountains. Still a mountain view, not as stunning but far more affordable. A small ranch with a 1,400 square foot house in perfect condition. It would work for the intended purpose. The deal was made.

We returned to Atlanta, and I began the process of selling my house, which was easy. I also gave notice at work. It took a little bit of time, but it all worked out as if it was meant to be.

A new venture was about to begin. My vision was taking shape. My new dream of raising Great Pyrenees, away from city life was

becoming a reality.
   A city girl turning into a country girl.

COLORADO

A couple of months later, we settled in Colorado. The first week we were there will never be forgotten. It was morning and we received a phone call from Oliver's mother.

It was September 11, 2001. She said with a trembling voice full of fear, "America is at war." She was not coherent. We turned the TV on and heard the terrible news. Commonly known as the 9/11 attacks, it was a day of unprecedented shock and suffering in the history of the United States. Almost 3,000 people were killed that day as four commercial passenger airplanes were hijacked and carried out suicide attacks, two on the World Trade Center in New York and one on the Pentagon in Arlington, Virginia. The fourth airplane was targeting Washington DC but crashed into rural Pennsylvania. The shocking events of September 11 were televised globally and left much of the world reeling in horror. A day marking a turning point in America and setting an entirely new tone for the future of this beautiful country. It took a while to absorb the full impact and meaning of what had happened and the consequences.

As the days and weeks went by, we fully settled in. We found a female Great Pyrenees puppy from a faraway breeder who flew her in. When we picked her up at the Colorado Springs airport and opened the crate, I was ecstatic. The most adorable white fur ball, eight weeks old looked up at me terrified. She was away from her family for the first time and the trip by airplane had traumatized her. Completely taken over, I named her Sabine and immediately felt protective. Sabine is a feminine given name of ancient Roman origin popular in continental Europe. She was a show quality dog like our male, Katu, who immediately demonstrated his dominance. He was the alpha and made sure she understood from the beginning the implications of her new status.

Katu confirmation – April 2000

A fence was quickly put in place around the house to confine the dogs.

We eventually adopted another Great Pyrenees, a rescue this time. A shy female who had not been welcomed in her previous home and placed in foster care. She was spayed so no worries about an undesired encounter with Katu. She too realized quickly who was the boss and she submitted to him without resistance.

We also had a female Golden Retriever and two cats.

Many mouths to feed. A lot of training was involved. Over the next few months, I became heavily involved in local dog shows. Katu and Sabine received their conformation and first prize entitling them to the status of Champion on their pedigree. This was the end of their career as show dogs. It proved to be time consuming, expensive, traveling was involved but most of all I quickly realized the world of dog shows is highly political as many other disciplines.

On another note, and to say this as gracefully as I can, Oliver had, before we left Atlanta, solemnly promised me he would quickly find work in Colorado. I was never going to have to work again, he said. He intended to take care of us. He was in the construction business, a booming industry where we had moved. He wanted to land a big job to start with, such as building a new house for someone. I was suggesting he started out with small jobs so the locals would get to know him. My idea of success was to establish trust first and build relationships which would open doors to bigger jobs. He did not share this perception, which led to major decisions on my part as time went by.

I began to do translation work from home for the company I previously worked for in Atlanta. He took a part time RV sales job in Colorado Springs three times a week paid on commission. After a few months income was not coming in and my savings were depleted. I was stressed and worried about the financial future. In the end, we discussed his return to Atlanta where he still had multiple contacts and the assurance of work opportunities. He promised to help me from afar. The dogs were bonded to him as much as they were to me, but I kept them at the time. He left.

ALONE TO THINK & MORE SOUL SEARCHING

I was now living alone on a small ranch at the foot of the Wet Mountains in Colorado with four big dogs and two cats, two miles of dirt road to get out of the community and a lot to think about.

It felt wonderful at first. A feeling of freedom. A great opportunity presented itself to reevaluate everything in my life. I had time to recover from many years of exhausting work responsibilities. My schedule was now mine. I loved to explore my new surroundings. I enjoyed the dogs tremendously even though it was difficult for me to handle them physically since all of them were big, strong with a mind of their own, a known trait of the breed.

They originally bred in the Pyrenees mountains of France and Spain to be guardians of livestock where they are commonly called *Le Patou*. Back in the days, they were known as fearless protectors of flocks from predation by wolves and bears. Powerful dogs, a breed striving to work independently as a team. They were left an entire summer alone with the sheep in the mountains without any human supervision.

In the seventeenth century, they were adopted as the Royal Dog of France by the Dauphin in the court of Louis XIV also known as Louis the Great or the Sun King, in French "*Le Roi Soleil*," the same king who had Versailles built to his glory. They subsequently became much sought after by the French nobility to guard their *chateaux*, particularly in the south of France near Foix and Pau in the *Occitanie* region. Each dog was counted equal to two men, be it as guards of the castles. While their royal adoption is interesting, the dogs' main fame was from their ageless devotion to their mountain flocks, shepherds, and shepherds' family. When not guarding the flocks, you would find *Le Patou* laying on a mat in the front doorway of the shepherds' humble dwellings.

My dogs were highly protective of me. Walking them together on a leash proved to be challenging and I had difficulty controlling them. I did not worry too much about it in the beginning, but this changed with time. They required a lot of grooming since I kept them in the house with their long, thick, white double coat. Shedding was no small affair. They gave me a lot of work, but I loved them dearly. They were my companions and family in a way.

Overall, I was happy to spend time alone. Solitude felt good and my four-legged companions were great company.

My outlook on life was going through a profound transformation. The values imposed on me, or my personal choices, no longer brought me satisfaction. I aspired to peace, tranquility, serenity, and identification with a force far greater than myself. I would sit outside, taking in my beautiful surroundings, sunrise and sunset. Stargazing at the dark night sky was beyond description and filled me with awe and wonder. I lived in an area protected from the prevalent effects of light pollution thus I was blessed with exceptional starry nights. I felt communion with the silence surrounding me, and a gentle calling I could not define.

Oliver's many references to his faith as a follower of Jesus Christ came back to me. I began wanting to know more about Christ in a deeper way than ever before. The thought of God's mighty power filled me with wonder as I gazed into His sovereign creation, undistracted by the outside world.

Meanwhile, Oliver kept in touch and occasionally sent money. He missed the dogs and offered to take them if I ever decided to let them go. Apparently, he was getting work and said he could afford them financially. I told him I would keep his offer in mind. They were a handful. The rescued female Great Pyrenees would jump the fence and disappear. My big male was unruly and hard to control. One day he ran out on the neighbor's property and scared her horses. I got a phone call from her, and she warned me I better get my dog back quickly otherwise she would have no hesitation shooting him. I found out later this was perfectly legal where I lived if a dog is considered attacking livestock. Everybody except me owned guns and threatening to use them did not seem to take much provocation. Domestic pets can be fair game in some rural areas if they intrude on someone else's property and create disturbance or damage.

I consequently had to take measures and keep my animals indoors unless I stayed with them outside. Another time, while walking all four on a leash, we came across another walker with a dog. I lost control of my menagerie, and two attacked the other dog. I could not hold them back. We had to separate them forcefully. I was lucky. No damage was done. But the warning was clear. I could no longer take a chance without risking being sued.

So, from that point on, I did not walk them together but only two at a time.

Upset, I had to accept the constraints I was now subjected to as reality. I was not physically able to control my dogs, probably not firm enough either. The big male was the alpha, not me, and he knew it. For a while, we walked alone in town, just the two of us. He enjoyed it and behaved well for the most part when it was just me and him.

This was a time when I resumed reading books related to metaphysics, New Age, and Christianity. Bridging science and spirituality were topics of high interest, hoping to find answers to my quest for Truth. I read into the wee hours of the night while my menagerie slept.

The New Age books presented Jesus Christ as one of the great teachers of wisdom in contrast to the Christian faith as the Savior of the world. He intrigued and fascinated me. I related and identified deeply with His teachings, but it never occurred to me He was the answer to my spiritual pursuit and my Savior. There was confusion in my mind. I was not reading Him from the Bible but learning about Him from other sources. The only close encounter I had with a Christian was Oliver who now lived in Atlanta. I either do not remember or maybe did not pay attention, but the sharing of his faith never led me to realize Christ was far more than a teacher, but God incarnate both fully human and fully divine. I could not understand why He was our Savior and Redeemer.

I felt drawn to Jesus Christ. I constantly returned to study Him more. Disappointed and chocked while reading the Old Testament, I was blind to the fact the Bible was indeed the "book" I needed to dive into and by studying the Word of God, I would find all the answers I longed for. No one directed or educated me until I met a wonderful couple who enlightened me years later.

I focused on reading about Jesus anywhere and everywhere. Unknowingly, I missed out terribly by not reading His Word straight from the Bible in the original context intended. He had become my champion and hero.

A few months went by. I began to feel lonely by myself with my menagerie on my isolated little ranch. I concluded it was time to meet other people and expand my minimal social life consisting of occasional greetings with my neighbors.

I knew human beings were not created to live alone, and I started to feel the effects of my self-imposed solitude. I socialized with a couple who lived a couple of miles away. Nice neighbors knowing I was French put me in touch with a French Artist painter who lived in nearby Westcliffe. This encounter created the beginning of a social life. I met a few more people through him.

Speaking on the phone was not enough. I needed to share with others in person.

Soon, thereafter, I had a dinner invitation from the French artist who wanted to introduce me to his friends. I accepted and was glad I did. The dinner was good and the conversation interesting. I met several people, men, and women, all single. Two of the guests had extensively traveled the world, one for pleasure and the other for business. French wine flowed. I had a fantastic time and enjoyed engaging in conversation with others.

There was a Japanese lady who described a matcha (powered green tea) tea ceremony and explained how this tradition remains ritualistic today in Japan to promote wellbeing, mindfulness, and harmony, as well as showing hospitality. She said she would love to invite me to her home for this unique experience and I gladly accepted.

There was another woman who clearly embraced closeness with nature and spoke about the relationship she had with plants and trees and how she would hug them and speak to them. She assured us there was a real bond and open communication between her and her natural surroundings.

An American Indian guest spoke about his culture emphasizing the importance of harmony with nature, endurance of suffering, respect and non-interference toward others.

I received questions about the French people and was put on the spot by someone who had traveled to Paris and found the French to be rude. I agreed the French and especially Parisians have a reputation for rudeness not entirely undeserved. I pointed out other large cities in the world are no different in this respect.

There was also a man present who to the contrary had traveled extensively to France especially through the countryside and had been impressed by the kindness and hospitality he received everywhere he went. Not to mention the charm, wealth of history, art, monuments, and the incredible food experiences he enjoyed.

After dinner, he suggested we take a walk together with my dog, my male Great Pyrenees I practically took everywhere with me. We exchanged phone numbers.

Within a couple of days, he called me and asked if I would be interested in letting him show me some unique local sightseeing. He had been a resident of Colorado for many years and knew the area inside out. He offered a day trip, and all my dogs were invited as well. I thought about it for a while and decided, why not. We had an interesting conversation. He was a globetrotter. The group reunited at dinner were his friends and all seemed to like him. The fact he included the dogs was intriguing. He was older than me and his behavior indicated no interest other than sharing his knowledge and beauty of the area while pursuing conversation about his worldwide travels.

As we got to know each other better, I admit enjoying the worldly conversations we shared, and his attitude was of a gentleman, always.

We solidified our friendship as time went by. He was protective of me, attentive, and most helpful. He would help with the maintenance work needed on my property I had neglected. There was no romance between us. We enjoyed each other's company and laughed a lot. He loved cooking and specialized in Italian recipes which were delicious. We would watch movies, go to dinner, but most of the time it was outdoor outings including my dogs. They behaved better when he was around. They looked at him as the alpha and even my big male had a dose of respect for him.

One evening, having dinner in a restaurant, he began explaining he had rarely spent such quality and fun time with a woman and how delighted he was I had appeared in his life. The fact I was from Europe was important to him because my outlook was different from most American women, he said. He thought I was far more open-minded and worldly, and emphasized how my demeanor and mannerism enchanted him. He wanted to take our friendship a step further revealing his hopes to find a female companion, no romance, no marriage. Someone who would accompany him in his world travels and enjoy life with him. He was in his late sixties. I was in my mid-fifties. Retired and well off, he was convinced I was the perfect match for him, if all this appealed to me. He specified I did not have to worry about the physical part of the relationship because he no longer had a drive. He gave me time to think it over, never pressuring me.

I had never considered this type of partnership. In a way, it appealed to me because I was tired of the "traditional" approach to men/women relationships as it had always carried stress for me. I shared this concept with friends. They were not shocked. As a matter of fact, they were intrigued and curious to meet him. Even my mother thought it was a great idea.

After a couple of weeks of thinking it over, I accepted.

Meantime, Oliver in Atlanta desperately wanted the dogs. He was ready, he said. He was prepared to rent a van and come pick up the entire menagerie.

I knew the time had come to let them go. Controlling them had been a challenge. This new lifestyle would not allow the pets to stay with me. Oliver loved them dearly and was ready to dedicate himself to them because they were indeed his life.

The new plans went into motion. The day came when I relinquished all my pets. They were full of joy reuniting with their master again and could not contain their excitement. For them, it was the best decision I could have made, all things considered. The actual separation caused me tremendous hardship and sorrow. The day they left was the hardest of all, I literally screamed in emotional pain with an acute sense of loss. I sobbed uncontrollably and kept crying for days.

My friend was concerned, offering to get them back if I could not live without them. I would call Oliver often to see how they were doing. Everything was fine. I eventually let go. The departure of my pets left me with a void, grief, and a feeling of betrayal on my part. They had been my world and my comfort for a long time. My consolation was knowing they were in good hands with someone who loved them as much as I did. I saw them several times over the course of the next few years while visiting my daughter in Atlanta.

ON THE MOVE AROUND THE WORLD AND THE US

I ended up selling my little ranch. My friend gave up his place in Westcliffe. We moved to Colorado Springs in a beautiful condo right off a golf course with a stunning view of Pikes Peak. Soon, the traveling began. Long trips overseas lasted a couple of months or longer once or twice a year. In between, we would take shorter trips to tour the US and Canada.

Extensive travel in Europe took place over the course of several years. We first landed in France and visited with my mother. She and my friend hit it off right away. They liked each other and, in many ways, had similarities in their thinking. After a week at my mom's and visiting Juliette, we drove through multiple European countries.

Europe offers incredible historical sites, important cultural landmarks, and beautiful scenery. With each of its forty-four countries, home to different people, languages, and cultures, however, it can be hard to decide where to start.

Besides its world-class cities, overflowing with amazing art and architecture, Europe has a myriad of historic towns and idyllic villages waiting to be discovered. Tucked away in scenic mountains, valleys, and countryside, you will find astounding archaeological sites and magical fairytale castles. Add in picture-perfect beaches and coastlines, as well as exciting culinary and nightlife scenes, and it is easy to see why Europe attracts more than half of all the tourists in the world.

We selected a few countries. On the list were France, Italy, Germany, Austria, Spain, Portugal, Ireland, Scotland, Poland, Romania, Bosnia, the Czech Republic, Montenegro, Slovakia, Hungary, Serbia, Croatia, Switzerland, and Greece. Not in this order and certainly not on the same trip or the same year.

The clear winners were France, Italy, Austria, Greece, and Croatia.

France: A delight to explore, impressive landscapes include such stunning sites as the Loire Valley, French Riviera, Normandy, and the awe-inspiring Alps. Most cities regardless of their size abound with historical treasures, markets, and restaurants offering a variety of delicious and unique regional culinary specialties. Tucked away among its picturesque countryside, you can explore regal chateaux, quaint villages, and verdant winelands. Two of my favorite areas in France are the Pyrenees mountains separating France from Spain and the Dordogne Valley known for its world class delicacy *foie gras*.

Italy: Home to not only Rome, Florence, Venice, and romantic Tuscany, but a staggering array of equally alluring smaller towns and cities. Italy is like nowhere else on Earth. Replete with stunning art and architecture, ancient historical sites, and cultural landmarks, its many riches and treasures veritably sparkle before your eyes. Add in fabulous weather and divine food, and it can be hard to tear yourself away.

The Dolomites Mountain range connecting Italy and Austria is an endless postcard scene. Towering, jagged peaks stretching into the sky, meadows, valleys, and glassy lakes undoubtedly unveil some of nature's most magnificent masterpieces.

Austria: Home to some of the most heart achingly beautiful scenery on the planet, Austria's many mountains, valleys, and lakes need to be seen to be believed. Austria is defined by the majestic Alps, showcasing arresting views wherever you go. Tucked among alpine valleys and glimmering lakeshores, stumble on charming villages. Vienna, the nation's capital, is one of Europe's most elegant cities.

Croatia: Alongside the glimmering Adriatic boasts a breathtaking rugged coastline, and idyllic offshore islands. Explore unique seaside towns such as Dubrovnik, Split, and Hvar.

Greece: Astounding archaeological sites dating back millennia. From Delphi, Olympia, Knossos and the Parthenon, the country is littered with impressive historical attractions. I regret not having visited the lovely laidback islands of Crete, Mykonos, and Rhodes. The world-famous Santorini, known for its whitewashed, cubiform houses, clings to cliffs above an underwater ancient caldera.

In other travels, a few cities stood out such as Edinburgh in Scotland. Prague in Czechia, Budapest in Hungary, and Bucharest in Romania.

Ireland offers jaw-dropping natural landscapes like the Giant's Causeway. Scenic road trips, rich heritage, and Blarney castle is a must see.

Some of the Eastern countries were depressing particularly Serbia torn by political unrest in recent wars. Visiting the Auschwitz concentration camp in Poland was a melancholic and poignant experience. A reminder evil is real. The atmosphere was oppressive and reminiscent of all the suffering that took place there.

CHURCHES IN EUROPE

Ifelt drawn into visiting many churches, from imposing cathedrals to tiny village churches and lost chapels in the mountains.

Depending on where you travel in Europe, the representation of Christianity takes on different flavors defined by historical, cultural, national, and local influences.

The Catholic church is predominant throughout European countries. Eastern Catholic, Eastern Orthodox, Oriental Orthodox, Protestant, Anglican, Calvinist, Presbyterian, Lutheran, and Methodist churches to name most. Judaism and Islam are also represented.

Non-denominational churches are far and few but gain more popularity as many denominational churches have lost countless believers for a multitude of reasons. Evangelical revivalism is rapidly proliferating. More and more European countries welcome Evangelism. An increasing number of souls are focusing on the "good news" of salvation or the "gospel" and believe in Jesus Christ as Savior and Lord.

My search for answers in my quest for spiritual Truth was alive. It is my firm belief God guided my steps. I was given the opportunity through my exploration of churches and religious monuments to immerse in the Christian world heritage of Europe.

The Vatican must be listed first because of the overwhelming stature of Saint Peter's Basilica and renowned work of Renaissance architecture. Marveling at Michelangelo's dome and standing in the famous Saint Peter's Square was undoubtedly a highlight. Joining the long queue to see the basilica's treasured Pieta sculpture was another high point.

I will cherish forever the Sistine Chapel. The ceiling, painted in fresco by Michelangelo is a cornerstone of high renaissance art. I literally could not leave the chapel. I sat on a bench admiring this great work of art until my head spun and my neck hurt to the point, I couldn't look up anymore. *The Creation of Adam* fresco illustrates the divine breath of life with God's and Adam's fingers almost touching. The Creator's index finger is ready to strike a spark upon contact with Adam's hand. A great deal of emotion stirred up in me and brought tears to my eyes. First insight and glimpse of my human origin. A powerful spiritual message asserting God as Creator of Humanity. I was never the same when I left the chapel. I knew to my core I had the immense privilege through Michelangelo's creation to feel God's presence. This moment in time was a turning point in bringing me closer to a transforming choice.

Saint Mark's Basilica in Venice, best known for its Byzantine architecture, proudly stands in Saint Mark's Square.

Sagrada Familia in Barcelona Spain, a famous landmark, a basilica like no other with both Art Nouveau and Gothic architecture featured on its unique exteriors. An imposing historical testimony of creativity by Antoni Gaudi.

I visited several other grand cathedrals, all stunning works of art and admired as such. I perceived most of them as impersonal, dark, domineering, and intimidating. I personally sensed no warmth or love, nor welcome within their imposing stone walls. The lack of brightness due to translucent light diffused through the stained-glass clerestory, lancet and rose windows contributed to my impression. Dimly lit churches purposely created a sober environment inviting contemplation, silence, and prayer. The light entering the sacred space through a stained-glass window strongly suggests a supernatural presence. Many of the marble statues so predominant in Catholic churches, especially tall statues caused uneasiness in me. I never liked being close to inanimate human-like figures.

All churches in Europe have carillon bell towers or massive bronze bells. They still are, to some degree, the voice of villages and many small towns. They had multiple functions and played an important role in people's daily lives. Not only did they mark the passing of time, but they punctuated the lives of our ancestors. The call to prayer still resonates today. In the past, they announced the angelus three times a day, funerals, baptisms, solemn masses, festivities, alert in case of danger, and when it was time for villagers to return from the fields. I feel a sense of nostalgia at the sound of church bells. I miss hearing it in the United States.

Churches are always the highest structure easy to spot in all towns and villages. From afar, the spire points sharply toward the sky as an attempt to reach the heavens.

From imposing cathedrals to secluded chapels, I have mixed feelings. I truly admired the architecture and beauty of them all. My favorites remain the small village churches and secluded chapels for their intimacy, warmth, luminosity, and the spirit of humbleness and simplicity depicting the original message God intended for humankind.

I remember a tiny modest chapel on a mountaintop in the striking Dolomites range. Built by shepherds, there was something so special about it. The spirit of God could be felt. It emanated love, light, and glowed in opposition to the dark cathedrals. A wholesome atmosphere, bringing feelings of compassion, serenity, and peace radiated. A comforting embrace flowing from the cross behind the altar filled me with unconditional love and a sense of acceptance. I did not want to leave.

SOUTHEAST ASIA

My friend had not been kidding when he said he needed a traveling companion. Traveling was a serious hobby, and he certainly enjoyed exploring the world and its diversity. A round of memorable trips to Southeast Asia took place. Numerous countries were visited. Vietnam, Cambodia, Malaysia, Singapore, Macau, Thailand, and Hong Kong.

Southeast Asia offers fascinating diversity due to a wide variety of ethnic groups and cultures, converging land and sea routes, pristine beaches, compelling history, sprawling rice terraces, rich, ancient customs, and traditions remarkably different from those of the West. This region offers an abundance of activities causing anyone's head to spin.

The largest ethnic groups of Southeast Asia are the Thai, Cambodians, Vietnamese, Burmese, Laotians and Indonesian. They share cultural characteristics. In 2019, the total Southeast Asian population stood at 655 million representing over 100 ethnic groups speaking more than 1000 languages and dialects. Their rich colorful traditions of cuisine, and folklore vary across regions, a source of great pride to many. Specifically, Indonesia, Malaysia, and Singapore are considered as Southeast Asian diverse nations, ethnically, linguistically, religiously, culturally, socially, and politically.

No matter where you visit, the food is tasty. The myriad combinations of textures, heat, and flavors leave your pallet longing for more.

Open air farmers markets and street vendors are everywhere it seems.

Displays of fruits and vegetables offered an abundance I had never seen before.

The selection of exotic colorful fruits was endless:

- mangosteen, rambutan, longan, langsat, pulasan, salak, pitaya, pomelo, jackfruit, guava, durian, sapodilla, goji berries, kumquat, starfruit, breadfruit, passion fruit, soursop, sugar apple, tamarillo, tamarind, noni, Asian pear, yuzu, mango, coconut, papaya, lychee.

I did not have the opportunity to taste most of them and was familiar with only a few.

Also, an explosion of vegetables and herbs to feast your eyes on:

- luffa gourd, yardlong beans, bottle gourd, snow peas, winged yam, lentils, daikon radish, Chinese celery, winged beans, broccoli rabe, bok choy, napa cabbage, mizuna greens, tatsoi, gai lan, peppers, thai eggplant, lotus root, ginger, galangal, turmeric, taro root, cumin, Vietnamese coriander, thai basil, mint, leeks, lemongrass to name a few.

Some of these fruits and vegetables are getting popular in the Western world as we commonly use them nowadays. Asian markets have made their appearance in the US a long time ago and their popularity is ever increasing with a growing consumer demand.

Southeast Asian recipes incorporate the organizing principles of Chinese cuisine and the complex flavors derived from Indian herbs and spices. Food can be sweet, sour, salty, spicy, and bitter all in the same bite. Through modern influences, the area has embraced certain aspects of Colonial French cuisine, and to a lesser extent, Spanish and American cooking. The result delivers an experience you cannot find anywhere else on the planet.

There are subtle differences in food culture between each

country. While Thai food, for example, is often characterized as sweet and spicy, Vietnamese food is considered light and refreshing and Filipino cuisine is heavy in comparison.

Some of the tastiest is street food, inexpensive, delicious, readily available anywhere round the clock. Many are traditionally from street food carts vendors, a form of open-air dining establishment pervading most of Asia.

Influenced by the French, sandwiches called *banh mi* are a popular quick lunch option. Noodle soups are also considered snacks, or a quick breakfast or lunch fare. Street vendors offer a wide variety of satay-skewered and grilled morsels including pork, chicken, duck, shrimp, squid and more. Street foods can be curries, green papaya or green mango salad, cabbage salad, coconut tapioca soup, raw beef salad (spice-and-salt cured), rice noodle soups, sour soups, spring rolls, summer rolls, and stir-fried leafy greens. All this accompanied by a variety of pickled vegetables, sweet chili sauce, Vietnamese fish sauce, peanut dip among many popular dipping dressings.

The locals are a joy to behold with a unique sense of hospitality never ceasing to amaze. The people of Southeast Asia are fun loving, gentle, open-minded, laid-back, and friendly. There is a prevailing sentiment: life should be lived in the present moment and problems should not be taken so seriously as to disrupt enjoyment. Most people have a strongly developed sense of courtesy and respect. Important values include high regard for elders, reverence for their government, and loyalty to friends and family. Polite and non-confrontational, their behavior is much derived from their Buddhist belief system.

The value of a smile, friendliness, community spirit and, more importantly, finding happiness in the simpler things in life was demonstrated to us daily.

The younger generation, however, is now regarded not as polite and gentle as their parents. The influence of modern urban culture has been said to have given young Southeast Asians a rougher, meaner, more streetwise attitude. We never encountered unpleasant behavior during our travels in this part of the world.

The history of Southeast Asia is unique as it pertains to foreign occupation, colonization, trade, war, and religion. European colonialism particularly the French influenced the region contributing to the uniqueness of this incredible melting pot. French Indochina was a grouping of French colonial territories until its demise in 1954. It comprised Cambodia, Laos, and the Vietnamese regions of Tonkin in the north, Annam in the center, Cochin China in the south and the Chinese territory of Guangzhou Wan until 1945.

The ancient capital of Laos is a host of French colonial buildings and was listed on the UNESCO World Heritage Site for its remarkably well preserved architectural, cultural, and religious heritage. During the French colonial period, there was a visible shift and transition of traditional residential buildings into French-style edifices within various parts of Southeast Asia. As such, Southeast Asia now has a harmonious split between traditional and French colonial architecture.

The landscapes are no slouch either. No shortage of picturesque postcards sceneries. Each country offers a variety of rural and urban sightseeing.

Unique topographical features, flora and fauna will surprise you. The landscape is characterized by intermingled physical elements: mountain ranges, plains and plateaus, and water in the form of both shallow seas and extensive drainage systems. Southeast Asia's tropical rain forest is home to at least thirty-five thousand vascular plant species. Tropical forests grow there year-round because of the region's warm temperatures and plentiful rainfall.

A considerable diversity of wildlife thrives throughout the region. Bears, gibbons, elephants, deer, civets, and pigs among others are found as well as a diminishing number of tigers.

As the pace of development accelerates and populations continue to expand in Southeast Asia, concern has increased regarding the impact of human activity on the environment. A significant portion of the region, however, has not changed greatly and remains an unaltered home to wildlife. The nations of the region, with only a few exceptions, have become aware of the need to maintain forest cover not only to prevent soil erosion but to preserve the diversity of flora and fauna. Indonesia, for example, has created an extensive system of national parks and preserves for this purpose. Even so, certain species like the Javan rhinoceros face extinction.

Large cities such as Kuala Lumpur, Hong Kong, Singapore, and Bangkok showcase phenomenal state-of-the-art modern architecture and do not mirror the West.

I loved Hanoi, capital of Vietnam, known for its centuries-old architecture and rich culture combining French, Chinese, and Southeast Asian influences. The French quarters offer a lovely stroll through early 20th century architecture, art deco designs, and some 1930s modernism. I recall the nostalgic colonial homes still standing from the long-gone "Indochina era." The Hoa Lo Prison Museum well known as the "Hanoi Hilton" during the Vietnam War is a landmark.

Being in rush traffic anywhere in the region was a feat. With barely any driving rules, roundabouts everywhere, no red or green lights, it was a wonder to watch. I remember riding in rickshaws, called *pousse-pousse* in French, being terrified and at the same time amazed on how they always manage to zigzag with few accidents. I understand today, with the afflux of automobiles, the situation is far more prone to accidents and the local governments are trying to bring in some regulations.

While in Hong Kong, we took a turbo-jet ferry to Macau and arrived in about 50 minutes. Macau located in the Western Pearl River Delta by the South China Sea was formerly a Portuguese colony for 442 years and was transferred to China in 1999. It became a special administrative region of China which maintains separate governing and economic systems from those of mainland China under the principle of "one country, two systems."

The unique blend of Portuguese and Chinese architecture in the city's historic center led to its inscription on the UNESCO World Heritage list. A remarkable conservation of heritage. Macau, referred to as the "Las Vegas of the East," has become a major resort and a top destination for the gambling industry said to be seven times larger than Las Vegas.

Macau has a turbulent history and was of strategic importance during the opium trade in the 18th century.

The mixing of Chinese and Portuguese culture and religious traditions left Macau with multicultural celebrations all year round. The cuisine mainly based on both Cantonese and Portuguese reflects a unique culinary blend after centuries of colonial rule.

The entire Southeast Asia region is a blend of old and new, a land of multiple contrasts. Its cultural diversity is unsurpassed. It is perhaps the most diverse region on earth.

Upon returning from this amazing trip lasting over six weeks, we were in dire need of rest and stayed put for a while.

CANADA

In between long trips overseas, my friend and I would fly somewhere in the US and Canada, rent a car, and explore different states and provinces at our leisure. Driving is the most flexible and thorough way to travel. You can stop where you want and go at your own pace. Some of the most wonderful sceneries are found right here on the Northern American Continent.

The list of stunning world-famous landscapes, attraction sites and natural landmarks is long indeed. I have had the immense privilege of seeing many of them. North America is a paradise for nature lovers.

Here is one of my favorites.

British Columbia, defined by its Pacific coastline and mountains ranges offers some of the most breathtaking sites on our planet. Vancouver despite being the second-largest city in Canada feels strongly connected to nature and the great outdoors. The city is surrounded by water, fringed with beaches, and watched over by distant mountains. With a healthy number of parks and gardens, the best known is Stanley Park, at the tip of a peninsula. I spent a whole day exploring the park walking, hugging a narrow seawall path, then headed inland to follow trails through hemlock, fir, cedar trees, and admire the parks nine replica totem poles inspired by those carved by the indigenous Coast Salish people. The Museum of Anthropology, housed in a concrete and glass structure, holds thousands of archaeological objects, artworks, and textiles from the region.

The food in Vancouver is scrumptious and it is not surprising the city is emerging as one of the top-ranking cuisines in the world, particularly their seafood. It is not food to just fill your belly but to appreciate the textures, mouthfeel, flavors, and aromas.

Salmon candy is impossible to stop eating once you try it. Made by smoking salmon and glazing it with their famous maple syrup, salmon candy oozes out the flavors of salty, sweet, and smokey all in one and can become an addiction. It will turn a non-fish lover into a fish-lover! Sushi is king in Vancouver. I remember the B.C. roll, simple and elegant, made with cucumber, smoked salmon, sweet sauce, and then grilled with the skin on, this dish is crispy and moist at the same time. Dungeness crab prepared by roasting the crab in butter, white wine, parsley, and other aromatic spices, the appearance of the final dish itself will make mouths drool. Chinese cuisine and Dim Sum are also wonderful staples. All my friend and I could think about while visiting this fantastic town was eating.

The pedestrian-friendly city of Vancouver consistently ranks as one of the most walkable cities in Canada with a compact downtown, easy-to-navigate neighborhoods, and plenty of natural attractions. Granville and Robson are vibrant and popular streets for shopping and restaurants.

We absolutely loved going there and did more than once.

We also took a ferry to Vancouver Island, just a short journey from Vancouver. Home to the provincial capital, Victoria, with its museums, parliament buildings, and manicured gardens, is worth a visit. Driving through the island's sheltered bays, glassy inlets, old-growth forest, and wildlife-rich coastline was captivating.

A short but scenic adventure was an epic road trip from Vancouver to Whistler. The town of Whistler was the Host Mountain Resort of the Vancouver 2010 Winter Olympics. Top ski resort but also an outdoor adventure paradise. We only stayed overnight. A world-class resort yes but it came with world-class price tags.

The road trip was the objective, the British Columbia Highway 99, also known as the Sea-to-Sky Highway winds along the Howe Sound, with mesmerizing mountain views, provincial parks, waterfalls, small towns, trails, and unique attractions. It has been said to be one of the most beautiful scenic drives in the world. It really gave us a true feel for what the Pacific Northwest is all about.

Then, we flew to Calgary before leisurely exploring the Canadian Rockies by car, stopping in places piquing our interest. A magical area of endless natural landscapes, plenty of opportunities for spotting wildlife and sweeping views of snow-capped peaks, azure lakes, and pristine forests.

We started with Banff National Park staying in the city of Banff considered to be the main hub of the Canadian Rockies. Canada's first and world's third national park. The spectacular scenery makes Banff, along with its neighboring national parks, Yoho, Jasper, and Kootenay UNESCO World Heritage Sites. The town of Banff is quaint with famous photography spots, also known for its Upper Hot Springs.

Lake Louise and Lake Moraine are popular destinations. The world-famous Chateau Lake Louise, built right on its shoreline, gives a perfect view of towering mountains and glaciers. Moraine Lake is a stunning turquoise lake, cradled by the Valley of the Ten Peaks. The impressive Plain of Six Glacier is one of the most pristine wilderness area Canada has to offer. We were blown away by soaring peaks and frozen glaciers and took lots of pictures.

Lake Louise marks the start of the Icefields Parkway all the way to Jasper and encompasses the heart of the Canadian Rockies. We traveled past monumental glaciers, icy blue lakes, enormous mountains and stretches of road which simply must be seen to be believed.

At the end of the Icefields Parkway, we ended up in the townsite of Jasper, central hub of many beautiful spots in the Jasper National Park region. We took the gondola and enjoyed spectacular 360-degree panoramic views from the top.

As we returned to Calgary, we felt like we only had scratched the surface and faced the fact we just could not see it all. So much more to explore but we did not because of immense distances to be covered and lack of time.

Upon returning from this trip, we slowed down the traveling because my companion was not feeling well and had to address his health issues.

We would occasionally take a few days off and concentrate on visiting various US states.

As we stayed home for long periods of time, I took a part time job in a department store in Colorado Springs where we lived. The management agreed to my request for nonpaid time off as I explained my frequent travels. They apparently did not mind as long as it was not during the peak holiday season.

REFLECTING

A s I reflect on my traveling days, I cannot help but feel immense reverence, gratitude and give all the glory to God. All creation points to God as the Master Designer. He gave us a richly created world to help us know Him better. Through His creation, He affirms His magnificence, His power, His kindness and generosity. I was blessed to have had the opportunity to see the unparalleled beauty of His handiwork, the magnificent environment He designed for us to live in, our planet earth.

(John 1:3 *ESV*)

Through Him all things were made, and without Him nothing was made that has been made.

RETURNING TO FRANCE

I had been keeping regular contact with my mother. She began hinting she had reached a stage in her life where she needed help. She was in her late 80s and I was her only child.

I remembered how frail she looked walking us to the train station at the end of our last visit a couple of years ago.

Since I was not traveling much anymore, I called her regularly. She would tell me how difficult it was for her to go to the market and carry her groceries. She did not drive anymore and either walked or took the bus, which is very common in European cities. She emphasized a lack of focus when doing paperwork because her head was not solid. She complained of a constant lack of energy and health concerns. She felt isolated and fragile. She was thinking of getting someone's help but thought it would make sense for me to take on the role.

On the other hand, my relationship with my companion was getting stressful. Other than sharing our traveling, we were not compatible and had serious differences of opinion on many important subjects.

Some were significant such as my intense and growing need for spirituality and God's presence in my life, which he systematically criticized, mocked, and considered a weakness on my part. It seemed I never did anything right and was frequently judged and unappreciated.

How interesting … in many ways, he behaved like my mother towards me.

Intense traveling provided distractions and a common purpose. Staying home changed the dynamics. Our disparities, disagreements, and irreconcilable differences surfaced and clashed.

It became obvious we had little to share or say to each other. The friction between us was constant.

When my mom suggested I come to France to help her, I felt touched she solicited my presence when she could have hired professional help. She was my mother. I had always wanted to get close to her. In my mind and dreams, I truly believed this was perhaps our last chance. I imagined because of her frailty, and of what seemed like helplessness, she had realized I was the only one she could reach out to. I genuinely thought she had mellowed out and desired closeness with me as much as I did with her.

It took me a while to make the decision. My strong desire to reconcile our differences had not faded away. It was not just my duty as her daughter to respond but it was a calling, I sensed from a higher realm. Not about to miss out on the opportunity to finally build a relationship with the human being who gave me life, I decided to give it a try.

My living companion and I agreed separation between us was necessary and to a degree, I think he understood my intent and respected it.

It was December of 2015 when I flew back to France to reunite with my mom.

After a long overnight trip, several connecting flights, buses, and trains loaded with luggage, I arrived at the small railroad station of Arcachon. It was late in the evening, dark, cold, windy, and raining. There was no cab available, so I dragged my suitcases for about a mile walking to her place. I arrived soaked, aching, and tired. Ringing the bell of her apartment building, she released the front door. I took the elevator to get to her floor, managing the best I could with all my luggage.

I will never forget the "welcome" she gave me. She looked at me and said, "Evelyne, I don't believe this is going to work out between us. You are not going to fit in considering the lifestyle you had in the US. This is a mistake."

The shock I felt in that moment is indescribable. Her words hurt me to the core of my being. She did not even realize what she had just done. I wanted to cry out.

Her pessimistic comments impacted me greatly. What a self-defeating statement on her part, setting the tone of our mutual interaction negatively from the very start. The following days were awkward.

I instinctively acted as if nothing had been said. I did my very best to be cheerful, helpful, and enthusiastic. I took on my role of helper and assistant seriously. She did not have internet. I made it happen. I accompanied her to the grocery store, holding her arm to help her walk steadily. This detail is important to me. She had difficulty with her knees and walking could be challenging. She was disciplined and walked twice a day without fail to maintain her mobility. I went with her everywhere and found myself being protective. If we had to take the bus, a local little bus free of charge, the driver could go fast and we had better hold on to a pole while turning street corners, especially when standing up when no seats were available. I always kept an eye on her and was ready to intervene if needed. I felt a strong sense of responsibility.

Her frailty was only physical. Her will and mind were as strong as ever. She could not focus for long, but while she could, she made it clear she was in charge. No softening of personality.

She was tired in the evenings and when I went to say goodnight to her, she would speak about the past and share family stories I did not know. Those were important moments, a sharing of events she remembered related to her own life.

Her apartment had two bedrooms but was small. We had little privacy and managed as best we could.

We set into a routine. In my free time, I would take long walks. I also decided to get involved in some of the town community activities. The town hall sponsored a variety of free programs for the residents, educational, cultural, sports, etc.

Arcachon is a popular seaside resort in Southwest France known for oyster harvesting. It boasts four districts named after the seasons. The *Ville d'Ete* (Summer), quarter to quaint shopping streets and restaurants. The town's sandy main beach and a casino built in the 19th century. The *Ville d'Hiver* (Winter) with extravagant 19th-century villas. The *Ville d'Automne* (Fall) and the *Ville du Printemps* (Spring). South of town is the *Dune du Pilat*, the largest sand dune in Europe.

Arcachon historically was a health resort for the upper class and nobility. Napoleon III and his wife Eugenie de Montijo from Spain visited several times. It added to the reputation and allure of the town. Illustrious residents included Alexandre Dumas and

Toulouse-Lautrec who lived in houses by the seafront.

Many retirees have elected to live in this charming resort, known as a prime destination for weekend visitors and second residence owners.

A lively resort all year round hosting a variety of events.

I needed to get involved in something besides dedicating my time exclusively to my mother who did not need me all day and liked to nap in the afternoons. I decided to meet new people and have some form of a social life. I mentioned it to her, but her reaction was not encouraging.

Despite her lack of enthusiasm, I pursued my interests and signed up for a couple of classes in the afternoons twice a week. It was not long before a few of the people I met, asked me if I would like to tutor conversational English once they knew I had lived in the US many years and was fluent. The organizing staff approached me about offering a class once a week on a volunteer basis. I was excited at the prospect and accepted.

Telling my mother was not easy. She did not like the idea. She reminded me for the first time I had not moved in with her to have a social life. She spoke in terms of a "contract" between us and full commitment on my part.

We discussed it. She did not need or even want my help most of the time. It seemed as always; I did not do anything right according to her rules. The way I cleaned windows, floors, or washed dishes was criticized because it was not how she wanted it done. Going to the grocery store by myself was an issue because I would occasionally buy foods, she did not need for herself. She complained about the space I used in her refrigerator and demanded I return some items at times refusing to keep them. Conflicts over trivial matters became daily occurrences. My patience was constantly being tested. The fact I was in my 60's did not faze her. I had to abide by her rules to keep out of arguments.

She also did not hide how much she enjoyed having her apartment to herself. The fact we were on top of each other and had no privacy contributed to the growing tension.

Her statements were contradictory and confusing. It seemed she was not pleased with my outside activities but at the same time she missed her solitude.

Nothing flowed naturally or easily between us. I was walking on eggshells and more and more felt I was intruding on her privacy.

I concentrated on preparing for my English conversation classes. A welcome diversion. I gathered different materials on current actualities especially lifestyle in the US and the multiple differences defining the United States versus France. I wanted to test the waters first as to what would be of interest to my students. I was not sure of the levels they had. About 25 people signed up. My professional background came in handy and being familiar with cross cultural training was a plus. After all, I was a naturalized American citizen by choice and had adapted to many of the American ways.

The first day of class everyone showed up. I was apprehensive knowing my first challenge was figuring out how much English each participant knew. I could feel the excitement in the classroom. I knew the previous teacher focused on grammar and was more familiar with British English. I jumped into action and began by introducing myself, who I was, where I lived before, how many years I spent in the USA, and my professional background. I spoke slowly and clearly while at the same time observing everyone's reaction and whether they understood me or not. Clearly by the expression on various faces, it was obvious some got most of what I was saying to various degrees and others had their hands up in the air or a facial expression indicating they did not comprehend.

Then, I proceeded to have each person introduce themselves in English and explain how and where they learned. We had one hour and thirty minutes class time total. It took all of it for each person's turn. Some had a basic conversational knowledge, others clearly struggled, and a few could only spurt out a few words. It was clear if we kept them together, it was going to be disappointing for those who could express themselves because I would have to make sure everybody participated. Conversation is conversation and if one could not converse, they could not participate.

It took a couple of sessions but eventually it worked itself out and a few people dropped out. The remaining students became active participants and were thrilled I was not focusing on grammar, but rather on world events and particularly on the US. A few had either been to the US or wanted to visit. Some did not like Americans, so they decided to challenge me. I welcomed their comments and questions. We made it as fun and light as possible. In the end, I socialized with a few people outside of the classroom.

In the meanwhile, the mood and ambience at my mom's apartment was not getting any better. The situation between us continuously degraded. The atmosphere was tense, and I knew we could not go on much longer. I started to react to her verbal attacks. I had always been passive, but a change was taking place in me. I needed to assert myself and could no longer hold back.

I told her to sit down one day, and for the first time, I vented a lifetime of piled up frustration. My reaction had nothing to do with my previous mild attempts at getting through. I told her everything weighing on my heart and mind going back to my childhood. I was specific. I gave examples. I was filled with an overload of destructive memories, and they all came out. She tried to stop me a couple of times, but I became so focused and intense that what I had to say flowed like a dam needing release. There must have been something about my determination and forcefulness causing her to remain silent after a while. She sat there listening with a smirk on her face which said a lot about how she was receiving me. I could see I was not getting anywhere and if anything, I was signing my own condemnation in her eyes.

I realized then my hopes and dreams would never come true on building a loving relationship with the human being who gave me life. When I stopped talking, exhausted and heartbroken, the sentence came.

Are you finished? She reminded me of all she had done for me and how ungrateful I was. She asked me to leave her apartment. She suggested I return to the US to my previous relationship. She indicated she wanted me as far as possible from her. For some reason, my reaction was to tell her I was going to stay reminding her even if things were not good, I still had left everything behind to be with her because she needed help. I was not giving up so easily. I asked her to reconsider trying to make this work because after all she was my mother, and I was her only child. I emphasized she was nearly 90 years old and had difficulties with her health and mobility.

All my life, I had avoided confrontation. My hopes of reconciliation and bonding, after this epic encounter, were evaporating.

Shortly thereafter, I was provoked again while washing dishes in her tiny kitchen. She stood behind me making comments I don't even remember. Out of desperation and unable to contend with her verbal provocations, I handed her a small kitchen knife and told her this was her chance to get rid of me if she hated me so much. A dramatic reaction on my part I must admit. It bore final consequences.

I was told to move out as quickly as possible. According to her, I displayed mental and emotional issues requiring medical attention and medication. It was now unsafe to be around me, and she was going to call her lawyer to find out how she could protect herself from me.

This time, the light came on. In order to keep my sanity, I had to go. I also wanted to leave as soon as possible. I walked out in the streets with my phone and called a couple of close friends.

Adeline, the daughter of my dear Juliette who had passed away a few months before, immediately suggested I move into her mom's apartment. She was getting ready to put it on the market. It was still furnished, she said, and told me where to find the keys. Literally, a Godsend. Our Lord Almighty intervened in my favor.

I packed my belongings the same day and moved everything to Juliette's apartment about a mile away. All on foot of course, dragging everything behind me.

With my last suitcase ready to go, and mother watching me, she accompanied me to her front door and wished me good luck. She asked if I was flying back to the US. I answered with the truth and witnessed her angry reaction as I told her I was staying in Arcachon. I reminded her of my legal right to remain in the same town and she could not tell me where to live. She asked for her keys back. She also specified she never wanted to see me or hear from me again unless it was an absolute emergency.

It had been less than seven months since I had moved in with her all the way from Colorado. What an unnecessary and sorrowful outcome for both of us.

I still don't know why she called me a couple of hours later as I was settling down in Juliette's apartment to ask me if I was okay. I broke down in tears on the phone, telling her how in the world could I be okay after such destructive events. After all, I no longer had a mother. She said I would eventually get over it.

THE PATH TO GOD

I had no family anymore. Rejected and abandoned, where was I going to turn?

At first, I was in a state of shock. I had to assimilate and accept the facts. My own blood did not want anything to do with me. This realization crushed me. I went through multiple stages: distress, an acute sense of rejection, and uncontrollable heartbreak. It was a process I was going to have to go through. It brought me into a whirlwind of emotions, soul searching, self-examination, turning inward. and reevaluating my entire life and purpose.

Mercifully, I was privileged to be in a quiet, peaceful, and private setting in the apartment of my dear friend Juliette, feeling grateful to her daughter who so graciously extended her help. The apartment, though small, was welcoming and homely. Not only did I feel comfortable there to do all the personal work I needed to do, but I sensed my late friend's warm and soothing presence floating around me. I spent countless hours sitting on her sofa looking out of her window offering a glimpse of the bay of Arcachon. Staring out for hours at times, I identified my despair as an illness to overcome and had little energy if any. Beaten down and weak, it was going to be a long road to recovery.

Mourning, grief, and hopelessness followed the initial shock. It resembled what I felt like when I lost my first daughter. Feelings of irrepressible anger at myself and my family would surge. Why was I rejected? What did I ever do to deserve such injustice? I even envisioned visiting my mother and bargaining with her for another chance or at least an explanation I felt I deserved but quickly abandoned the idea. It was ludicrous as I knew deep inside it was a self-defeating hope.

Introspection and self-reflection succeeded. What was it about me I needed to understand? I looked at my behavior with my closest "blood" relatives throughout the years. Yes, I had not always done right by them or been perfect. I made mistakes, no question about it. But my intent was always good, I never intentionally did anything to hurt anyone.

I had been valued and loved as a "daughter" by three women, two of whom in a close relationship with my father and the third, Juliette, my dearest friend. I relished my close bond with every one of them. They had never been critical of me but had supported and defended me on multiple occasions. I also remembered how close I was to my grandmother and my aunt Liliane in my youth.

I had a couple of dear friends who gave me emotional support, always present and available. Adeline, Juliette's daughter, rescued me and, to this day, remains a close friend. There was never any judgment, only acceptance, support, and words of encouragement.

Slowly, and after some counseling, I began to come to terms with and accept what was. The choices my mother made were hers alone. I could only account for my own behavior, and I had to let go. I realized we must take ownership of our lives. We are accountable for the decisions we make and resulting action or inaction.

This was a pivotal point for me, and I emphasize pivotal. It is not every day you are forced to terminate your relationship with your own mother and divorce yourself from all possibilities. My patience, understanding, and willingness snapped. It became apparent she had underlying issues I was never going to solve.

I found myself almost every day, walking into a couple of nearby churches, spending time there, kneeling on a pew, staring at the cross behind the altar. I asked questions to God, specifically requesting His guidance. Was I being heard? Would I receive a sign showing I mattered to Him?

What did I know about God? Each church I walked into displayed Jesus Christ nailed to a cross behind the altar. It was devastating to see and be reminded of such suffering and humiliation. I knew from history Jesus was the Messiah, the Son of God, crucified for the sins of humanity. His death and resurrection formed the cornerstone of Christian faith.

I remembered, while living in my little ranch alone in Colorado, how I had been drawn to Jesus through reading mostly New Age books. They presented Him as a great teacher holding supernatural powers leaving a profound and lasting influence on humanity. Reading randomly parts of the Old and New Testaments on my own volition over the years had left me with no clear answers. Nothing made sense. I was unable to connect the dots to the story line because I had not read the Bible from start to finish. This prevented me from grasping the big picture. I pleaded with God for answers through a sign, a truth revealed, a godly presence felt. I knew in my heart I was on the right path.

More books were absorbed. I went back to the Bible and again without guidance read at random. Unbeknown to me, my approach was counterproductive. It confused me, preventing me from bringing to light the very revelation I yearned for. It never occurred reading the Bible in chronological order would have helped me grasp the meaning of the incarnation of Jesus as prophesized multiple times in the Old Testament.

Nevertheless, the messages I received through the parables of Jesus spoke to me in a profound way. It was heart felt and resonated within the deepest part of my being. His words were fulfilling, empowering, and comforting. I found myself reading His teachings over and over. His words pierced through my soul. I would focus on His sermons and disregard the surrounding context.

I could not grasp Who He really was and Whom He fully represented. I shared my impressions with friends for feedback. They only agreed to the fact He had been a great teacher along the lines of Buddha and other famous "avatars," incarnated deities embodied in human form throughout history. After a few attempts to explore with them my search for Truth, I concluded it was best to keep my ongoing transformation to myself. I knew they were wondering what was happening to me.

Through His teachings, Jesus Christ became my friend, my comforter, and Whom I would reach out to for emotional support.

When going to a church, and looking at Jesus on a cross, I was heartbroken and apologized for the cruelty we showed as humans toward Him. I felt ashamed, my ancestors participated in such destruction of the highest representation of wisdom and hope humanity had ever witnessed.

I was so far from the Truth in my interpretation. The true identity of Jesus Christ would be revealed later and transform my life at the deepest level. I was off to a good start and surely on the right track. Not quite ready for a full-blown "revival and renewal of the heart" and God had His reasons.

What I so sadly missed:

(John 3:16 *NIV*)

For God so loved the world that He gave His one and only Son, that whoever believes in Him shall not perish but have eternal life.

IDAHO

A reconnection was made with my former travel companion who, in the meantime, had moved to Idaho. He suggested I go for a visit.

It was winter of 2016. A full year had gone by since I had returned to France to "help" and "lovingly connect" with my mother in the hope to build a relationship and care for her to the end of her life.

I agreed to fly to Idaho and spend a couple of weeks there. We did what we knew best together and took off for a few days of driving and exploring Idaho.

I was impressed by the swath of wilderness and endless sweeping vistas through the mountains and valleys of Idaho's vast landscapes. I noted Idaho has 31 scenic byways offering breathtaking scenery of lakes, mountains, glittering rivers, waterfalls, immense plains, old mining towns, and more. A mystical wonderland in the mist of winter. Nicknamed the Gem State, it is known not only for its scenery and famous spuds but also for the abundance of rare minerals having been found in all corners of the state. There are seventy-two different precious and semi-precious gems recorded in Idaho. The state gemstone, the star garnet, is by far the rarest and can only be found in India and the Idaho Panhandle.

My old companion and I reconnected during this trip. He showed no surprise regarding the outcome with my mother. He even mentioned he had wondered why it lasted so long. He was happy to see me again and even showed some compassion. He suggested I come back and resume living with him again. He was getting older and did not hide the fact he could use some help and company. He was looking forward to taking some trips again.

Requesting time to think it over, I went back to France.

After a few days upon my return to Arcachon, something in me began to feel quite unusual. I identified a strong pull and urge to return to Idaho. It did not make a whole lot of sense. I knew I would be returning to a precarious situation by moving back with my old companion. As much as we enjoyed our travels together, we were clearly on a different path. My need for spirituality was getting stronger and I knew I was not going to share this crucial part of my life with him. Nevertheless, the powerful attraction for Idaho was undeniable. My inner guidance kept pressing on. I reasoned with myself. What could be the significance of this captivation? I took some time to think it over but the more I resisted the idea the more overpowering it became.

I finally chose and agreed to return.

We moved into a brand-new house he had built with a view of the Snake River in a little town in Southeast Idaho.

Slowly, we settled in and began a new routine. Across the road, was a beautiful, paved trail by the Snake River with miles of walking. I explored it every day. The Snake River, 1078 miles long, rises in Western Wyoming, flows through the plains of Southern Idaho where I now lived, through the rugged Hells Canyon on the Oregon-Idaho border and the rolling Palouse Hills of Washington, emptying into the mighty Columbia River. I remember the water's rushing sounds, the abundance of vegetation and migrating birds. I enjoyed my walks and would sit on a bench looking at the scenery in contemplative meditation.

I met a few of my new neighbors on my walks and shared greetings with them. A lady, by the name of Angela, whom I met along the way, also exchanged greetings. We eventually started to talk. She suggested we walk together whenever possible. I enjoyed speaking with her.

She exuded kindness, compassion, and authenticity. I rapidly felt comfortable in her presence and looked forward to our time together, walking, talking, and getting to know one another. We eventually began sharing our life stories. Hers was amazing, filled with events and situations revealing much about her character. As a young woman, she chose to move to South Africa dedicating her life to help kids who lived in extreme poverty-stricken ghettos. How she eventually adopted a couple of these children and brought them back to the United States.

She described an existence of dedication, abnegation, wanting to make a positive difference in the life of others in a giving and selfless way. I had never quite encountered anyone like her. She spoke about this like it was the most natural choice one could make. What was the driving force behind her actions? She invited me to her home. I met her husband. I will never forget how drawn I was, when stepping into their living room, to a magnificent painting above their fireplace depicting Jesus Christ. His hands were outstretched extending His grace in a gesture of love as if to lift us from darkness capturing us into His light.

This is when, still unconsciously, I began to realize why I had felt such a strong calling to come to Idaho.

Both Angela and James were living their faith by simply acting on God's Word. Their life choices reflected their beliefs. I felt at home with them and as we sat down in their living room, we spent countless hours talking about Jesus Christ. For the first time ever, I was with a couple who welcomed my curiosity and endless questions. The tugging on my heart grew stronger.

They understood my misconceptions based on my past and my solitary search for the Truth. They explained the significance of the Old Testament helping me to connect the dots with the New Testament. They revealed the Truth with great enthusiasm in simple words supported by an open Bible they knew by heart. The Jesus I was drawn to, the Son of God Himself, fulfilling every prophecy about the coming Messiah in the Old Testament, brought forgiveness, life, and hope to all of humanity.

Angela and James glorified God by being faithful stewards and disciples, sharing the love of Christ Jesus with everyone. They were touched by my eagerness to learn. I was like a child in a candy store, embarking on my greatest spiritual journey. We developed a strong bond. I took a deep dive into the Bible with them. All my questions were answered beyond my wildest dreams.

For the first time I began to make sense of the third Being of the Trinity, the Holy Spirit. From my background with the Catholic Church, the Holy Ghost was undoubtedly the least understood member of the Godhead. Without a body and a personal name, the Holy Ghost seemed a distant entity. God's spirit dwelling inside every true believer as a constant companion in the walk of faith was wonderful news to me. I began to long for Him to dwell within me too.

Angela and James helped me open my eyes to the Holy Spirit existence throughout eternity sharing attributes with God the Father and Jesus, His Son, such as omniscience, omnipotence, and eternality. Likewise, He is all-loving, forgiving, merciful, and just. I marveled at His steadfast readiness to transform us from the person we are today to the person He created us to be, ever closer to the character of Christ. This is what I had been searching for all my life.

These revelations profoundly impacted me. I felt gratefulness and thankfulness for the new awareness slowly taking place. I found true friends in Angela and James, and they became the brother and sister I never had.

While all this marvelous transformation was taking place, I had committed to a trip to Italy with my roommate, and we were scheduled to leave in the coming fall.

This was about the time I felt compelled to write a letter to my mother. I had attempted to call her the previous Christmas and the interaction between us barely lasted a couple of minutes. She was not happy to hear from me and reminded me to leave her in peace. Still, something in me was not giving up. It felt vital I wrote her a letter. A reflection of my sorrow for our failed relationship, thanking her for having brought me into this world. Expressing my love for her. Nothing more, nothing less. I left her my contact in case she would have a reversal of heart.

ITALY IN THE FALL

We flew to Italy and landed in Bologna. The plan was to spend time in Tuscany, the Northern Lakes region, the Italian Riviera and possibly the Amalfi Coast.

Tuscany, an achingly beautiful region of Italy, is a touchstone of art, food, and culture. Made up of stunning countryside and distinguished cities, it is a perfect escape for gastronomes, nature explorers, and fans of the Italian Renaissance. Florence or Firenze in Italian, the cradle of Renaissance, is a true enchantment. Home to numerous museums and art galleries, such as the Uffizi Gallery exhibiting Botticelli's *The Birth of Venus* and Da Vinci's *Annunciation*. One of the most iconic sites is the Duomo, a cathedral with a terracotta-tiled dome engineered by Brunelleschi and a bell tower by Giotto. The Accademia Gallery displays Michelangelo's *David* sculpture. Florence was declared by UNESCO a World Heritage Site in 1982. Tuscany is my favorite part of Italy. I could not stop taking pictures. To give justice to Florence, a minimum of three days is a must to visit the most popular landmarks.

We drove to Siena, a city in central Tuscany distinguished by its medieval brick buildings. The fan-shaped central square, Piazza del Campo is the site of the Palazzo Pubblico, the Gothic town hall, and Torre del Mangia, a slender 14th century tower with sweeping views from its distinctive white crown. Interesting fact, Siena is home to the world's oldest bank, the Monte dei Paschi Banca, still in operation since 1472. The university of Siena, originally called Studium Senese, was founded in 1240, making it one of the oldest universities in the world. Siena was one of the most important medieval towns of Europe, and its historic center is a UNESCO World Heritage Site, showcasing several buildings from the 13th and

14th centuries.

Then we leisurely drove through the Tuscan countryside, an endless source of delight and postcard scenery. From Siena, we took the direction of Montepulciano. We were on the most scenic road of Tuscany with the highest concentration of typical landscapes seen in travel magazines. The countryside of Val d'Orcia is nothing short of spectacular. Charming villages and hidden abbeys are well worth a visit. Medieval towns such as San Gimignano, Volterra and Lucca are all highlights. I found it difficult to prefer one over another.

The area is also known for its award-winning vineyards producing Chianti wines. Eating is another pastime, and a work of art. Tuscan cooking is based upon using the freshest and simplest ingredients of the season including many legumes, cheeses, vegetables, and fruits. The food is simple, rich in flavor, hearty, and quite filling. Some of their specialties include the *bistecca alla Fiorentina* or Florentine steak, *buccellato* a popular sweet bread, *cantucci* a *biscotti* filled with almonds, *crostini di fegatini* made of chicken livers, *gnocchi di castagne* or chestnut dumplings. *Lampredotto*, a traditional sandwich dished up from street food made with the fourth stomach of a cow slowly cooked in a broth if you can "stomach" it. These are samples of the most typical Tuscan dishes. My favorites remained pasta dishes and pizzas found everywhere on the Italian soil.

One could spend months wandering through the rolling hills and towns of Tuscany, still finding more to love.

Then we drove to the scenic and spectacular Italian Riviera, a narrow coastal strip which lies between the Ligurian Sea, and the mountain chain formed by the Maritime Alps. It is known for its beaches, colorfully painted towns, natural environment, food, luxury villas and hotels, and scenic views of centuries old farmhouses and cottages. We started the exploration of the coast by first staying in Genoa, city in the center of the Riviera extending westwards to the French Riviera and the Riviera di Levante between Genoa and Capo Corvo. Several streets and palaces in the center of Genoa and the Cinque Terre National Park are two of Italy's 58 World Heritage Sites.

We explored the Mediterranean coast from Genoa to Cinque Terre National Park. Cinque Terre is the smallest and oldest National Park in Italy. It covers an area of only 15 square miles but packs plenty of gorgeous scenery, a mix of rocky cliffs, scenic coves, clear blue waters, terraced vineyards, and olive groves linked by a network of footpaths. Made of five separate villages, Monterosso, Vernazza, Corniglia, Manarola, and Riomaggiore, each one is a charmer, featuring pastel color buildings tumbling down the hillsides and sparkling sea views. No driving is allowed in the park, so we stayed in the nearby town of La Spezia and caught the train into Cinque Terre. There is also a ferry connecting the villages. A lot of walking was involved with many opportunities to sample local seafood such as a cone of fried calamari which goes brilliantly with their local white wine. We took our time and stayed in the area for a few days.

We stopped in the city of Pisa famous for its leaning tower and nearby monuments particularly the Square of Miracles also listed as World Heritage Site by UNESCO. We only spent a couple of hours there simply because the whole experience was marred by street hawkers harassing tourists selling fake Rolex watches and trinkets. To us, it ruined Pisa and all its charm.

We also visited the old fishing village of Portofino, now a glamorous spot, with fancy yachts in the harbor, high-end hotels, restaurants, and upmarket boutiques. It did not seem much of a fishing village anymore. I much preferred the traditional simplicity and authenticity of Cinque Terre.

The next leg of our journey was the remarkable and memorable lake region of Northern Italy. A group of large lakes located on the south side of the Alps, formed after the retreat of glaciers at the end of the last ice age. From west to east, there are Lake Orta, Maggiore, Varese, Lugano, Como, Iseo, Idro and Garda. The three largest are Lake Garda, Magiorre and Como.

We saw two. The most popular is Lake Como in the Lombardy region. The whole area is an upscale resort known for its dramatic scenery, set against the Alpine foothills. It is shaped like an upside-down Y with three slender branches meeting at the resort town of Bellagio. At the bottom of the Southwest branch lies the town of Como, home to Renaissance architecture and a funicular traveling up to the mountain town of Brunate. Glamorous Lake Como is the deepest lake in Europe at 410 meters. This gorgeous spot also earned fame as home to Hollywood star George Clooney. Lake Como is one of those dreamy places exceeding expectations, a veritable stage set of fairy tale villas and garden follies. Como is the most "James Bond" of the Italian lakes and it is not unusual to watch shiny red Ferraris weave through narrow lakeside towns and neoclassical villas. Parts of the 2006 Bond movie *Casino Royale* were filmed here and many of the fancy lakeside hotels have a 007 price tag.

From the town of Como, a former Roman city, we hopped on a ferry to Bellagio. We agreed, Bellagio is a small jewel. The town boasts unparalleled shoreline and Alpine views. Add in boutique-lined cobblestone streets, Italian villas, and fragrant gardens, and it's no secret why Bellagio is known as the Pearl of Lake Como. What a romantic town even though I did not experience it in such a way.

Lake Garda is another world apart, more rustic, not as glamorous as its cousin Lake Como. Lake Garda offers a different atmosphere. This long, narrow lake is surrounded by mountains to the north while the southern part is flatter and much less dramatic. We drove around the entire lake and stopped at several small towns doting the shorelines.

- Riva Del Garda is picturesque with colorful buildings lining narrow alleyways and wide piazzas. I climbed the medieval bell tower walking through ancient city gates. My companion did not as he was feeling tired.
- We stopped at Arco, a small town sitting on the north end of the lake tucked away in the mountains. Its medieval tower, Torre di Arco was the highlight.
- Villa Canale, a medieval village entrenched on a mountain slope was recently included in the list of the most beautiful villages in Italy.
- Punta Larici boasts the most spectacular lookout point on Lake Garda.
- Malcesine, an elegant resort, is considered a gem with great shopping, dining and stunning views.
- Bardolino is celebrated for its vineyards and olive groves.
- Sirmione, a dreamy village, a true joy to wander through. This medieval town surrounded by its castle, gardens, thermal spas, beaches and aquamarine waters, is the most popular site on Lake Garda. I took a tour of Scaligero Castle,

a 14th century fortress, one of the best-preserved castles in Italy.

- Rocca Di Manerba features an Archaeological Museum and churches rich with frescos, witnessing the antique religions and cultural traditions passed in this area along the centuries.
- Salo, one of the pearls of the shore of Lake Garda, is an elegant location full of stately residences and palaces of great historical and artistic value.
- Limone Sul Garda is a place of terraced lemon groves, a picturesque fishing village with wonderful views.
- Santuario Madonna della Corona, built over 2,000 feet above sea level into a vertical cliff looks as if it is nearly suspended in mid-air.

This had been another voyage unveiling God's revelation of Himself through the physical universe. The beauty of the natural world is only a reflection of supernatural divine imagination.

We thought of going to the famed Amalfi coast but did not since it was quite a drive, and my friend was not feeling well. We shortened our trip and flew back to Idaho. We had been gone for four weeks.

As we landed in Idaho Falls upon our return, the news came. My mother had been found unconscious in her apartment and was in a coma in a hospital. The next day my daughter informed me she had passed away. She was 92 years old, and we were in October of 2017.

I flew back to France where I met my daughter in my mother's apartment.

SAYING GOODBYE TO MOTHER

I felt apprehensive reuniting with my daughter under the circumstances. She insisted on me not getting inside my mother's apartment before she did, upon the request of her late grandmother. She said there was something she needed to do there before I came in. Clearly her grandma had left something for her I was not supposed to know about making her jittery and uneasy with me.

We met in the apartment once I got the green light. We spent the next few days addressing what we needed to do together. Our priority was to take care of the last wishes of my mother.

My daughter, who was the last one to speak to her, had a message to relay to me. My mother's last words to me: "Tell your mother I read her letter but could not respond to it. I wish her well." It was a form of acknowledgement and would have to do. It was better than nothing. I was relieved, she wished me well.

We got her urn at the funeral home and had a little ceremony late at night before dispersing her ashes in the ocean per her request. My daughter felt it was my responsibility. We went on the beach right across from her apartment when the tide was at its lowest. Barefoot, holding the urn, I walked slowly into the water up to my knees. I gently dispersed the ashes saying goodbye. The tide was low but rising. The waves rolled back to the shore. What manifested next never occurred to me or crossed my mind as a natural phenomenon. The ashes rolled back with the waves and covered my feet and legs. My daughter walked away and sat on a bench at some distance. This symbolized my last contact with my mother.

The next day, we met her *notaire*, a public officer appointed by the French Minister of Justice with whom previous arrangements had been made to handle her estate and started the procedure. It would last well over a year. I was the legitimate heir and therefore, according to French law, it was my duty to handle all formalities.

The reunion with my daughter overall went well and she returned to her job back in the US after a few days while I stayed in France. She had a busy life back home. My attempts to deepen our connection did not materialize. She was pleasant but kept her distance.

I spent time getting the apartment ready for sale and took care of all administrative tasks needing to be addressed.

Staying alone in the apartment was not particularly pleasant or easy for me. The energy lingering there was far from uplifting, and I took it upon myself to stay focused on the tasks at hand. Going through my mother's belongings, personal papers and photos triggered old emotions, but I dealt with them to the best of my ability. Somehow, it was easier than anticipated and I never felt alone or overly anxious. There was a loving and encouraging presence surrounding me. I felt supported and guided. An angel must have been by my side.

The time came when all was in order. I had picked a realtor who could work with me from a distance. There was nothing more I could do. I returned to Idaho, knowing I would come back when the apartment sold.

BACK TO IDAHO

Iresumed my routine with my companion. More importantly, I resumed my visits with Angela and James, whom I felt comfortable with. They met my roommate. He did not like them and quickly tried to discourage me from associating with them as they were a bad influence in his view.

They shared their faith in Jesus Christ creating a source of conflict and rejection for him. I was being transformed in front of his very eyes and was becoming a new creation he could not identify with. Instinctively, he knew it would bring me to reconsider our living arrangement. Day by day it became more and more intolerable for me to be under the same roof.

He spoke about moving out of Idaho and relocating somewhere where the climate was warmer. I did not contribute to the idea and left him to his own decision. He put the house for sale. I encouraged him in his new plans.

Meanwhile, my mother's apartment had not sold and my contact with the realtor was uneasy and limited. We were in late spring. I decided to return to France because matters needed my attention, and I could not count on the realtor.

I was sharing all this with Angela and James, and they suggested I move in with them until the time I returned to France. This was an easy and joyful decision leading me to the most important choice of my life transforming me forever.

FOREVER AFTER

Amy and James's invitation to stay with them was heartwarming. It felt like a reunion with a long-lost brother and sister, who wanted nothing but the best for me. They treated me as a welcomed family member. We studied the Word of God, we prayed, we laugh, we grieved as one when referring to deep-rooted and sad memories in our lives. We spent quality time and enlightening moments together. They showed me through their actions what a true believer does. I accompanied them to their church. James who had been a pastor would sometimes give the sermon when the leading pastor was not available. His teaching style revealed fire and passion when quoting scriptures, challenging all who attended.

And it dawned on me, this had been God's plan all along. Angela and James ... Idaho! They inspired and encouraged me to open my eyes to the Truth I had been longing for. I repented a life of sinful ignorance. I was ready to receive Jesus Christ as my Lord and Savior.

I heard the "calling." I wanted the commitment. What I felt in my heart goes something like this:

> "Lord Jesus, I believe You are the Son of God. You died on the cross to rescue me from sin and death and reconcile me to the Father through Your sacrifice. I believe in Your resurrection on the third day after Your crucifixion. I confess my sins, repent, and ask for Your forgiveness. I surrender to You as my Lord and Savior. Take complete control of my life and help me walk in Your footsteps with the power and guidance of the Holy Spirit. Thank you, Lord Jesus, for Your

precious gift of salvation."

I asked James and Angela to be baptized as a formal acknowledgement of my new faith in Christ.

A couple of weekends later, after the service at the rural local Cowboy church, I was baptized in front of everyone outdoors in a horse trough. It was such an emotional moment, the beginning of a surrender to Christ.

The onset of a never-ending journey of self-renewal as a brand-new follower of Jesus Christ. I was given a new heart, a spiritual birth, and I had become a part of God's family.

The most profound and significant chapter of my life was emerging. The transformation was real. A work in progress and unending.

I prepared for my next adventure as a newborn believer. I felt ready to return one more time to France with no plans beyond other than God's blueprint for my life, led by the Holy Spirit.

This is when I received an offer for my mother's apartment. We had a potential buyer. The timing was perfect.

Angela and James understood I needed to go back to France and were already thinking to come and visit.

ARCACHON FOR THE LAST TIME

It was June of 2018. I flew to Bordeaux and got a cab driving me to Arcachon about an hour away. It was the middle of the day, and the heat was brutal. A little apprehensive, not knowing what awaited me in the apartment as realtors and potential buyers had been through it for the last few months. To my surprise, I opened the door to a clean, uncluttered home. Some of the furnishings had been moved around to make it more marketable and spacious. It turned out the lady who handled the maintenance of the building and had proven to be helpful on numerous occasions, took it upon herself to tidy everything up for my arrival. This kind gesture did not go unnoticed. It was the same person who showed compassion toward me while I was living with my mother a couple of years before. I remembered how at times she would cheer me up with thoughtful words when she saw me walking up and down the stairs or crying in the basement after an episode with my mom.

The apartment not only looked different but felt different. The energy had shifted and did not carry the darkness or heaviness I sensed the last time I was there. Looking out the window or stepping out on the balcony revealed a joyful scene. Sandy beach teeming with vacationers, colorful umbrellas and happy kids playing, people taking a leisurely stroll on the boardwalk, hang gliders showing off their skills in a graceful flight over the bay and sailboats drifted around each other on the sparkling sea of the bay of Biscayne. Summer by the seaside in all its splendor. What a wonderful welcome. I felt free, grateful, and thankful to our Lord for arranging such a favorable and positive arrival.

This immediately set the tone for what would follow the next few months.

There had been two offers on the apartment. I accepted the best one, of course. It turned out the buyer had a house to sell so it was a contingent offer which did not bother me at all. To the contrary, this was going to give me the time I needed to reflect, recover, and see what direction God lead me. I felt at peace. I was exactly where I needed to be.

The time spent alone proved to be precious. My schedule was mine. I did what I enjoyed most, walking, reading, going to the movies, eating when and what I wanted, spending time with my friend Adeline whom I went to visit in Biarritz where she lived and vice versa. At times, she would ask me to watch her dog, Foxy, for a week or two when she traveled. Foxy loved to play frisbee. We had a great time together at the local park or the beach. I socialized with the people I had taught English to a couple of years before. I was relaxed and happy.

Most importantly, I spent countless hours either in the apartment, sitting on a bench at the park, or on the beach connecting with God, meditating, reflecting, and praying. Overwhelmed with gratefulness and thankfulness, I acknowledged God with every breath. I felt a liberation, a freedom I had not experienced before. The energy filling me was one of unconditional love.

I reflected on my past: my upbringing, my family, relationships, life experiences, and world travels. How I was raised among unbelievers. How on my own, I was determined to find the Truth and relentlessly pursued my desire to connect to the source, our Creator. How this journey ultimately led to God, our Lord Jesus Christ, and the Holy Spirit.

I forgave myself, my mom, all those needing forgiveness in a way I never thought possible, with heartfelt understanding and compassion, praying they would, as I did, find the Truth, the Light, and the Way to Jesus Christ.

Blessed to have been touched by the grace and mercy of God, I wanted to share the good news with everyone. I must admit the people who surrounded me and whom I shared with, were not receptive to say the least. My friends respected and accepted my choice but did not relate. Others had a condescending attitude at best.

The apartment's buyer whom I met was a nice lady who worked with me eagerly. She really wanted the apartment, and I wanted her to have it. So, we made concessions to each other, and I got to stay in the apartment in the meanwhile, to my delight. It took over a year to close the deal.

Angela and James came for a week during the fall. It was a short, but wonderful reunion. We spent three days in Paris together. They hoped I would return to Idaho, and we discussed my future.

I had fully enjoyed my time while in France and grew in my beliefs as a new Christian despite the general lack of interest around me. I slowly realized I wanted to be near believers. People who shared my new faith were crucial to my Christian development. Clearly, this was not going to take place in my current surroundings.

I decided to go back to the United States. But where?

Idaho was not the answer, and I had another idea in mind. North Carolina appealed to me remembering how attractive the state was from my travels through the area. Southport near Wilmington on the Atlantic coast was not far from the Atlanta area where my daughter lived. Far enough for our mutual independence but easily accessible. A friend, who lived in Southport, was a successful realtor who provided me with tempting and good information. I could spend a few months there, short-term renting and testing the waters with my daughter. Through Airbnb, I found someone willing to rent me a part of her house.

I thought moving closer to my daughter would give us a chance to reconnect. I had the same hope of bonding with my daughter as I had for my mother in the past. I contacted her to share my impressions and thoughts. Her reaction left me no shadow of a doubt. She was not receptive, too busy, she said, with very little time available to see me. I felt rejected again. By the same token she was honest and as hard as it was, I respected her position. It was her choice. She suggested I move where I wanted without taking her into account in my decision to relocate to the US.

Reality sunk in one more time. I was on my own and family was still a remote fantasy of mine. The difference, it did not hurt me or make me feel guilty as it used to in the past. I had my faith, and God would guide me in my next venture.

Then, Hurricane Florence hit the Carolinas in September of 2018. It was a powerful and long-lived hurricane causing catastrophic damage on the coast and the flooding was severe.

This sad event made me reconsider my options. With climate

changes, it seemed investing in real estate on the coast was not the best plan.

I gave up North Carolina. Instead, I took an inventory of where in the US I had lived before and enjoyed enough to return to.

COLORADO AGAIN

I felt drawn to return to Colorado. The Rockies always appealed to me. North Carolina would have been a great choice had my circumstances been different.

February of 2019 was my target after finalizing all aspects of my mother's succession. I had a friend in Colorado Springs whom I kept in contact with. I told her of my decision and asked if she could refer me to a realtor to find a month to month furnished rental and help me buy a townhouse around Colorado Springs. It was easy, she knew someone and put us in touch. It must have been the right sequence for the next step of my life since all arrangements flowed smoothly. I found a lovely private cottage to stay in while my newfound realtor showed me different possibilities. It turned out I did not care for what she selected or was available within the confines of the city. On my own initiative, I did some research and spotted some new unfinished townhomes north of Colorado Springs in the little town of Monument. What really attracted me there was the fact they were facing the Front Range of the Southern Rocky Mountains and had a view not only of famous Pikes Peak but also Air Force Academy. A prime location and away from the hustle and bustle of the Springs. An ideal spot with numerous hiking trails nearby.

A month later, I moved into a beautiful brand new three level townhome with breathtaking Front Range views. I enjoyed furnishing it and limited the furnishings to the area where I spent most of my time. All levels exhibited a view, the highest level revealed even more spectacular scenery.

I must admit, it was cold. Very cold at 8,000 plus feet. I needed warmer clothes. My walks were few because of the ice everywhere and I did not venture driving too far given the slipperiness of my driveway. I got walking poles and ice cleats to affix to my shoes as I was concerned about a fall especially being on my own. I needed to be careful.

I decided to take a part time job and luckily found one close by in a department store, less than a mile away. I enjoyed meeting new people and settling into a new life. I started to go to church and tried a few different ones within a couple of miles. I also enrolled in a Bible study group.

Making new connections through church and work, a couple invited me to join their group of friends who met on a regular basis rotating through each other's homes. The objective was for each person to read either a short personal story they had written about a specific event or select a topic from a book of their choice which led to discussions and debates. This is when I met Camila and Noah who became friends and would play a role later in a major decision involving where to retire.

Then, I was invited to participate in another weekly meeting at a local breakfast place. This time the participants discussed various topics, mainly exploring the subject of near-death experiences (NDE) so heavily documented throughout the world. We had a physicist, a psychologist, a chaplain, a native American Indian, a psychiatrist, and my new friend Camila besides me. Quite a group, quite a weekly meeting. I always looked forward to the challenging exchanges brought about by the fascinating subject of NDE. As a new believer, I was captivated by the multitude of testimonies worldwide, stressing major changes in the lives of those who nearly died, came back, and testified. Accounts of NDEs most often reflect an indescribably glorious heavenly realm imbued with a mystical radiant white light, transcendent peace, pure bliss, a sense of unity, and unconditional love. Many say they do not want to come back. What a testimony to the Truth of the Glory of God. All praises to God were my interpretation. Non-believers in my group came to different conclusions.

The weather eventually warmed up, and I started hiking some of the trails surrounded by the awesomeness of God's creation.

I celebrated my 70th birthday kindly invited by the couple who initially included me in their social gatherings.

Life was good. I enjoyed every aspect of it. I particularly

appreciated one of the couples, both strong believers and joined them in their church. I remained connected with them as my life would take a new turn in the future. When walking with Nicole and hitting the trails together, we would share some of the challenges each believer faces, especially our own tests and trials.

Then Angela and James visited during the summer and brought me the belongings I had left with them when going back to France. A positive and joyful visit. Lots of prayers, laughs, and sightseeing took place.

In the fall of 2019, I took a trip to Atlanta to spend a few days with my daughter, grandson, and another family member, her stepmom Nathalie, whom I had not seen in a while and was visiting from France. We went to Asheville in North Carolina for a day with my daughter's boyfriend born there originally. I had traveled through the area a few years before and remembered finding the scenery breathtaking. Sightseeing the Smokies and the Blue Ridge Parkway left a grand impression on me.

Then back to Colorado and preparing for my second winter. I spent a lot of time working and my part-time job in retail became full time temporarily through the holiday season. I worked long hours and was on the clock during the madness of Black Friday. Then, Christmas and the sales after New Year. We were now in late February of 2020 and the working hours had considerably dropped.

I will always remember March of 2020, when COVID-19 officially transformed human lives across the world. I was working that day, when my manager announced the store was closing by government mandate due to a global health emergency. The WHO, World Health Organization, declared COVID-19 a global pandemic. We knew about it from January, when the first case was reported in the US. But March 11, was a turning point affecting daily lives not only in this country but worldwide. Things were never to be the same.

We were told to go home and stay there until further notice. The lockdown had begun.

In a way COVID-19 evoked the tragedy of the 9/11 terrorist attack, a critical and dark moment in time with unknown consequences.

As I sat in my townhome for several weeks, isolated, reduced to telephone or digital contact with others, another time of reflection began. I still went out for walks or grocery shopping with a mask on.

Everything stopped. My work life and my social life. If I ever enjoyed being alone, I got my wish. No church either. The TV was my only connection to the outside world, and the news was rather depressing.

A brand-new study Bible had been given to me, so I began to read the greatest story ever told again, and this time in the right order. My intent was to read all 66 books having shaped laws, influenced cultures, and inspired billions to faith over two millennia. The Holy Bible, the most read book in the world as unique as it is profound and as relevant today as it ever was.

I called my daughter to see how she was doing and how they were affected by the COVID situation. She was now working from home like millions of others and my grandson was being home schooled.

Somehow, I ended up speaking with her boyfriend on the phone. He showed concern for me and my isolation. He was a family man and close connection with family members was important to him. He genuinely offered for me to go spend time with them if I needed help or simply did not want to stay alone. He mentioned it was a time when we needed to support each other, and I was always welcome in their home. I could hear my daughter in the background approving and in total agreement with him. Stunned and extremely surprised, I thanked him and my daughter, assuring them I would consider their kind and heartwarming offer.

I called more often and found my daughter more receptive than she had been in the past. She sounded happy. I could tell she was in a relationship with someone who brought her stability and a sense of security. Her boyfriend gave her support in more than one way, and he uncontestably had a beneficial influence on her state of mind even in my regard.

I could not help but start evaluating my situation again. I enjoyed my townhome. I had made a couple of good friends here and certainly appreciated my life in Colorado until COVID 19 made its apparition. On the downside, the second winter was rough on me and long. The ice and snow represented a real safety hazard and restricted my daily walks and outdoors activities. Plus, I did not have a job anymore.

North Carolina came back on the map. Not the coast this time, but the Smokies and more specifically Asheville. This time, my daughter was amiable to my plan and told me her boyfriend was thinking of retiring to the Asheville area. The decision was made to move again, and the process went in motion.

I googled Asheville realtors and contacted someone who gave me preliminary information on real estate in the area. I was also in touch with a few local realtors about selling my townhome. I had only been in it barely over a year but given its prime location, selling it was going to be easy.

Amazingly, once the process of relocating to Asheville began, everything worked flawlessly with minimum effort despite the COVID 19 restrictions. A red carpet was literally unrolling in front of me. The experience was fun, joyful, and excitement was in the air.

The still small voice whom I know now was the Holy Spirit strongly suggested I find a different realtor in Asheville. I hesitated because the one I had so far dealt with was doing his job. Something was telling me to contact my realtor friend in Southport and ask her if she could recommend a good real estate agent in Asheville. She responded within the hour and told me to call a lady who in her opinion was the sharpest and most competent in the area.

I called her the next morning. Joanna impressed me immediately. I caught her driving. She said she wanted to take the time to listen to me asking me to hold while she found a parking place. Then she took her time, asked me a few questions, intently listened to what I had in mind and mentioned she had just helped her own mother relocate. She understood perfectly what my needs were and became a fantastic support in my transition. Her enthusiasm was contagious. I had found a pearl and an ally eager to assist me giving me her best. God encouraged my relocation by opening doors for me. The unfolding of my plan was effortless as if meant to be.

I repeated what I had done when moving back to Colorado from France. Finding a furnished rental in Asheville while I looked for my new home to be. Joanna found the perfect solution. A little cottage looking like a tree house. The owner was French, and the area was an established and desirable part of Asheville.

My townhome sold quickly. I had my car transported and my furnishings held in storage in Ashville. I flew there in July of 2020.

Thank you, Lord, for making this transition such a delightful and seamless experience.

ASHEVILLE, NORTH CAROLINA

July 2020 – All was settled in Colorado, and I flew to Asheville, landing a late afternoon in heavy rain. I picked up a rental car at the airport for a few days until my car arrived. The traffic was congested from the airport to my little cottage. The rain did not help, and it was stop-and-go driving all the way. I had a pleasant surprise upon entering the established residential neighborhood of north Ashville near Beaver Lake. The streets were lined with majestic oak and red maple trees creating a canopy of shade. Luxurious Victorian era architecture filled the landscape. I could tell walking was going to be pleasant.

I was delighted when I found where I was staying. A small tree house nestled between two beautiful mansions occupied by the owners on each side. Grandparents on one side and children on the other. I was kindly welcomed and made myself at home. A decorative bag awaited on the table with gourmet snacks, a bottle of wine, and a warm greeting note signed by my realtor. It was lovely and I felt appreciative.

Joanna gave me a couple of days to settle in. We met for lunch to get acquainted and had an interesting conversation on a more personal level. My time with her was productive. She genuinely wanted to know and understand what was important to me. The little bit I shared about my international travels, religious beliefs, and state of mind was listened to carefully. I knew her intent was to use the information to provide exceptional service with an individualized touch.

Two days later, she picked me up and started showing me around so I could first have an overview of different areas and what they offered. She made the whole process enjoyable.

She also invited me to a couple of social gatherings since I knew absolutely no one. Joanna went beyond her realtor's duties. She became a friend who cared about helping me blend into my new surroundings effortlessly.

I sincerely enjoyed my time with her. She strongly suggested I consider looking south of Asheville, in the Hendersonville area. We drove there, had lunch one day and looked at a couple of possibilities. Being and living alone, I did not want an older home requiring maintenance. I preferred a carefree lifestyle in a newer community where I could lock the door and take off for extended periods of time without worrying.

It did not take long to find what I had in mind. We discovered a newly built neighborhood amidst apple orchards in a country setting but still close to city amenities. There was one house left overlooking a waterlily pond backing to woods. Under construction, it would not be ready until mid-October.

Perfect. Waiting was not an issue. I signed the contract and planned to remain in the rented cottage in the meantime.

Having found a home, I had free time on my hands. I took long walks in my lovely neighborhood.

I spoke to my daughter and planned a few days' visit at her house a couple of weeks later.

I now had the leisure to slow down my pace and regroup. I spent time alone thinking about my near future. How did I envision it? What truly mattered in my life at this point?

Looking back at my short history as a believer and follower of Jesus Christ, a paradigm shift was taking place in my still new Christian life. Gratefulness and thankfulness overflowed my heart bringing joy and peace.

For a while now, I had been asking our Lord to direct me where He wanted me to be. Most importantly how could I give back some of the grace He so compassionately and generously had bestowed upon me. I felt, more and more, a strong need to meet others who were like-minded and on the same path. This was part of the reason why I returned to the United States. Not because I was lonely, but the time had come to expand my Christian Walk and to put it on speed dial. I was driven to walk the talk and be of service to others.

The need intensified as time went by. I had done some volunteering while in Idaho, working in a hospital and visiting patients. But now I felt compelled to fulfill God's purpose on a whole different level. I sensed this calling was essential to become a true follower of Christ.

What would my next step be? Joanna suggested a couple of charitable organizations. Finding a church was going to be a priority as soon as I moved into my new home.

I kept reading the Bible. The more I read the Word of God, the more I wanted to serve. I continued praying.

Little did I know, my prayers were about to be answered in a most unexpected way and Joanna had an essential role to play.

A few days later, she called me to ask if I would join her in the evening. She wanted to introduce me to her mother, and a couple of other friends. The plan was to have a drink first at a local brewery in Hendersonville and then go for dinner.

I hesitated because I was staying north of Asheville and Hendersonville was 30 miles south. I was concerned about driving at night due to poor vision, but at the same time I did not want to miss the opportunity to meet new people. If I was going to live here, socializing was important, and declining was out of the question considering Joanna had shown multiple times she had my best interest at heart and so kindly included me in her close circle.

She was there when I arrived and introduced me to her mom whom I liked instantly. A lady with a bubbly personality and distinct accent was present and like me from another country. We ordered our drinks and started to talk.

Then another friend showed up. A tall, slim man, who sat right across from me. Introductions were made. He knew Joanna's mom and I could tell they were old friends. I quickly noticed he had difficulty talking and frequently wiped his mouth with a towel because of excess salivation. Joanna's mom asked him how he was doing, and it was obvious talking was not natural and required energy and effort on his part.

Joanna introduced me and mentioned clearly, I had extensively traveled the world and was born in France. I could see this caught his attention and interest. We started to chat with each other. I had to focus and concentrate on what he was saying especially in a noisy environment.

He asked me where I had traveled. For some reason, I felt compelled to mention growing up in North Africa, both Morocco and Tunisia. He was curious to know where I specifically lived in Tunisia which I thought was a little unusual since most Americans I had come into contact with were not even sure where Tunisia was. I mentioned the little town of Metlaoui in the south at the edge of the Sahara Desert and he responded he had been there before. This intrigued me tremendously. What are the odds? I was a little kid when I lived there about 65 years ago. The town is practically unknown and has nothing to offer.

My curiosity was engaged. He attempted while struggling through his speech to tell me why, when, and where he lived in Tunisia with his family while working in the petroleum industry many years ago. We also discovered he traveled through Morocco.

We had topics of conversation. But speaking wore him out in this loud environment, added to the difficulty I had understanding him already. It resulted in cutting the conversation short. He mentioned his dog was alone, waiting for him and left.

We continued our evening between ladies enjoying our time and dinner together.

I went back to my little nest. A couple of days went by when Joanna called me and asked if I remembered the gentleman I had met, whose name is Homer, and would it be okay to give him my phone number. Knowing I was new to the area, he proposed to help me discover my new surroundings if I was interested. The next couple of days, I was a little hesitant to accept his offer because I knew communication would be difficult and challenging, but at the same time, I was curious and interested to continue our conversation. Eventually, I said yes. I received a text message from him quickly thereafter.

In his first text to me, Homer explained he was in the area for another couple of weeks since he currently lived in Louisiana and was staying in an RV resort in Hendersonville. He mentioned he had lived in Weaverville north of Asheville for over 15 years, knew the area well and would be delighted to show me some beautiful spots outside the city. He suggested different options and asked which one appealed to me the most. I picked Mount Mitchell, the highest peak of the Appalachian Mountains about an hour away from where I was staying. We settled on the following Sunday at 9 in the morning, he would pick me up.

The day before, he asked me if I would mind having a couple of his friends join us. It was a great idea for our first encounter and would facilitate communication between us.

He was on time, and we spent a few minutes greeting each other before his friends arrived. This is when I met Hannah and Lucas for the first time. We drove in their car, and per everyone's request, I sat in the passenger front seat. They wanted me to have the best view. Homer and Hannah sat in the back. We were on our way leisurely driving through the lovely countryside and soon on the Blue Ridge Parkway.

Everyone made me feel welcome and put me at ease. I sensed a curiosity about me and soon enough, they asked me a few questions.

I knew I was an unusual case and had a story to tell, and they were eager to find out what I was about. We spoke briefly about my French origin, my numerous travels, and the fact the only thing Homer and I knew about each other is we lived and visited some of the same countries. Then, I don't remember how it came about, but I did what I like to do best, to emphasize where my lifelong journey and story led me.

I summarized many years of yearning and searching for the Truth. How of my own volition, being raised as an atheist and spending most of my life around non-believers, I became a Christian and follower of Jesus Christ in Idaho a couple of years before. I shared my excitement on how my brother and sister in Christ, Angela and James were influential in my decision to become a Christian. It was obvious I had the full undivided attention from all passengers in the car as I made my case describing my surrender to Jesus Christ as my Savior and Redeemer late in life.

When we got back to Asheville, Homer left, and I had a late lunch with Hannah and Lucas. We enjoyed our time together.

A couple of days later, Homer suggested riding for the day to the Highlands, another beautiful spot. I accepted gladly and drove down to meet him at his RV Resort. This was when I met Cali, his little dog. Her friendliness, excitement, and joyful behavior were contagious. She was adorable and a good-looking dog. An unusual mix of Australian shepherd, schnauzer, and poodle.

This was the first time we were alone and while he drove, I did most of the talking. I could tell he was intrigued by me, and eager to hear more about my story. I gladly obliged sensing more than curiosity but a genuine interest on his part. Even though he was driving, he listened to me intently and kept on asking questions.

Cali sat in the back observing me. She attempted to come and sit on my lap. I let her and we quickly became good friends. It was obvious she was Homer's dear companion. We had a great day and thoroughly enjoyed our time together. Upon returning, I visited for a while and sat with him in his RV. I was curious about him too.

This was the first time I noticed he was on a feeding tube as he was eating his formula. I had never seen someone on a feeding tube before and naturally wanted to know why. Homer opened up for the first time and despite his difficulties speaking, did his best to describe how and why a couple of years ago, it became necessary for him to have one put in.

He also explained why his ability to speak was compromised. I focused intensely on his eyes and facial expressions as he revealed the story of his health. The multiple cancer battles, autoimmune disease, partial removal of his colon, Lyme disease, French polio, and there was more. His last cancer surgery had necessitated the removal of his tongue. I felt sad, fully realizing how blessed I had been with my own health. I had never been exposed to someone who had experienced so many ailments and suffering.

This man was a survivor, and a true miracle. He was calm and matter of fact while disclosing extreme hardships so deeply impacting his quality of life. I was assuredly humbled by his quiet acceptance and peacefulness. I sensed the strength of character behind the apparent physical weaknesses. Compassion and empathy overwhelmed me, and I did not know how to respond.

I was already asking myself, was it fate or what could have happened in his life causing such drastic deterioration of his health. But it was not for me to interpret. I had a strong desire to hear more. I experienced a mixture of feelings intensifying as he described some of the events which took place over the course of his life.

Our next exchanges were profound, depicting life tragedies, sorrows, but also times of joy and happiness.

Homer had lost his first wife to cancer when she was 45 years old, and I had lost my first daughter to crib death when she was 11 months old. We had similitudes in our lives forming the beginning of a kinship between us.

We both traveled the world and lived in some of the same countries. We both went through adversity, losses, obstacles of all sorts like most of us do, but also lived unique and exhilarating experiences. We both had children, two daughters for Homer and one on my own and shared the same estrangement with them. Whatever their reasons might be for refusing to grow up and get over the past, the fact is our children had no interest in being a part of our lives.

Homer mentioned he had written his biography as a legacy to his daughters in the hope they would, after reading it, discover the man behind the father figure. He was in the final stages of completion and editing before publication.

Neither one of us had given up hoping our daughters would mature and want a relationship with us as much as we did with them. Regarding our children, we undoubtedly had much in common. Ironically, a couple of years before, Homer had moved closer to where his daughters resided to facilitate a reconciliation with them and here, I was buying a home a couple of hours away from where my own daughter lived in the same hope.

Speaking of my daughter, the time had come for my trip to her home, and it was an important reunion since it had the potential to reopen the channels of communication between us.

We had a good visit for the most part. At the time her boyfriend lived with her, and being true to his word, he sincerely and warmly welcomed me, making me feel right at home. My daughter was working all day and my grandson homeschooled. The evenings and weekend were the only time together and we made the best of it. She was stressed and preoccupied, but nice without engaging too much. Her two dogs were stressed too and demonstrated behavioral issues. My grandson stayed in his room with brief appearances in the kitchen and remained distant.

The following Saturday we all hopped in her boyfriend's truck and took a beautiful ride to the countryside. We had a pleasant day, and I got an opportunity to take a couple of snapshots with my daughter. The last picture of us together went so far back in time I could not remember. I had reached the end of my visit and invited them to come and see me. On a Sunday afternoon, I left to drive back to Asheville.

The entire week I stayed at my daughter's; Homer texted me regularly twice a day inquiring on how my visit was. We also shared more about each other, and the topics included political views but far more importantly our spiritual journeys.

I was still reading the Bible from the beginning to the end and was in the Old Testament. It was a challenging read. I shared how hard it was for me to grasp the abyss of disobedience and sin separating God from His people and how they brought His wrath upon themselves. It shocked me to see their lack of understanding despite the endless testing and patience from God.

It was the first time I could openly allow myself to discuss the Bible with a man who was receptive instead of being resistant, unresponsive, or worse, criticize me. This was extremely important. I soon found out Homer was a Christian, had been his entire life and was raised by parents who had devoted themselves to evangelism and shared the Word of God for many of their years. Especially his mom who had dedicated her existence to the cause of Jesus Christ. What a sharp contrast with my own godless upbringing.

I was so joyful and grateful I had found someone, besides Angela and James, who shared my enthusiasm for Christ, welcomed my questions and encouraged me in my endeavors. We had in common an inexhaustible topic not just for conversation, but we were opening a window for growth and expansion of our spirituality together.

For the first time, he mentioned in one of his texts an open invitation to visit with him when he returned home to Louisiana at the end of the following week, and if I would be open helping him edit his biography.

Knowing I was coming back on Sunday evening, Homer suggested I stop on my way to have dinner with him. I did not respond to the suggestion to visit him in Louisiana and kindly declined the dinner invitation. I did accept another dinner invitation for the next day. This time, he was going to cook a muscovite duck at his best friend's house. I gladly accepted.

Early the next day, it was a Monday night, I met Homer at his RV and from there we drove together in my car to his friend's house since his truck had a flat.

This was a different couple from the one I met before. William and Brooke were Homer's closest friends and they also had lived in Tunisia where he met them originally many years ago while he was on a work assignment with his family. We made a positive connection and Homer's cooking was delicious. I do not like duck, but he made it irresistible and cooked it to perfection.

We had a fantastic and memorable evening. Again, I received a warm and cordial welcome. The conversation included memories of Tunisia for all of us. I felt observed that evening, but approvingly.

On the way back Homer asked me again if I would return with him to Louisiana. We would drive down, stop at his niece's house in Florida overnight and then go to his home where I would stay a couple of weeks to help him edit his bio.

I kindly said not yet. It was not something I was ready to do. I just wished we had more time to get to know each other. I wanted to deepen our connection but in neutral territory not in the privacy of his home traveling with him out of state while I was waiting for my house to be built. He asked the RV resort if he could prolong his stay but there was no space available. He only had a couple of days left. We said good night, not knowing if we would ever see each other again.

It did not feel right to walk away but at the same time it did not feel right to go with him either.

I knew without the shadow of a doubt I had to see him again before he left. The small voice in me was crystal clear. The day before his departure, I texted him and asked if I could stop and say goodbye in the afternoon. He said yes and we decided on 2pm.

We spent time in the RV discussing a variety of topics. This time the conversation was mostly led by Homer who shared more information about his past relationships particularly with the opposite sex including his daughters. and in essence what remained ingrained in him. The word stress was highly and repeatedly emphasized. He seemed to have painful and destructive memories. He described how women in his life brought drama, strain, and tension. He was emphatic on the subject. Therefore, he had concluded it was safer to keep all sources of unnecessary pressure and trouble away because of the negative impact on his health.

Having endured traumatic experiences myself, family, and relationships, I could relate. Luckily for me, my body had not been attacked and suffered such devastating consequences.

Homer also touched on how God tamed him through breaking his body down and how he learned lessons of humility and true forgiveness.

He spoke again about his biography and went into more detail.

He had spent a year writing it for the benefit of his daughters in the hope they would understand their father, who he was, why he made some critical choices after the loss of their mother. He shared how his decisions were guided by the Holy Spirit and surrender to the will of God.

This was compelling sharing and deeply touched my heart. What could I say but feel a strong sense of sympathy, sensibility, and solicitude towards him. I wanted to read his biography. Intense and deep-seated emotions stirred up in me. A wave of empathy submerged me, and tears flowed uncontrollably. Something beyond my control was happening as I attempted to resist the outpouring.

Somehow, I managed to regain my composure and thought it would be best if I left.

I had an appointment to go check on the progress of the building of my house anyway. Reluctantly, I said goodbye, promising to stay in touch.

As I drove away, I still felt emotionally present with Homer in the RV. It was difficult for me to drive away. All I wanted to do was comfort and support him instead of just leaving. I checked on my house with my mind still connected to him.

When I was done, the only thing for me to do was drive back to my little nest. I got close to the freeway entrance and at the last minute turned around and drove into a parking lot nearby. I sat in my car with a heavy heart and an acute sense of unfinished calling. I could not make myself get on the freeway. The "calling" overwhelmed me.

The small voice finally said, "I want you to go back." I found myself starting the car and followed what I sensed as a command from above, out of my control, I knew instinctively this was exactly what the Holy Spirit asked me to do.

A few minutes later, I parked next to the RV again, got out of my car, and knocked at the door.

Homer said, "Come in, what took you so long?"

"THE DOWNLOADED DIVINE"

The next couple of hours determined the course of my future. I was functioning on a different level of perception. The energy running through me felt heavenly. Indeed, I was vibrating on a higher frequency level.

I sat down and we looked at each other. There were no words for me to say really. The moment held nothing ordinary. I was transported in time and space.

This is when the "download divine" began. My body was shaking and my lips trembling, I could not help but laugh while crying at the same time and my heart burst with intense joy.

An indescribable feeling came upon me, and I was filled with the purest light. Powerful waves of unconditional love flooded through me. I felt like an open vessel being emptied of what was no longer needed and replenished with pure divine undying love and a surge of absolute devotion. I burned in a fire of refinement.

A sense of belonging, ecstasy, and perfect peace overpowered me. I received the outpouring of the Holy Spirit, like a flowing river through my heart and soul.

For someone observing me, it could have been construed as an emotional breakdown or some form of mental disturbance. It was not for Homer who witnessed this momentous episode. He recognized this unique phenomenon and held my hand for the longest time while all slowly dissipated, and I returned from the most enlightening journey ever.

The next moments were spent in silence as if no one wanted to break the enchantment.

I had been blessed with divine grace. I beamed gratitude, thankfulness, and holy love I had not known before.

There was a sense of communion floating in the RV. It was a sacred moment. The Holy Spirit was present, and both Homer and I yielded to His power.

Nothing was more vital than receiving the divine outpouring of love and devotion I was graced with and passing it on.

A heavenly gift meant to be shared.

How does one walk away having experienced with another human being the most unforgettable and significant divine breakthrough of one's life? No less than the supernatural immanence of the Holy Spirit.

(John 9:25 *KJV*)

He answered and said, "Whether he be a sinner or no, I know not: one thing I know, that, whereas I was blind, now I see."

The full version can be read in John 9:13-25.

HOMER

It was Homer's last evening in the area, and we both knew I had to stay. So, I did until the next morning. He asked me to reconsider driving with him and offered to fly me back a couple of weeks later. He mentioned again I could help him edit his biography before publication. The temptation was strong to accept but something held me back. What had happened between us was extremely powerful. I needed time to absorb and process the significance and impact of the last evening's events.

We said goodbye to each other and went our own ways.

As I got to my apartment and settled in, the first text from Homer came in. He was halfway to his niece's house in Florida and had stopped to eat his formula. He texted the next day and jokingly commented on how he was relaxing at his niece's swimming pool having a drink, describing the property, and pointing out what I was missing. Ha-Ha. Cute sense of humor.

This is when I read his biography. "If you want to know what kind of a man I am, he said … read my story, it will answer most if not all your questions. I poured my heart and soul into it for the benefit of my daughters. It is not published, and I could use some help finalizing the editing." Textually, the comments on his email said "Here is the bio. There may be some edits left to scrub. I haven't made my final review yet, but it is close enough. Have a read. We can discuss any time."

It was September 6th of 2020.

I began reading the same evening practically all night until I finished. I could not stop. Compelling story with real life trauma, tragedy, and comedy. A captivating attempt to describe the many human and spiritual experiences shaping his life and an account of his own physical, mental, and spiritual development. Lessons learned by trial and error under controversial circumstances.

Touched to the core of my being, I experienced multiple emotions, crying, smiling, laughing as I turned the pages. I deeply related to every emotion and lesson learned. Universal lessons intended to benefit a reader who has eyes to see and ears to hear. By the time I was done, I was stunned. It echoed my own journey in many ways. Different life events and pathways certainly, but the writer's inspiring experiences mirrored my own. Profoundly impacted, the best way I could give an impression was to write a letter to the author:

What did I see in You, Homer Adams, after reading your bio:

"A beautiful and humble spirit. Analytical and heart felt. Soul moving. Courageous and uplifting. Sensitive and sensible. Straight forward and unapologetic. Someone who overcame his many challenges with dignity and uncompromisingly high standards both in his personal and business life. Someone who paid and was still paying a high price for events and circumstances he was not responsible for. A being filled with the Holy Spirit teaching universal truths through his own story.

Someday your daughters will realize what they missed.

I did see some typos and caught a few things needing revision.

I will be happy to go spend the time needed to help you with the final editing and publication.

Yes, I found what I was looking for and already knew intuitively."

If there had been any doubt in my mind about visiting Homer and helping him with the completion of his biography, it was gone.

He did not have to ask anymore. I bought an airline ticket and three days later flew to Baton Rouge where he picked me up.

LAFAYETTE, LOUISIANA

My ticket was booked for a duration of almost three weeks, giving us plenty of time to review and complete the bio. It turned out God had other plans for us.

Reviewing the bio took up a part of each day and some changes were made. I contacted a publishing company I thought would be interested in a story ultimately about a spiritual journey.

I quickly got involved in Homer's daily life. I could not just be in his house, review the bio, and ignore every other aspect of routines taking place. Every morning, when I got up, I realized he had a regimen to follow regarding his health. He also had several doctors' appointments to catch up on. Things had to be done and he visibly was not feeling well. By nature, I pitched in and helped. In his case, it was beyond a desire to help. I naturally contributed to various tasks such as housekeeping, gardening, cooking with him, and more while reviewing the bio. A couple of weeks went by in a flash.

His energy level was low. Something was going on. His blood pressure mostly on the high side resulted in his primary doctor sending him to a specialist. It turned out he had plaque in his carotid arteries blocking circulation. A high risk for a stroke anytime. He needed an angioplasty followed by the placement of a stent on both sides of his neck requiring two separate surgeries at one week interval. The first surgery was scheduled after my departure.

By this time, I had become an active participant in his daily routines and because he had such difficulties with speech and could not make himself understood on the phone, I found myself making his calls and managing his appointments. I felt guided. The more I did the more I wanted to do.

The still small voice within my conscience was saying. "You are where I want you to be doing what I want you to do." I felt like I belonged. A sense of knowing was upon me. My compassion turned into a deep loving devotion. Homer became a priority, in turn giving me a great sense of joy and accomplishment. I understood God had placed me in these circumstances for a purpose bigger than myself. My visit turned into a commitment to this man. I was going to be there for him and support him in every way I could.

The settlement at my house was three weeks later. My time to return to Asheville had come, I decided to stay through his first scheduled surgery. It was not hard to convince him. I am not sure how he interpreted my position and decision, but he did not fight it. I called the airline and changed all flights schedules including my return to Louisiana after setting up my new home.

I was there at the hospital with him for his first stent surgery and because of COVID, only one person was admitted with the patient. I made sure it was me. We got closer to one another while at the hospital and when he returned home the next day, I cared for him, and still the wee small voice motivated my actions.

His second surgery was scheduled on the exact same day as the closing on my house. It was October 15, 2020. This time I had to go.

I spent a little over two weeks in North Carolina. We communicated by text several times a day.

He also had two cataract surgeries a week apart. His sister helped when she could so he would not be alone.

All I did in Asheville was pray for Homer's recovery and send him positive healing vibes along with loving energy.

I could not quite relate to my new home or even think of my near future now having reached my goal of moving to North Carolina. Looking back and sharing my situation with friends and my daughter, most of them could not understand the choices I was making.

Nothing made sense to me. I had moved from Colorado to settle into a new home in North Carolina and instead of concentrating on building a new life for myself, I joyfully felt compelled to help this man whom I had met a short time ago.

My daughter got upset reminding me I barely knew him. She was adamant. I should give more time to the situation. She made sense and I intellectually agreed.

The still small voice kept guiding and reassuring me I was on the right track doing what I had been called to do. The Holy Spirit showed me the way. I listened.

I flew back to Lafayette the first week of November 2020, the day of his second cataract surgery.

About a week later, after a routine visit at his primary doctor, a blood test revealed his PSA was high resulting in a visit to a specialist for further testing and a biopsy. I was with him when he found out he had stage four prostate cancer metastasized into his lymph nodes. It came as a shock to both of us. We contacted MD Anderson Hospital in Houston where most of his previous surgeries had been performed. He felt comfortable going back to doctors he trusted. It was scheduled for January of next year.

Christmas approached and we decided to spend the holidays together in my new house in Asheville. It was a wonderful idea. It would give us a much-needed break, a time for reflection.

Homer had survived cancer multiple times, and he was on his fourth round. His response and reaction amazed me. He took the news stoically and with grace, accepting his fate and determined to fight back. He used the term "being under attack from the evil one." We prayed about it. Homer emphasized to me the power of the Armor of God prayer as his foremost line of defense against the unseen forces of the enemy. He explained how spiritual warfare is real and how by wearing the Armor of God, we can stand strong. I admit to not having given much thought to the reality of spiritual battle and the protection available to us.

We decided to enjoy our time together for the holidays and made it a well-deserved vacation.

This is when I began to tackle learning how to play golf and accompanied Homer, who is an accomplished golfer. We had fun and he patiently taught me the basics of the game.

We spent a lot of time outdoors on golf courses, walking the dog, visiting the area, and appreciating quality time with his friends, who now were becoming mine too.

The month went by quickly and we returned to Lafayette the first week of January.

The time had come to consult with doctors at MD Anderson, do more testing, and see what his options were.

Stage four prostate cancer was confirmed. His treatment options were limited due to the lymph nodes metastasis and devastating consequences of previous cancer radiation and chemotherapy. He agreed to begin a hormone treatment to shrink the tumors, understanding side effects would follow. Sure enough, they kicked in after a couple of weeks and were debilitating. The most pronounced side effect was extreme fatigue leaving him lethargic. He described it as, "I feel like a zombie."

This was especially taxing on him considering his "fight back" personality. Finding himself unable to practice any of his normal activities such as working out and playing golf depressed him. He experienced mood changes, hot flashes, difficulty controlling his emotions, etc., all known side effects of hormone therapy.

We somehow managed to complete the biography and ended up self-publishing it. A copy was given to each one of his daughters in the hope they would come to know their father, thus stimulating a change of heart and a sincere desire to mend their relationship. The completion of the biography was a crucial step.

I remained at his side providing all the support I could muster and praying to God for his recovery. Going to church was comforting. His friends demonstrated how much they cared for him. His daughters showed no interest or concern, much less empathy following an ongoing pattern started many years before after the passing of their mother. The biography he wrote for their benefit generated no reaction from them to my dismay.

By mid-February, Homer was at a low point and distanced himself from me. He struggled physically, mentally, and emotionally. His future did not look bright, and he was in the process of analyzing and determining what was to be his best course of action.

In the midst of battling another round of cancer for the fourth time, he needed what little strength was left in him to rebuke evil. He kept on referring to this new cancer as being "under attack" again.

Prayers for me had become a way of fighting back. At this point, my mind was made up. I was going to help him through this new ordeal.

Waves of unconditional love and healing energy washed through me as I channeled to Homer what I sensed to be pure white healing light. Blessed recipient of a divine gift, I had become a conduit of transmission. Reverence and praise for our Creator swept over me.

I was also overwhelming Homer I presume. How could I explain to a man who is withdrawing from me the wonders taking place in me.

And then, one evening as we were having dinner with a couple of his friends, I specifically remember on February 19th of 2021, Homer made a shattering announcement. He said to me in front of everyone present at the dinner table, "You must leave and move back to your home in North Carolina. This is over, I need to be alone. This is "my" battle, not yours, I want you out of my house tomorrow."

Well, for a bombshell, could he have done any better? Complete silence followed in the room. We left shortly thereafter and drove back to his house. It was very cold that February night in Lafayette. Once parked, he went inside, and I remained in the car. My body felt cold, but it was insignificant compared to the shock paralyzing me. I called my sister in Christ, Angela, in Idaho. I had to hear someone's voice who cared. She picked up the phone and comforted me for the next couple of hours.

I finally went inside and spent the remainder of the night sleepless. A knife had pierced my heart, and I did not know how to remove it.

The next morning was awkward. As I absorbed the reality of my situation, an odd feeling began to unfold. Dualism was taking place. As I watched Homer attending to his morning routine, a part of me wanted to leave on the spot. After all, he had publicly crushed me but something else was emerging. The wee small voice always guiding me in times of joy or crisis began manifesting. At first, it was a consoling and soothing presence reassuring me I was going to be fine, and I was not to take this rejection personally. I felt calmer. The other part, the self, my ego, I presume, said, "You are not wanted here, pack up and go. What are you waiting for?"

I went for a walk with Cali, Homer's little dog. She had stayed by my side all night. Walking has always been a miracle cure. How many times in my life did I go for a long walk when distressed and it always made me feel better and brought clarity.

When I came back, I found breakfast on the table, and Homer had left.

I knew I had to leave and could not fathom where my hesitation was coming from.

I started to pack and get organized. My belongings were all over the place. I did not have my car so I would need to rent one. I began to assemble everything I had in the same room. I would need to rent a van most likely if I was to take it all. There was no coming back.

Nothing made sense to me. Homer's reaction felt like he had missed the whole point of my presence. I was dismissed, tossed out like something no longer needed nor wanted. Like an open wound, my heart physically ached within me. My mind raced. I needed comfort, reassurance, and most of all discernment after investing myself heartily and without any reserve in this relationship. His disconnection was incomprehensible emotionally.

I prayed fervently for an answer to lessen the pain weighing so heavily on my heart. I was not seeing clearly. My emotions clouded my judgement and reactions. I repeatedly asked God for solace.

Meanwhile, I went through the motions of getting ready to leave. I realized I could not just walk out. It would take a couple of days to be ready. I had practically moved in to stay permanently.

Consequently, when Homer returned, I asked him if I could spend a couple more nights, three nights in fact since I had rented an SUV for an early morning pick up on the fourth day. This allowed the one-way rental rate to drop, making it more affordable.

He accepted my request, but obviously was uncomfortable with the idea. He had severed this relationship and my staying a bit longer was not easy for him.

A long couple of days began. I was piling up boxes. Homer was not around most of the time. We had little interaction, but he prepared meals for me since I was still a guest in his home.

I stayed in a separate room. Cali comforted me with her loving presence. I fell into a slumber the first night. A night filled with dreams and agitation. The next morning, I felt calmer, and my emotions were more manageable. A long walk with Cali proved to be beneficial as usual. I spoke to a couple of dear friends on the phone to bounce things back on them. I was switching from reacting to analyzing. Awareness of another reality was arising. I began pondering on Homer's side of the story and what brought him to the decision of asking me to exit his life so abruptly.

This man had been tested repeatedly for many years with a deteriorating health condition leaving him fragile in many ways. He had fought battles where most would have given up. He had proven he could rebuke the enemy, the dark forces of evil attacking him relentlessly. He had close friends, a loving sister while his daughters had chosen estrangement.

He always made it clear to me from the time I met him that protecting what was left of his quality of life was paramount to his survival. He could not withstand chaos, drama, nor carry other people's emotions. Any unnecessary stress endangered his very existence. A shield to preserve peace, harmony, and further degradation of his body had to be put in place. Part of his decision towards me had taken the above into account.

But more importantly, he had considered the quality of my own life. In his physical condition, what did he have to offer other than a life of sacrifice as I eventually would become his caretaker as time went by. He cared enough for my well-being to end our relationship, albeit coldly and sternly, instead of letting the situation become irreversible. Thank you, Holy Spirit for detaching me from my own emotions allowing me to be rational and see the facts.

Now, I could see his side of the story. What did it provoke in me? How would I react if the situation had been reversed? Likewise, but being a woman with a high level of empathy, I would have approached him more gently taking his feelings into consideration. An explanation and justification would have been offered to soften the full blunt of rejection.

Still, in spite of all, walking away did not make any sense. It would have been the easy way out and Homer by his attitude had given me all the reasons to do so. But it is not how I felt. It was not my heart's inclination nor response. I knew the choice I made to be with him was not based on a romantic attachment. Our interconnection and alliance were not a random coincidence.

Ever since I became a Christian and a follower of Jesus, I had been asking God to direct my life to serve Him by heightening and manifesting unconditional love through my actions in honor and praise of Him, the Almighty.

My intuition suggested our encounter was a supernatural response to my pleas. Was I supposed to walk away knowing my prayers had been answered? Does one walk away from God's plan?

This knowledge explained everything I had done, every action I had taken since meeting Homer. I followed divine guidance. I could not leave without clarifying my position and my heartfelt convictions. Giving up at this point after all that had been accomplished was foolish, pointless, and against what I recognized as a sacred mission. I decided to have a talk with him, two nights before my departure. I had no idea how to approach him, so I asked the Holy Spirit to bless me with the right words.

Homer agreed to hear me, I think more for my benefit than his because his mind was made up and he had closed all channels of communication. We sat down and he waited politely for me to speak. I did and the words came, pouring out, without holding anything back. He had to know my real motives.

I was driven and able to express the depth of my unwavering commitment and devotion to him as a divine purpose. I was serving God in a beautiful relationship with a likeminded follower of Jesus Christ. I asked him to reconsider allowing me to remain in his life. Not only was I not sacrificing anything but my decision to support Homer drew me one step closer in building my relationship with God.

He requested a full day to process what he had heard. I agreed. I had given him a lot to digest. It is not every day that someone will present their case so boldly and candidly. From the expression on his face, I knew I had reached deep down.

The last evening preceding my departure, Homer returned to give his verdict. I was anxious, not knowing what to expect.

As we sat down, I could see he had made his decision. At first, he acknowledged how much he appreciated what I said, how genuinely I expressed my thoughts and the profound impact it had on him. He emphasized how wholehearted and compelling my words were and the context of faith in which I let the Holy Spirit speak through me. The wee small voice had spoken to him as well.

I was encouraged and touched by what he had noticed, not only the content of my speech, but also the truth inspiring my words. He agreed I had made my case and deeply moved his heart. Therefore, he offered me to stay.

He took the time to explain what had led him to his decision to ask me to leave. He did not feel it was fair or right to sacrifice my life since he had nothing to offer me other than a future filled with uncertainties. I reassured him I had considered what my position would be, and he did not need to say anymore. The fulfillment of our relationship was for a higher and greater purpose.

I was overjoyed when he embraced and accepted what was not a sacrifice on my part, but God's plan in answer to my prayers.

We resumed our life together. Our setback resulted in a stronger bond and a much deeper connection between us.

What more beautiful role divine providence could have given me, and I was elated.

We were now on the same page and could make plans for our future.

****

Homer had his house in Louisiana, and I had my house in North Carolina. We thought it would be a great idea to spend time in both locations. A couple of months here and a couple of months there. We could avoid the miserable summers of Louisiana and enjoy the coolness of the mountains of North Carolina. He had been a resident of North Carolina for 15 years and missed being there. Poor health had prompted his return to Louisiana to be closer to family for help.

The dynamics in his life were changing. We were going to be together, and he had my full support.

We decided to drive to North Carolina and spend some time in my house. It was Spring of 2021. The weather was outstanding, the scenery beautiful and we enjoyed the outdoors as much as we could. Despite his fatigue, Homer was determined to pursue golfing, working out, and walking together. We enjoyed drives visiting the countryside.

He was still under hormone treatment therapy to fight his prostate cancer. The side effects remained challenging. The treatment provided the benefit of reduced tumors but poor quality of life. For an active man who used to play golf and workout several times a week, slowing down was hard. He had survived the terrible side effects of his previous treatments through his faith, drive, and surrender to God. I made sure I did my best every day to bring sunshine into his life. We prayed together. We read the Bible together and always remained positive and as stress free as possible. Relaxation and rest were included daily.

One evening, I decided to show Homer pictures of me in my

younger days. As he went through the photos, I noticed he was putting a few aside and kept on looking at them several times over. I also observed his facial expressions changing. Something was happening. Showing excitement over some photos, he asked me to reproduce and frame them for display in his immediate surroundings. I was not sure what motivated him. At first, I attributed his reaction to my appearance as a younger woman.

The next day, my curiosity got the best of me. I had to know what effect my pictures from the past were having on him. His input proved rewarding although unforeseen.

Yes, I looked attractive he said, but it was not the reason driving the impressions and feelings he experienced. For the first time, he saw a vulnerability and innocence of character in me he had not yet recognized. My pictures somehow revealed to him a side of me he had not perceived with such depth before. It touched him profoundly, giving him much to reflect upon. He added, "The camera always tells the truth."

A couple of days later, I was in for the biggest surprise ever. We went as usual to a nearby field to let Cali free to run. As we got out of the car, Homer came towards me and grabbed both my hands.

The next thing I know, he knelt in front of me making the most incredible statement, "If you want your prince, here he is. I am fully committing to you for the rest of my life. I want to protect you, support you, grow with you, and be here for you always if you will have me."

Naturally, my heart melted right then and there. It was the most joyful and elated moment of our relationship. The bond between us was cemented and we could move forward without reservation. It was a time of celebration, the best decision we ever made.

I had already been fully committed. His reciprocal commitment opened a new dimension, a higher level of trust and intimacy between us.

Praise the Lord for Homer saw something in my pictures fanning the flames of his heart prompting him to pledge himself to our relationship without reserve nor holding back.

ARKANSAS

A few days later, Homer came up with an idea and suggested we combine our financial resources. Sell both our homes and buy one together somewhere. I believed it was a solution that made a lot of sense. The question was where?

Being resourceful he suggested we take a ride to Tennessee and explore the Tri-Cities area comprised of Kingsport, Johnson City, and Bristol. He had considered moving there before and remembered it as a beautiful location with much to offer.

It was not far from Asheville, and we could make it a day trip. It was indeed an attractive area consisting of rolling hills and pastures reminiscent of European sceneries reminding me of France. A realtor showed us around. We did not care for what she presented us with. We spoke to a different realtor who grasped quickly what we had in mind and knowing our budget, she honestly felt our price range would not allow the type of property we had in mind.

During the same time frame, friends of mine from Colorado, Camila and Noah had just moved to Northwest Arkansas, to a small town called Bella Vista and absolutely loved it. They felt it was the best decision they had made for their retirement, strongly recommending we come and visit before deciding where to move. Their enthusiasm was contagious, so we planned a trip to Northwest Arkansas.

We returned to Louisiana first and within a couple of weeks we were on our way to Northwest Arkansas with the RV. We spent a week there and loved the area. It had scenic beauty, a four-season climate, and wonderful amenities such as several golf courses, a big draw for Homer, lakes, a multitude of trails for biking, walking, and hiking, a big draw for me. Lots of activities for everyone's taste and apparently real estate prices were within our range.

The decision was made. This is where we wanted to be. The realtor we contacted told us houses were hard to come by and when they did, they were snatched up quickly. She only had one home for us to see and by the time the showing was scheduled, an offer had already gone through. This was day two of our stay.

We did a lot of driving around and the more we saw, the more the area appealed to us. It felt right, the energy floating in the air was positive, welcoming, and we were both drawn to move there.

Our "wee small voices" approved of our choice and left us with no doubt we had found our retirement spot even though there was nothing on the market.

On the morning of the third day, our realtor called. A home had popped up we might be interested in. We saw it but it would not work for various reasons.

Time was flying. On the fourth day, we received another call about a house just listed. We were the first to see it. It was perfect and just what we had hoped for. The owners wanted to combine offers over the weekend before deciding. We put our best foot forward and came up with the most tempting deal. We clearly had competition. But it was meant to be, the following Monday, we were picked as the new homeowners.

The rest is history, everything flowed like a red carpet unrolling in front of us. No obstacles and a flawless move ensued.

We sold our homes quickly and a month later moved into our new house knowing we had made the best decision and time was going to prove it.

Our common goal of pursuing the Truth under the guidance of the Holy Spirit has opened new doors for us. We met likeminded Christian brothers and sisters driven by the same aspirations, following and celebrating God's Son together, our Lord Jesus Christ.

This is the journey we are on, one day at a time. An incredible and rewarding exploration of God's Words, Attributes and Promises. A gift available to all who choose to believe, repent and surrender.

I have reached the point where I am now turning over the writing to Homer who in his own words and style will contribute to our story together.

The three of us – September 2022 -

INTERFACE BETWEEN CONTENT

The content of Evelyne's Biography will pause before concluding. The pause will allow for the interface and incorporation of a collection of other memoires by Homer Adams. The interruption in the rhythm and cadence of the two writing styles is conceptually a way to bring into the dialog a different interpretation of the circumstances and perception of the events bringing us together.

We had an experience charged with energy and emotion at various times, it was hard to deny the presence of something far bigger than ourselves at play. My written account may or may not mirror that of Evelyne's but should shed some light on the outcomes and motivations we were to follow.

These events are characterized independently by both writers and attempt to tie up the life stories of both while at the same time introducing the overriding theme of the Holy Spirit and Ascension to be brought into our lives. The decisions we made due to this melding together of our spirits caused significant changes for both of us as well as others.

BOOK TWO

Homer Adams

DREAMS

Carl Jung, "The Undiscovered Self" (Signet 1957) suggested "dreams" are part of the psyche of the individual, the interworking of the mind and the unconsciousness within. He insists we should pay close attention to them especially if they are recurring.

On most mornings, I wake up between 6am and 7:30am depending on what time I went to bed and what was on my mind the night before. Over the last few years an overriding factor crept into my dream-state. An urgent need undeniable because of its metabolic origin. A 74-year-old bladder doesn't have much tolerance.

On this morning, the urgency was stimulated by a recuring dream causing anxiety and tension. Of course, the tension separated the unconscious nature of deep sleep from a state of awareness long enough to become totally awake. Then sleep ends.

Since the anxiety came during the unrestful hours before dawn, it could have only been created by the unconscious mind since the cognitive mind slept. The biological processes while dreaming increased the pressure and resulted in all the "red lights" going off signifying an emergency. I had to either end the dream and wake or worse case - get up.

Sleep data and scientific testing shows everyone experiences dreams differently. Two dreams have been recurrent, both cause unrestful, and stress filled nights. A third resolved an existing problem I was unable to solve in the conscious state. Remembering dreams has never been something I have been good at doing. I was surprised, in these two cases, I could remember them and the stress I was going through while it was happening.

I began contemplating what caused these dreams. In one, I kicked my feet and uttered stressful noises. Evelyne was concerned as she informed me of this unusual behavior the next day. In the other, I found myself wrestling with the sheets, pillow, and breathing heavily.

April 12, 2021: I dreamed a male figure in a white suit with "no tie" was following me. I didn't understand the significance of "no tie," but it must have meant something. When I awoke, this detail remained, despite his facial features fading away. As he pursued me at an ever-quickened pace, he tried to grab my arms. It was more of a half-hearted effort or maybe just plain clumsiness. Whatever the reason, I wasn't waiting around to find out. Moving quickly and managing to evade his grasp by zigzagging through the crowd of people who appeared in front of me, I wondered why this guy was chasing me. Why was I running at all? What did I fear? Stop, turn around, show some backbone, and face this guy. I abruptly stopped, swinging my left arm in a large swirl over my left shoulder so I could hook his outstretched arm. I made an aggressive turn from right to left, 180 degrees, while moving toward whomever lingered behind me. I also thought to make myself as big as I could to bring up the energy level. A change in thinking turned the tables on this dream by using clear thinking and a willful energy to engage my fear. Now, I had his arm tucked in a standing armlock under my own and my right hand was free to become a hammer or weapon. The dream ended the moment before thrown blows made contact with his body and head. I suppose the dream woke me from REM sleep causing the twitching and thrashing. The movement of my feet became a rapid kicking, or it may have resembled the footwork used in a fight. In either case, it was a demonstration of the struggle going on in my mind. This dream was not recurring and left only impressions of meaning, and more questions than answers.

April 13, 2021: The second dream was recurring. I found myself in a large pool with distinct sides much like a swimming pool. I was under water but near the surface. My arms were restrained which restricted my ability to swim or stay afloat. As I fought to free my arms, I could see in the distance a large Great White shark headed straight for me. At this point, I imagined his mouth open wide and all its teeth bore down on me. It was evident it meant me great harm. I continued to feverishly struggle with the restraints to get away, to no avail. The extreme anxiety created fear, helplessness, and more struggles with the bed and pillows. I eventually woke up before being eaten.

The dreams alerted me to something of significant importance – a message from the recent past or not too distant future. The future would eventually converge on a choice or decision I would have to make.

Based on the severity and intensity of the dreams, the fork in my road would become a significant change to my life (in-the-near-future and maybe forever). I would need to pay close attention to the details to decipher the dreams for clues to help make the correct decisions. My thought processes began to grind on the possibilities. Apparently, I would have to wait for my complex life to unfold a bit more and look for the forks. I mentally noted the dreams seemed counterproductive and negative. It was too soon to analyze the dilemmas they would bring. I don't like negativity in any form.

April 23, 2021: The following dream was positive and productive. I struggled for 9 months with my golf swing. I practiced hard, one and a half hours a session 3-4 times a week and played as often as I could. Yet, my game seemed to worsen. Trying harder created more frustration. I couldn't figure out what caused such terrible ball striking and missed hits. The dream solved the problem instantly. By seeing in my mind's eye, I had begun to close the club face down. In the dream, I clearly saw the mechanics and lack of a correct address club face to ball. I woke up in delight and great awareness of what was needed to correct the issue. That day, I went to the driving range to test my awareness and, low and behold, it was 100% correct. Problem solved!

I don't know if the unconscious mind connected these dreams in some way or if they were mutually exclusive to each other. Surely the stress associated with the first two couldn't have been only a mental operation to set up an unconscious solution to a golf swing. Or could it?

My intuition says "no" to the connection, and I will have to wait on time to usher in the future chain of events I believed loomed over the horizon.

For the continuation of Evelyne's Biography and the continuity in the merging of our two stories together, the narrative around events and the forces which brought our two lives together will hopefully tell a story of Hope and Love emerging from a Force outside of ourselves. Giving way to the spiritual journey we were to embark on together!

For the sake of consecutive events and correlation, I believe it is helpful to provide the following timeline in a chronological order of movements, locations and some of the more impactful events which shaped our lives:

Oct – Dec 2018: Tongue cancer surgery extraction; followed by partial colon extraction.

Feb 2019: Relocate from Asheville, NC to Berwick, La; purchase home in Lafayette, La.

March 2020: Purchased the Montana RV.

June 2020: Elevated PSA to over 38.

June 2020: Utilize RV for 6-day voyage with Ashley and Adrien to Asheville, NC.

June – Sept 2020: Spend 3 months in Flat Rock, NC. in RV.

August 2020: Met Evelyne in Flat Rock.

October 2020: Surgery to implant stents in carotid arteries.

November 2020: Cataract surgery.

December 2020: Drive to Flat Rock and spend Christmas at Evelyne's house.

January 2021: Return to Lafayette.

January 2021: Biopsy prostate.

February 2021: 1st (one month) hormone injection.

March 2021: 2nd hormone injection (3 months).

May 2021: 3rd hormone injection (6 months).

May 2021: Trip to Bella Vista Arkansas to survey the area and look at real estate; Put offer on house in Bella Vista; Return to Lafayette.

June 2021: Drive to Flat Rock and prepare Evelyne's house for marketing; Ship household goods to Bella Vista; Returned to Lafayette; Evelyne's house sold in 1 month.

September 2021: 4th hormone injection (4 months).

June 2021: Put house on market; Lafayette house sold in 1 month.

July 2021: Pack up household furniture and ship to Bella

Vista.

August 2021: Close on house in Bella Vista.

As I reflect on these previous events leading up to the dreams and the unanswered questions, it was apparent the issues I faced would certainly add to the complexity of life. The forks in the road led to profound changes. The timeline helps sort dates and times of the events in order to emphasize their spiritual connectivity and how they played out during periods of serendipity and centricity. And as a matter of answered prayer.

It seemed overwhelmingly obvious all the things required to ultimately move forward from another round of cancer would take on multiple complexities and demands on the human spirit.

THE ROOT CAUSE & RESURRECTION

Chinese Proverb #35 – He who returns from a journey is not the same as the one who left.

In late October 2018, with the resurrection of cancer diagnosed on the tongue, this would be the second time cancer attacked my tongue and my third battle overall. Unfortunately, the tongue would be sacrificed to rid myself of this new outcrop of cells.

We must honor the "causes and effects" bringing Evelyne and I together in the first place. At the core, the influence my biography had on Evelyne would play a significant part in how things eventually played out. Had I not written it and she had not read it, things would have taken a different course and led to a different outcome. Writing the bio ended up changing both our lives, even though it was written for another purpose all together. As a special footnote, I often marveled when rereading and editing sometimes weeks or months after writing it, it bore no resemblance to what I perceived as something I would write. It doesn't carry the voice of its author. Where it came from, God only knows.

Returning to my third encounter with cancer. Another threatening fight for life! After two long weeks at MD Anderson, going through evaluation, I faced the results of the tests and the medical team's recommendation. I found myself sitting at the medical facility, again, with the surgeon and assistant in the examination room. I expected to absorb the details of the test and their meanings going forward. I needed to make a decision while trying to concentrate on the facts as I heard them. My conceptual mind desperately tried to whisk away the fog my brain seduced me into. It became surreal and dreamlike. In the scene, the patient is watching himself and others discuss results of the tests and implications for survival along with the recommended treatment and outcomes. It was like an out of body experience.

Obviously, there would need to be surgery to extract the affected part of the tongue by one surgeon. Then, a second surgeon would take over mid-operation and reconstruct the tongue using tissue from the thigh. The surgery would have its own set of consequences and a recovery of 6-8 weeks. The second part of the team's recommendation was chemotherapy.

The consequences of the original treatment for cancer in 2007 using chemotherapy and radiation left severe damage and scars which will never go away. The chemo was intolerable, and the radiation caused tissue and structural damage which would remain and continue to deteriorate the radiated area with time. Both treatments caused significant distress for years to come. It became painfully obvious extending lifetime vs quality of life as an outcome should be carefully considered before accepting treatments. I continue to face speech, swallowing, and breathing damage forever and a day. Deterioration in all three areas progressively worsened, despite the treatment, 11 years ago.

The previous three rounds of chemotherapy had more than an immediate effect. It was more devastating during the actual treatment, but the residual effects on the immune system over time could never be determined. Recovery time after each was like going into the boxing ring with George Foreman wondering when the bell would finally ring. A near death dance with chemistry or poison is more descriptive of the process.

The radiation left the tissues in my tongue, throat, and neck in an irreversible state. The severe fibrosis and hardening over time left me with breathing, swallowing, and vital functions I could not overcome. I learned the grave difference between "aggressive treatment" as opposed to "quality of life" the hard way. The treatment added little to my quality of life. Little did I know, at the time, what the ultimate outcome would be. The doctors didn't go into great detail of what to expect. The best they could do is sum up what they thought the life expectancy would be. In the end, I endured the regimen with nothing but a fist full of willpower and the need to make my own decisions about therapy in the future.

I proceeded to take a more active role in my health issues and solutions as a recourse with medical personnel rather than present myself to them and say, "fix me." I needed my decisions to be based on more extensive research and intuition rather than people I barely knew. They say if the treatments didn't kill you, you might have a chance. The treatments felt like I died multiple deaths.

After about two weeks of research and with the help of close friends, I was able to develop an extensive spreadsheet of the facts as I had found them. I gathered a second opinion from another surgeon and patient I knew who was going through the same diagnosis with a tumor on his tongue. He had to make the same decisions and endure the same processes I was now navigating. I submitted the facts and data I had gathered to numerous trusted friends for opinions and insight. We compared notes and experiences within the medical field and focused on grasping the risks. Always looking for the least of two evils. We mapped out issues with the cancer itself. We compiled a list of complications from the first cancer treatments.

We tackled the extraction of the tongue issues and how much of the tongue would have to be taken out. We looked at some of the implications it would have on breathing and swallowing, but in most cases, we could only filter out hints of what was to come. All risks would ultimately have to be taken to get the tumor out. Surgery would have to be the primary choice in everyone's mind. The outcomes - post recovery - would have to be dealt with as they came.

By a process of elimination and risk evaluation, the decision to remove the tumor was made and the surgeon accepted the decision without reservation. How much would have to be removed was unknown and would be determined based on the margins of the tumor while in surgery. They seemed to think at least half of the tongue would have to be surgically removed. How this would affect my speech would be anybody's guess, but it boiled down to the right choice and lowest risk in search of the maximum "quality of life." More importantly, quality to life in general. Hopefully, the surgeon would get it all.

The tongue reconstruction was the most important part of the procedure I needed to wrap my head around. It was shaded with much less straight forward understanding for what to expect as a result. If I had to sacrifice my tongue, reconstruction using tissue from elsewhere on the body would be a foregone conclusion.

Consultation with the plastic surgeon was necessary to understand the process. Trust in the surgeon would have to be the only way to grasp the risk. His part in reconstruction was purely technical as he would have to tie all the blood vessels and muscles back together and hope the tissues would grow in their new location. At this point, I would already be committed to the extraction, so I hoped the risk of reconstruction was minimal.

All this brought into focus the emotional prism, before even considering chemotherapy. I remembered chemo from my first experience with great reservation, swearing never to undergo such torture again. The poisons used had severe consequences and reduced living to managing the awful side effects. At first, nothing seemed abnormal. Then, you lose your appetite, and the weight starts falling off. Everything you try to eat tastes like axel grease and cardboard. Your hair falls out – all of it. You find yourself without a lick of energy and can barely get out of bed. For 9 weeks your life is no life at all. It's a nightmare! I took three rounds of chemo each over a period of three weeks. About the time you come back to life, you are up for the next round. It was a mental, physical, and emotional battle all the way to the end.

The results of the therapy were good, and the tumor shrunk to non-existent during the first two rounds. They decided to push on to a third round as insurance and my wellbeing. It seemed like the most logical thing to do at the time. The third round nearly killed me, and I promised myself to never take chemotherapy again, even if the cancer were to return.

My memory retained all the horrors of chemotherapy from 2007 in every detail. I was bound and determined (this time) to decline chemotherapy.

When my research and contemplations concluded, I found myself facing the oncologist with one final direct question, "What statistical evidence did the oncologist have to support taking chemo." She hesitated, then said, "there is no statistical evidence. It would only be insurance over and above surgery to remove the cancer."

The answer to my question was the smoking gun needed to resolve the dilemma. No Chemo! I would have to manage risks and accept the outcomes: win, lose, or draw.

I went on to have the surgery. When I woke up in the recovery room, I was told all went well. I had been on the operating table for nine and a half hours, but it only seemed like minutes with the help of anesthesia. I was still under the influence as I lay there with the fog lifting, but I knew the pain would eventually come as I awoke. Whatever the risks were, I would be expecting them to manifest themselves soon.

The cat had my tongue which had been replaced by a piece of my leg (inner thigh). How funny it would be, I thought, if my mouth started running all the time? I could blame it on the leg. The thought made me laugh. I use this line about running my mouth at every opportunity, until the joke wore out and wasn't funny anymore.

After 5 days in the hospital with no sleep, I was discharged cancer free once again, minus a tongue and facing a 6–8-week recovery. A dear friend in Houston welcomed me into their home for the initial recovery time. I began by walking a little each day as far as my energy would allow and then just a little more. After the first week, I started going to the gym and weight training, again as far as my stamina would allow. After 5 weeks, it was time to return to Asheville. I talked my sister into coming to help me through to full recovery which would take a lot more time. She agreed. Bless her.

Six weeks after returning to Asheville, I found myself in the final stage of recovery but weakened by the procedure and fatigue associated with cancer. At this point, I was cancer free, but soon discovered how vulnerable I was to other attacks. While playing golf one day, I teed off at Asheville Municipal, and as I swung the club, I felt a twinge in the lower abdomen. A few days later, I learned the ugly truth about the twinge. Rushed to the Emergency Room, I discovered my colon had wrapped around itself and caused a blockage. According to the medical personnel on hand, it would require immediate surgery to remove the blockage.

Another surgery. How lucky could one guy get? I faced another long recovery, one on top of another. There was no time to discuss it or even try to reason with the diagnosis. It was critical. I was critical. As I lay in the emergency room in severe pain, it was plain as day surgery would be necessary. Away we went to meet the surgeon's knife and suffer the new consequences on an aging body.

Three weeks into recovery, the body I respected for its endurance and tolerance had deteriorated to a meager 170lbs of bones. Not much left to look at and not a spark of life left to find. I must admit, there were moments of numbness and a fade in what was once a confident and strong-willed person. I couldn't find motivation. The two things I always relied upon in desperate times were motivation and perseverance. Going the distance. Going the extra mile. Pushing and driving myself to the limits of endurance and pain. The two most essential character traits I relied on and trained into my persona were nowhere to be found.

My mind drifted off to some far away sorrowful and negative place of woe throughout the day as I sat waiting for something to happen. As if something was going to pull me out of this ditch. I consciously pulled myself back into my inner-self and reflected on who this shell of a man was. I conversed with myself on several occasions. This is something I do in dire occasions facing low points in life. But these conversations were unlike the previous. They were not talks of simple persuasion. They were more demanding in tone. One involved a little bit of shouting and anger. A struggle against something I didn't want to do. After a couple of rounds of talks and pointed conversations with myself, I finally faced the reality of my situation. The reality led to deciding to sell the home I dearly loved in Asheville and move back to Louisiana because I no longer had the stamina nor energy to care for the house nor the grounds. I needed outside help and assistance. It had become a matter of survival.

It was a move to be closer to family support not only for recovery, but long-term relationships. The kind of support only family could give. I had quickly become someone else's problem, not just my own. Since I had been a self-starter, I don't remember when and never depended on anyone, this was a hard realization with which to come to terms.

The series of events began, starting with "wham bam thank you ma'am" and there was more to come. The cause and effect had also begun. "For every action there is an equal and opposite reaction." I was about to learn and understand the law of physics controlling causality.

The circumstances beginning in October 2018 set up a fork in the road forcing me to consider moving back to Louisiana. I could not conceive of possibilities for the future, but I had to move and accept the outcomes with grace and humility.

I packed up, moving at a snail's pace, with the help of my sister and daughter, we improved by a factor of 10 and finished 4 weeks of packing, selling, and giving away in about 1 week. We had a loading crew fill up a 26-foot U-Haul and off we headed to Louisiana.

I hadn't had time to locate a home or make any decision except to prepare the house in Asheville for sale, the first priority. One thing at a time was my only thought, considering the amount of energy I could muster. We drove straight to my mother's old house in Berwick, LA.

My sister had cared for our mother until she passed a couple of years before, which left her house vacant. My sister did it without any concerns for herself or the living conditions at the time. But God bless her, she made it work. The final years of mom's life were spent with her daughter and the majority of her family members at her beck and call. For that, I will be forever grateful. Giving her my share of any inheritance (50% equity in the house) couldn't compensate her enough for her service to mom.

No one had lived in mom's house for 12 months, and it was in bad shape when we arrived, filthy, and in need of major repairs and construction left unfinished, but it was shelter and could be used as my transfer/holding point until I could sort out where I wanted to live.

My sister was obviously someone I wanted … needed to stay close to until I could get back on my feet. We teamed up on the projects and repairs the house needed and started working on restoring it to acceptable living conditions. It was a long road back to regaining a new life and getting reestablished. It took equally as long to regain good health.

I would never be the same, physically, as I once was. My life had taken a major change in direction, but I was determined to make the best of it. I followed my heart and brain working in tandem in a state of cohesiveness rather than on impulse. I slowed everything down to the lowest common rhythm and let things flow. I waited for the answers from my inner being and the Spirit to guide me. I let all emotions subside before making any decisions. I surrendered my will to Divine Providence and guidance from the Spirit.

These realities and experiences drove me to an even greater need for spiritual connection with God and the Holy Spirit to get me through. I called on the Triad for help many times in my past and it seemed to be much more frequent lately. I felt the Spirit now more than ever guiding my every move. I surrendered to the Omnipotent power from above without reservation.

The more recent calls for help occurred when I needed guidance to get through the valley of the Shadow of Death and find still waters. The history of my recoveries was always filled with gratitude and determination. The survival instinct was primeval and came from some unknown part of me!

REVISITING PAST

Tao Tzu (Chinese Philosopher): when I let go of what I am, I can become what I can be.

The unfolding of my new experience started with a journey to the past: people I once knew, places I had lived and attached to, and the life I lived in my youth. It was soon to be reborn in the present and relived in my memories. I never wanted to return to my hometown for any reason, surely not to live. Circumstances and the spiritual guidance being given to me now presented harmony and humility, as if those had been my own virtues all along. My footsteps became more interesting and serendipitous. The synchronicity appeared almost daily with each step forward providing the spiritual evidence I was on the right track. Of course, I interpreted the evidence and emotional uplifting as God sending it. There was no other way to interpret the euphoria and energy coming down around me.

I was able to reestablish contact with old friends I hadn't seen in a lifetime. I played a lot of golf and worked out 4 days a week. I finally got my strength back. Life seemed to give me one more chance, but this time with a little less intensity. I had lost a step or two. More than the steps lost, my sense of balance left in the surgeries as the breakdown of the parasympathetic nervous system set in.

The aging processes could be as much at fault in the latter years since I had been diagnosed with Chronic Inflammatory Demyelinating Polyneuropathy (CIPD). This autoimmune disease left me with neuropathy in the feet and calves, altering the feeling in the feet with a kind of numbness and tingling so I no longer felt the ground. My feet felt heavy and dangling, not firm and foundational. The surgeries seem to compound the effects.

During this 4-month interlude, I spent a great deal of time with my sister, who proved to be vital in my rehabilitation. She helped me find my way back to the possibilities ahead. We talked a lot over the days and nights while we were at mom's house. We worked on restoring the house inside and out and reacquainted ourselves with each other. I cherish this time spent with her.

In the beginning, she had a hard time showing any affection towards me. I understood the reluctance which stemmed from sibling rivalries. I didn't treat her well as a sister and for this I was ashamed. Every time I tried to hug her, she would shy away and resist the hug. This went on for weeks, maybe even months. I persisted in showing her affection and eventually she gave in to my persistence and began hugging me back. Thank God for second chances and forgiveness.

After 5 months of recuperation, I began looking around for someplace to live. I settled on Lafayette, where I previously lived. I finished a Petroleum Engineering degree at the local State University, got married, and started a family. Going back to Lafayette had to be inspired by a higher power. I never wanted to go back due to the memories. My children's mother passed away from cancer here. This was where most of my troubles in life began and I did not want to suffer the pain again. If, however, this is what I was being asked to do. So be it!

I, eventually, found a great house, for the money, in an area I knew well. I closed in record time and settled in. It reminded me of my home in Asheville. The living room was the exact same size and shaped as the living room in Asheville, 14-foot cathedral ceiling and all. Asheville had a blue bedroom, so did this one.

It was easy to reestablish myself in the city because I knew the area and had friends. It turned out to be a lot less troublesome and emotionally easier than I expected.

Here, I thought about writing my biography. It was going to be a project taking me on a reflective journey into the past on a scale bigger than my own imagination. I had no idea once I started if I would finish. Beginning the bio is always the problem. How would it be structured? What should I write about? How would the tone resonate with the reader? I wanted to write the bio to and for my daughters, leaving an account for them of who their father was. Some account and understanding of what accountabilities and responsibilities I thought I had in raising them to a higher standard. A standard requiring a steady hand and a thoughtful poise. There would always be decisions a father would make leaving children unsatisfied or frustrated. I offered them a perspective from my point of view as a father and parent. Writing a bio would mean treading on ground laden with pain, tears, and sorrow. The task took courage and tenacity. I wasn't sure I had enough of either. I began to tell my story and the bio was written and self-published.

The first month of writing and editing didn't yield enough substance, structure, bylines, or vision working toward an ending. As a dear friend put it, "it reads like a textbook." It was matter of fact, the words lacked flow or feeling. After I considered the voice of his first impressions, I found myself empty, searching for something more. It was an honest and fair estimation. I could not hide behind self-pity or bias. I was not shocked by his opinion; therefore, I embraced it, knowing I could do better.

I took off for three weeks to lick my wounds and let the emotions subside. When I sat down and began to pick up the pieces, I found the story of my life became intertwined with hidden messages of knowledge, spiritual guidance, and wisdom. This time it came to me without struggling with the content. It came by releasing myself and surrendering to whatever emerged. I think the greatest lesson learned from writing was surrendering and letting it flow. Ideas came and were captured. Substance was born by connecting the dots and framing them into the story. Somewhere in the mix, creativity entered the picture, as well as humor. It started to take on a life of its own. All I had to do was sit down and write.

I often thought about the men and scribes who wrote the Bible and how they might have received their inspiration. Could that be how they downloaded the history of events through divine connection?

By June of 2019, I had been writing for 6 months and completed the first draft. I contacted an editor to review the bio for a nominal fee. I had written, edited, and reread the bio numerous times catching error after error, and rewriting numerous pages to improve the readability and content. By the time I made an agreement with the editor on a price, I was exhausted with editing. It never seemed quite good enough. The more times I read, the more changes I would make. I found myself rewriting the whole bio. It was time for someone else to shake it out.

For about a month, he would edit and forward me the edits for approval. At the end of the editing, the book read much better, even though it wasn't perfect. But perfect enough for my budget. I never intended to have it professionally published. After all, it was really written for my daughters and close friends.

In March of 2020, I had an urge to buy a Fifth Wheel RV. One day on the way home from Baton Rouge, I saw two RV sales and service businesses. I hesitated but eventually found myself taking the exit off the interstate and arriving at Camping World wondering why I was doing this. I didn't need or even want an RV. I was not sure in my physical condition whether I could handle it. I looked at some new and used RVs, to get an idea of what a 32-foot Fifth Wheel would look like. Coincidences started to fall into place. The first RV I looked at was a 2006 32-foot Montana with two slides. It was in pristine shape with 13 years on it. After canvasing the rest of the lot, I came back to the Montana, because nothing else compared. The dealership didn't have it on the books yet, and it hadn't been serviced or detailed. They couldn't give me an asking price. After surveying it inside and out, it was apparent it would eventually need a new roof within the next couple of years. Still, it would be a great way to enter the world of RVs at a minimum cost and see if this lifestyle was for me. At least this is how I rationalized it to myself. I felt confident I was going to buy it, and I knew what I was getting. As I stood there with the sales agent, my brain ran through all the justifications, advantages, and disadvantages of ownership. Most of all, I questioned the wisdom and compared it to impulsive behavior entering my thoughts for unknown reasons. I was going to commit to the cost of the RV as well as purchase at least a ¾ ton truck to tow it. Spending the money on the RV and a truck at a time when the vision for my future was in doubt didn't make any sense, but, somehow, it felt right as I surrendered to the positive possibilities. I felt something irresistible drawing me to make the deal with complete confidence.

A couple days later, I found myself the proud owner of a 32-foot RV Montana Mountain Edition. I didn't have a truck with which to tow it. As I started a search, I realized they were over the top expensive. My sister called at one point and put me in touch with a friend who had a used Chevy 2500 HD, 4X4, Dura Max for sale in Baton Rouge. I went to see it and what a miracle, doctor's order fulfilled. It was the biggest diesel, standard bed, four-wheel drive GM makes. It had a towing package installed to include a B&W goose neck ball in the center of the bed. What synchronicity it turned out to be. I bought a one-year-old truck worth $60,000 for $35,000. This was taken as another sign my future was shaping up. The reality was it made no sense to have acquired an RV and a truck to go with it. It was not in my nature to be impulsive, and I was in no physical shape to have made such a decision. I had succumbed to an urge I could not explain logically to myself.

It became apparent, life was taking me in a completely different direction and on a new adventure not of my own making. It was easy to surrender, after all I sought after the divine power to reveal itself to me for many years. The Grace pouring down on me was Grace I knew as a child.

During my mid-adult life, I left no stone unturned in search of purpose and meaning. Many great minds and reasonable theories were pursued for understanding. I consistently tried to connect the dots, the mysteries and science revealed in our blessed existence on planet Earth. Each concept guided me to the end of a dead-end road to nowhere. The rabbits I chased and the many rabbit holes I went down left me with a void. There were always more rabbits, and I was running out of time to chase them. There weren't any answers connecting the spiritual world with the material world we live in. I gave it a serious effort and strived to find one. I eventually came back to the Truth, inspired to believe.

Earlier in life, I decided, through inner guidance, to drop searching and quest for knowledge and wisdom, follow the inner voice I spoke about in the bio. As I lived out the present, day by day, the voice became a real light in the darkness and force within my will. Prayer became my daily consultation with the voice and the Creator, pausing to act on the inspirations I received. I soon found myself being guided with every thought in a way seemingly clearer and more decisive than ever.

The set of actions, buying the RV and truck, put in motion a series of events eventually defining the vision and future. I would never have considered buying an RV had it not been for the inner voice guiding me. It placed me on a course I longed to be on. It changed in a spiritual and material way the remainder of my life. A fantastic journey of the heart and soul began. The road led me to meet a real, living Angel.

After cleaning and doing some maintenance on the Montana, I took her out for a maiden voyage to Berwick to see my sister and stayed in a local RV park. The maiden voyage would put me through the paces of loading what I needed, hitching up to the truck, towing the big rig, parking in an RV park, setting up the RV, sleeping in it, and then rigging down and towing home. I admit my antennas were up on those two days. All went well and the voyage was a complete success. I built a lot of confidence and was satisfied with my performance in remembering what I researched and learned on YouTube. It would only get better from there.

I made some additional upgrades and minor modifications, I felt ready to jump off into the bigger world of RVing. I started planning my first real trip to North Carolina, in the Hendersonville area, near a golf course or two and within ear shot of a close friend. It took a while to find an RV park reasonably priced for long stays with availability. I, eventually, found one meeting the right criteria and booked it for late June. All I had to do was finish editing the biography. I wanted it completed before I left town. The next few months went by quickly. I worked in the yard in the day and edited the bio at night. It kept me busy. I completed the editing and decided to put it aside until I could figure out how I wanted to publish it.

I was fast approaching bon voyage time. The trip might be a good opportunity to see if I could coax a grandson into coming with me on a trip of discovery and relationship building. He hesitated but when my daughter decided to come along, he obliged the offer. The trip took us first to the Pensacola Beach area for an overnight stay and some beach time. Then, we headed to Tallahassee and spent a couple of nights with my niece and husband. From there, we hopped over to the Georgia low country to visit a friend and spend a night gearing up for the next leg of the trip.

The trip to NC with my daughter and grandson had been great. I enjoyed their company and sharing the experience together. The last stop was just outside of Savannah, Georgia. We took a day to drive to Darien, GA. I wanted to take the opportunity to show them where my mother's family once lived before the Great Depression of 1929.

We visited the area where she grew up and played as a young girl on what once was a 400-acre plantation. Located along the intercoastal canal in the "low country" with huge, moss laden oak trees all around, the historical marker/marque locating the "Hope Plantation" had fallen from its perch atop an empty pole. The property overlooked the endless blankets of sawgrass covering the entire basin, North, South and East of the plantation. The kids saw firsthand where their grandmother and great grandmother once lived. It was a memory I hope they will remember with fondness in the future. We tried to imagine what it must have been like at the turn of the 20th century in Darien. What it must have been like during the years of the depression could never be known by us, but I'm sure it was tough going. Family history reveals they either sold the plantation or lost it to taxes. In the end, they migrated South to Ft. Lauderdale, FL. during the great land rush. Mom finished the rest of the Depression and World War II living in Ft. Lauderdale.

The setting or maybe the experience itself must have left an impression on my grandson. Before we piled back into the truck for the trip back to the RV park, he laid down in the middle of the county road in front of the historical marker and shot a picture of the road going away under a host of large oaks with drooping moss. The picture captured the history and the ambiance. It was used on the cover of my biography. I think it captures the essence of the trip and the time spent together.

The final day of towing would take us up the Eastside of the Smokey Mountains to Hendersonville where I would remain the rest of the summer. It was a long but uneventful day. We arrived about 5:30 in the afternoon, in time to park the Montana and rig up before dark. Cali was having so much fun as she loves to travel.

Cali is 1/3 poodle, 1/3 schnauzer, and 1/3 Australian shepherd. But she has the markings and personality of an Aussie, as well as the best of the other breeds. Most of all she has brains. She was cross bred by design using a miniature poodle and schnauzer and then crossed with a full-sized Aussie to get a smaller short haired dog in the 25-to-30-pound range. The breeders got what they were shooting for. A perfect size dog with relatively short hair and tricolor pattern and Aussie markings on the face and ears. Aussies are shedders with long coats which makes owning one a little undervalued. Cali is a medium shedder and therefore somewhat unnoticed by the everyday eye. The shedding doesn't take anything away from her other attributes in the least. Her remarkable ability to be trained comes with little effort and shows significant problem solving and communication techniques when she wants something. The ability to communicate and learn from repetition and training quickly distinguishes her from other dogs in her class and to some degree even other Aussies. She continually performs at a high level in behaviors and is second to none with her affection and devotion to both Evelyne and me. She is quite a companion to both of us.

I initially got her as a therapy dog after the 2018-19 surgeries while recovering in Asheville 2019. She was 1 year old and owned by a lady in West Virginia. The owner kindly parted with her because she understood the need I had for a therapy companion, bringing her to me from Virginia. Another synchronicity at play, I wonder. Cali has been a very special companion ever since and I love her dearly. She is beyond companionship; she is totally devoted and extremely loving 24/7.

The kids stayed for a few days before flying back to Lafayette. I settled in for a nice cool summer in the mountains of NC. I was ready to enjoy my single life with Cali, my dearest companion, play golf as often as I could, and enjoy the outdoors only NC could offer.

A MOUNTAIN OF BREATH...
THE GREEN YOU COULD SMELL

Albert Einstein (German Physicist): You never fail until you stop trying.

Carl Jung (German Psychiatrist): The meeting of two personalities is like the contact of two chemicals substances; if there is any reaction, both are transformed.

The mountains were a sanctuary for me. A place to relax and rest comfortably in the coolness and freshness of the green mountains and fields abundantly present. The altitude gave me immediate relief from the labor of breathing considering the present state of my respiratory system. It was home for me. A place providing the happiest times in my life and where the outdoors and yard became my living room and kitchen, and the nature living there became my own personal tapestry. I longed to return when I wasn't there and hated to leave when I was. I lived there, off and on for 15 years, and I was home albeit now staying in a 32-foot RV.

The RV Park was well-established, offering long-term rental for those who lived there on a permanent basis. Or short-term rentals for the short-term travelers. We were going to stay from late June to early September, ensuring we would not have to suffer the entire heat of the summer back in Louisiana. Cali and I would go for walks around the RV park in the morning, afternoons, and before bed. Many other dogs were present so there was always some sniffing to do no matter where we hiked. A large field on the far side of the park was dedicated to dogs so she could run free from the leash. I could see a difference in her behavior when she was on the leash as opposed to being freed. More focused. More reserved. More mature. More suppressed. Anytime I took the leash off, she immediately bolted in an expression of herself to the world around her. She became more aware and self-assured. She became a puppy again, frolicking around, jumping in joyful bliss, and showing off her athleticism and running speed. She was something to behold.

On one afternoon, a dear friend called and asked if I would like to join her and a couple other people, including her mom whom I knew well and liked very much, in Hendersonville for a beer at one of the local ice houses. In North Carolina, an icehouse isn't just an open aired place to drink beer. They are considered a more sophisticated model of beer joints. They have become micro-breweries with their own variety of beer and offer other local designer brews, as well as serving food and other drinks. One of my previous neighbors opened one of his own and my friend recommended we all go over to celebrate his new business.

I agreed to meet them and was happy to oblige her invitation. She was a crackerjack real estate agent who helped me sell my home in Weaverville two years earlier. We got top dollar for it. Selling my home was painful to say the least as I loved living in my paradise.

When I arrived at the brewery, everyone who was expected to be there were already enjoying a brew. I introduced myself in muffled speech which was all I was capable of uttering after the surgery to remove my tongue. Normally, I would have to try to force out some garbled articulated slur not resembling any form of the English language two or three times and hope I was understood. Each time I repeated myself I would have to force more air across the vocals to make them vibrate to effect more of an articulation. This made talking laboriously intensive and the strain of forcing air wore me out over time. I found myself listening more and speaking less. Sometimes, I would make some kind of hand signal in an effort of recognition to a question but would avoid long dialogues altogether.

I came to meet with my real estate agent, her mother, and two other friends I didn't know, severely handicapped in small talk abilities. But I was willing to face my lack of abilities head on and have some fun anyway. I always like meeting new people.

I sat down across from one of the friends, who had short hair and wore a pair of eyeglasses with unusually large round frames – not frames expected to see on the streets of America in a beer joint. They caught me by surprise as did her beautiful unmistakable French accent. I instantly desired to engage in conversation but was not equipped to talk in an audible voice, especially in a noisy brewery. Not only could she not hear what I was trying to say, she clearly struggled with the noises in the bar too. This made talking tiresome and frustrating for both of us. After a few minutes of struggling, I understood she was born in Paris, but had spent numerous years in Tunisia and Morocco as a child.

As we sat in the noise of the bar, the struggle to communicate became even more difficult and it wasn't long before I was mentally fatigued and physically out of breath. I could see the pointlessness of continuing and felt the need to leave and find the tranquility of the RV.

I said my goodbyes and left the building without much thought about the event or the short nature of my visit. There was a small sense of guilt about leaving within 30 mins of my arrival, but I was sure they understood and appreciated I came.

Initially, I hadn't given much thought to the afternoon's social or the lady with the short hair and European glasses. I pondered the coincidence of meeting someone who had lived in Tunisia and Morocco as a young girl. The encounter with this French woman was the beginning of a longer conversation eventually capturing my imagination and led to matters of the Spirit and ultimately my heart. The intrigue wasn't one of infatuation or physical attraction in any way, but one of mystery and expression of the woman in Sophia Loren glasses. Inspired to find out more about who she was, and her experiences became overwhelming. Was it by coincidence or by design? Since I already followed the direction of spiritual guidance, I could not discount this encounter as something trivial. My own experiences in Tunisia and Morocco were interesting to me. We might share some equally tantalizing stories and discoveries. Whatever the brief encounter with Evelyne caused, a few switches flipped, which brought my time in Tunisia back into my mind, places and people I was blessed to have met. There might have been a precursor to this encounter. I tend to think in routines of connecting dots and experiences of life to a spiritual picture. I eventually asked myself, "What if everything was connected and one coincidence led to another until they became a reality?" This possibility only existed if I continued to pursue the French accented, round glasses person. It wasn't until the next day; I felt a small nudge to call the friend who invited me and explore the possibilities of offering myself as a tour guide to the lady from France. Since I was only going to be in Hendersonville for two more weeks, it was not something I would find threatening. Goodness knows, I didn't have anything to do that couldn't be rescheduled or changed. Besides, it was a great way to offer my services to someone moving to the area. It would be a nice gesture and neighborly thing to do. Even if she declined for any reason, it wouldn't be a failure, only a missed opportunity to be nice to someone looking at North Carolina as a new life unfolded. What better way than for me to share with them what I had come to love about living here?

The realtor friend thought it was a great idea and said she would pass along my number to Evelyne with the invitation to call me if she wanted to pursue an outing. Mount Mitchell, Boone, Highland, or Lake James would offer easy access and the drive would be fairly short – there were so many to choose from.

A couple of days passed but, eventually, Evelyne texted me. She had to consider what my intent was and how best to deal with the difficulties in understanding my speech. I am sure there were many other thoughts going through her head, especially since our brief exchange at the brewery wouldn't have impressed her. She must have felt I was harmless in the end and accepted. We exchanged texts on which destination she would like to visit. Mount Mitchell was the closest and the highest point on the US Eastern seaboard at 6,500 feet. From the top, you could see 7 states on a clear day. It had a restaurant on top offering a stopover for coffee or lunch. The day and time were set.

In the meantime, I called some friends I knew in Asheville for 12 years and invited them to come with us for the drive. It would help if there was someone in the car who knew me well enough to be informative about who I was and some of my history in the area. They also knew the region well and could share with Evelyne their own personal impressions and insight into the Mountains. They could express in their own words how they came to love the mountains and what there was to enjoy about living here. They could also help me speak when I needed to enter the conversation. They would have a better ear for what I was trying to say or anticipate what point I was trying to make. It would be difficult for me to even try to carry on a continuous conversation for 3 or 4 hours. They graciously accepted the invitation.

The trip became a milestone in the foundation with Evelyne even though at the time it was a simple gesture of friendliness and good will. "One" thing doesn't necessarily lead to another without the "one" thing to become comfortable. The process can be frail and subject to many outside influences. It is only a statistical probability of many possible outcomes. Going through the motion of helping someone was the only motive I focused on at the time. In the short term, however, it was the original jumping off place to a closer relationship than I could have imagined. It began a new relationship I didn't know I wanted or needed. It would be a grander enhancement to the Spiritual path I already pursued.

We all met at Evelyne's apartment in the lower part of the Historic District of Asheville on Sunday morning at about 9am. My friends offered to drive, which allowed time to concentrate on sentences and the conversation at hand. Right away my friends took over. Something they were prepared to do on my behalf, being talkative people, this wasn't an effort, simply a natural progression. The day went well from my perspective, Evelyne and I got to know each other through proxy. Both friends seemed fond of me and over the years have always expressed their affection. They were a good choice for the task of advocating for me or my history in Asheville.

We made the drive to Mt. Mitchell and spent time at the top to see the beautiful 360-degree scenery. We entertained casual talk at first, mostly on positive things we shared together and what there was to see and experience in the Smoky Mountains. Naturally curious about Evelyne, my friends encouraged her to tell us a little bit about herself. She graciously obliged giving us a brief summary of her history and enthusiastically emphasized the culmination of years of searching for Truth.

The conversations we shared shone a light on Evelyne's life and proved to be well worth a listen. She revealed how her mother and father moved to Tunisia when she was very young. While the experiences were monumental in her development, the family life and negative experiences overshadowed her memories of childhood following her around like a dark cloud. Most of all, Evelyne's memories were surrounded by relational issues. Not that any of the rest of us have experienced anything different in other ways.

Before the day was over, she took a courageous stance and told us about her recent conversion to Christianity and how it changed her life dramatically in the last 3 years. She went into great detail and did so without reservation or hesitation. This perked up my attentiveness to her story. All the negativity she mentioned suddenly melted away and she told us of how a new creature was born. It was a beautiful story to hear and take notice of - more in my heart than head. I empathized with her as a person, alone in this country, and finding herself in NC was compelling in many ways. It provoked my senses, but she was also a new babe in Christ. Developing a different dimension to the picture, my empathy turned into a desire to know more about her and offer my assistance while I was still in the area. This is a person I could identify to with this newly disclosed information. It put her within my sphere of influence, mentally and spiritually, and I felt the door opening for me to take notice of her in a different way, including additional sharing of ideas and past experiences. It occurred to me I should at least contact her and see if another outing was in the picture. I had about 10 days before I was scheduled to return home.

Since Cali had been in her kennel for 5 hours it was necessary to get back to the RV and give her some relief. I left Evelyne in the hands of my dear friends and went my merry way. It turned out they enjoyed their initial contact with her and invited her to spend more time with them by having lunch together to pursue the conversation, giving them time to explore new relationships on their own. I'll never know how the conversation went, but my friends thought highly of me, and I am sure, would give her a good report.

Later that week, after a follow-up text to Evelyne, thanking her for coming on the road trip and meeting my friends and hoping she had a good time, we discussed a second road trip to the Highlands, a group of mountains at about 5,500 feet, about a 2–3-hour drive in the opposite direction of Mt. Mitchell. It is an equally beautiful drive, and the town is quaint in its design and surroundings. It's a wealthy community which can be seen in the real estate and resorts tucked into the hills and valleys. We eventually went to the Highlands on a beautiful day, having lunch and a glass of wine, surveying some of the shops on the main street. We had a delightful day on the mountain and shared more of ourselves than I can remember. It was more difficult than I had hoped and there wasn't anyone else to fill in the conversation with small talk like the first road trip. The conversation as much as it was, exposed more of my speaking handicaps, but it didn't seem to bother Evelyne. She plowed ahead and enjoyed the day, delighted in the drive and the time spent in the Highlands. As we returned to Asheville, I mentioned continuing to text her while I was in the area to check in on her, but I was going to be leaving at the end of the following week. She had a trip planned herself to go see her daughter in Gainesville for a few days and would only return a couple of days prior to my departure. We texted regularly while she was visiting her daughter in Georgia.

Upon her return, having only a couple of days left, I invited her to join us the next evening to have dinner with me and my closest friends. I was going to cook a muscovite duck at their home, and I looked forward to introducing her to William and Brooke. The conversation flowed naturally and was effortless and smooth. They enjoyed Evelyne's company and rejoiced sharing their memories from Tunisia where they also had lived for many years. On the way back to the RV park, I felt compelled to suggest Evelyne come with me to Lafayette and help me finalize the editing of my bio before publication. I felt comfortable asking her and thought nothing of it but continuing our mutual discovery and building a friendship. She did not respond to my invitation and drove back to her apartment.

The next day she texted to let me know she was going to see her new home which was under construction about 3 miles from where I had the RV parked and said she would like to stop by and say goodbye since I was leaving the next morning. Of course, I said I'll be in the RV and would be happy to see her if she wanted to come by.

Early in the afternoon she arrived, and we had a great conversation capturing the events we shared the previous week. It wasn't long before we discussed our philosophies and all the venues of discovery, we obtained over the span of a lifetime – Eastern and Western, various religions, New Age, and more. She shared more details of her conversion to Christianity and her baptism in a horse watering trough in Idaho at a Cowboy Church. The story of her childhood which we covered in detail had not been part of any kind of Christian or religious background or training, but she was obviously inspired by her salvation and had an insatiable desire to learn and consume as much as possible and grow in the Spirit and the love of Christ. This was a hallmark of her strength in Christ as her Lord and Savior. She would share her story about her life and her conversion with everyone she met in short order. As I made note, she would follow this line of discussion well into the longer term and it supplanted her life story with her courage and tenacity for the Love of Christ.

It was amazing how close and parallel our life seemed to have been. The authors, books, and sciences we pursued in trying to understand our lives and answer our quest for Truth, Knowledge, and Wisdom. Her own appetite and pursuits were the mirror of my own on many fronts. I explained to her, in the end, all my pursuit had led back to my childhood and the roots of my belief system given to me by my parents. Founded in the Judeo-Christian faith. I gave her numerous reasons for arriving at this as an impasse in the journey of life because it was exactly where I began. Full Circle - The Energy returned to the Source, and I was on a path of ascension to spirit form. I detailed what this meant to me spiritually, metaphysically, and in my life story.

The events of my life were more than enough to plant a high degree of reservation in her mind. The health issues of the recent past clouded the future in a way even casual observers could plainly see and had taken their toll.

We shared all the predominant details of pain and joy we experienced to the point of exhaustion over the course of two hours. We found many points of comparison and parallel circumstances from which emotions flowed from places deep inside our soul. Could it be we each had a similar view of life and worldview, as well as a spiritual path? We covered all our accounts of coincidences accepting they were not coincidences at all. We also cited serendipity highlighting the mystery throughout our lives. The conversation was exhausting but joyous at the same time. Here is someone who knows me, thinks, and understands what I have come to learn and is articulate enough to speak sincerely and wholesomely. It was at this moment of time something miraculous began to unfold, a feeling. While the conversation continued tears flowed down her face and the energy overwhelmed her little by little. In a few short minutes, Evelyne entered a place she couldn't understand and began sobbing profusely. Agitated at not being able to control the magnitude of the emotional flow of energy and power overtaking her, she fidgeted around the sofa until the shaking set in. The tears went on for nearly 30-40 minutes. Not hysterical but getting close with no end in sight.

I was a little surprised by the outburst and not sure what or how to handle it. One minute we were having a deep conversation about ourselves and sharing experiences and the next minute we were in an emotional state of being. I barely knew her, and it was obvious she was an emotional person, as most women I have known, but this was highly unusual even for me. I sensed there was something more than my own senses could determine. I discerned her spiritual experience from somewhere other than within herself and I needed to let it play out without judgement or fear. It could be something I needed to participate in and to acknowledge. It seemed as if it was necessary to give her my support to reveal itself to her or the both of us. I acknowledged the Spirit and accepted my role should be supportive. I suppose we could also agree, this could be interpreted as a rant. However, it was something of uncontrollable beauty. The innocence and vulnerability on full display before me. It was a tearing open of her soul and something she chose not to resist.

After an hour or so, things settled down and it was obvious it was time to say goodbye. I said as compassionately as possible I would stay in touch, and she left.

I felt a sense of calm having observed her transformation, but the thought of her in this state of submission and vulnerability left me bewildered. Thoughts lingered on, and I wondered if it was truly a spiritual connection or emotions running away for no apparent reason. Somehow, I distinctly felt this was not over, and I halfheartedly expected her to return for reasons I didn't know. Nothing this powerful could be left to wither away. Sure enough, about an hour later there was a knock on the RV door and there Evelyne stood looking sheepishly. She said, "Can I come in for a few minutes and talk a little more? I need to find answers as to what happened." I responded, "I was expecting you to come back but couldn't figure out what took so long." It was a feeble effort to be funny and set her mind at ease albeit I did mean it.

After several hours of deepening our previous conversation into more personal experiences of growth, and development as an adolescent, we moved into more of the teenage years where the challenges became bigger to overcome. They were more complex and harder to understand. As she divulged her long-suffering relationship with her mother whose actions towards her appeared to be unloving and hostile, she sadly told me her parents divorced and sent her to a nunnery in France and left her to fend for herself. As she described her memories of a difficult upbringing, I felt my heart move from empathy to sympathy in a deliberate way.

Round two had gotten off to a different start than the first visit and was much more personal and painful. Evelyne wanted to share the marriages, how and why they ended in disappointment. The one discussion was about her children and then the tears began once again. Her first daughter had died at 10 months in New Caledonia (an island in the South Pacific) where they were living at the time. She shared with me how hard it was for her to survive the tragedy.

She shared the long saga of fighting years in the French courts for custody of her second daughter after a divorce from her husband. In the end, her daughter didn't want to live with her. As she described her internal conflict from this second loss and the rejection, it resonated with my own children. This time the emotional state rose even higher than the first time earlier in the day. I could see she was having a difficult time emotionally and moved closer to her, touching her hand in a consoling way. The same trembling as before returned as she nervously tried to control herself. Eventually she let it all out with no restraints. Once again, my first thought this time through her windowpane was what others might have interpreted as a nervous breakdown, but my inner self kept me out of speculation and focused on a spiritual awakening and a flow of Spirit through her. My own personal experience of years gone by, understood the signs and the presence of the Spirit in our midst. I remained reverent to the presence and what was being said.

The sympathy deepened to a point I could feel her sadness as I felt her pain. I felt my pain of the past and we sat there with tears flowing and me trying to hold back on my own until there was nothing left to say. The connection with her at some deeper level had been made and it drew me closer. I recognized the blessing of an outpouring of the Holy Spirit and was a recipient of a form of Love I had not experienced in a long time. An outpouring I understood, but Evelyne did not. By the time it was all over, and the conversations ended, midnight neared, and she was exhausted.

Since she is nearly blind in the right eye and was afraid to drive at night, I invited her to stay for her safety. I had a roll-a-way sofa in the living room where she could sleep. This was a wild and harrowing experience the day before leaving for Lafayette. It was a full day of unexpected encounters with a force of multidimensional nature seeking me out. It showed itself to me in unabated interactive exchanges and experiences, as well as unexplainable mystery found in real life. It was a case demanding me to see through spiritual eyes. It required me to feel rather than think about what I was experiencing. In the final analysis the download was powerful and real.

It overtook Evelyne's sense of thought and reason. She felt a need to draw closer to this source and investigate how she could help me. She went on to say she felt gifted as a healer and would like to pursue it. As she spoke, it came to me as the influence of the Spirit through her own feelings and showed me what her intent was and the sincerity of her heart. I couldn't help but feel humbled by this woman and her courage to feel so deeply and to engage it so innocently.

I was obliged to counter with my own personal story of death, rejection, and a troubled relationship with my in-laws and daughters for years. I discussed how much stress my body had been under with immediate family, but career related stresses, and controversies invariably came my way and often. Stress of any kind was something I needed to avoid at risk of further damaging my health.

I took her through the medical history of what the stress left in its wake. Cancer I, auto immune disease, Cancer II and Cancer III required surgery to extract the tongue, as well as the residual side effects remaining from chemotherapy and radiation. Then, a 9" colon extraction. I spoke of how my way to cope with a meaningless simple existence was to imagine what life could be by dreaming on a grand scale and running away from time to time. To taste it only for a little while, freedom. I told her about the first time I tried to run away at the ripe old age of 4 years old. Made it to the street and came back in tears. My mother was wise enough to let me go. I never forgot it.

While we were scratching the surface of our personalities and experiences, there was a closeness taking place and it grew deeper than the conscious mind sensed.

Again, I told her I had written my biography earlier and was in the editing mode. For some reason, I asked another time if she would like to come with me to Lafayette, help edit and publish it. It was an innocent offer with purely professional intention. She quickly said she could not. A typical response to a big decision and commitment. I really didn't expect her to accept the invitation on a halfhearted and weak justification, but deep down it was an idea/thought coming from elsewhere in my psyche, not an impulsive gesture. A deeper connection bonding her and I.

My own intuition suggested a good fit for her in her personal journey to grasp at a spiritual moment and maybe get a better understanding of why she was having these episodes and down-loadings from above. All I could do was follow this intuitive thought, feel, and see what would happen. In doing so, it would let her know the door had now opened to the existing possibilities. Possibilities for her to seek ascension on a spiritual path to a spiritual form. If she truly wanted to investigate, I wanted to let her know it was what I sought.

After all the power and energy expressed throughout the day came to an end, we were mentally and physically exhausted. We were unable to sleep, our minds in overdrive the rest of the night. I laid there wide awake, wondering what had happened. It was going to be difficult to say goodbye and leave.

Before she left the next morning, we recapped our experiences, and I again extended the invitation to come to Lafayette to complete the bio. Again, she declined on the grounds she would think about it. I offered her a copy of the unfinished, unedited biography and said, "If you really want to know who I am, it's all in the bio." I emailed her a copy.

This had all the earmarks of a brief encounter at its end. She was buying a house in NC, and I lived in Lafayette. Long distant relationships of any kind never worked in the past. Why would this be any different? I wasn't looking to have a relationship and surely didn't want to take on the stress. The simple truth was, I may never see her again.

I felt a deep seeded connection unfelt before and in a different way. I justified in my own mind it could be a real friendship. The beginning had enough substance worthy of a friendship, I made my mind up to remain in touch for as long as conversation and contact were pursued by both.

WELL SPRINGS OF LIFE AND HOPE

Albert Einstein (German Physicist): If you want to live a happy life, tie it to a goal, not to people or things. Only a life lived for others is a life worth living.

I pulled out the next day and drove 9 hours to Tallahassee to spend a couple of days with my niece and her husband. They moved from California the year before and bought a 10-acre estate previously set up for raising horses. It was a beautiful Victorian style two story home similar to the "painted ladies" from the era in the South. All the big oaks in North Florida and Georgia are moss laden, beautifully decorative and made a splendor of nature in the forests in which they stand. The moss gives them a kind of boldness next to other trees. The stopover would break the trip up into two towing days and provide a restful stop in this majesty before I drove home.

It was on the road trip Evelyne texted sent a written impression of the bio. She started reading it the evening of the day I sent it. She stayed up until the wee hours of the morning and completed the read around 5am the following day. She said she laughed and cried, but most of all she saw herself in all the experiences and development of my character, as well as identifying with all the tragedies. The letter she wrote was an extensive list of the emotional and some physical descriptions of how it affected her deeply. And, how much closer she felt to me as a result of her own revelations.

During the drive, I mulled over and relived the events of the past few days. The one persisting and reoccurring impression was the possibility Evelyne was actually an Angel. A real live Angel sent to engage with me in a spiritual way and help me focus on the inner voice I came to know through my life. At least by this time, the thought wasn't foreign to me, since I do believe in Angels and the part they play in manifesting the will of God throughout human history. But it was incredibly early in this encounter to assume too much of metaphysical phenomena such as an Angel in my world. Of course, I would have to find a way to accept it and bring it into my own reality! I didn't know if I was capable of making this jump. It was the beginning of a thought pattern, however, opening the door to evidence of a higher power and its presence actively influencing my life. This thought continued pursuing me and would be developed time and again over the next few months. Even my conscious mind noted this existential presence of Spirit entering my soul.

I made it safely back to Lafayette after a wonderful stay with my niece and didn't realize much of any road fatigue. I was glad to be home after being away for 2-1/2 months and changing gears yet again.

Life fell back into the normal routine around the house. It was early September and still hot and humid. I knew Cali and I needed to endure the heat and humidity for a little while, but fall was already in the air, and it wouldn't be long before cooler temperatures and lower humidity would arrive. I returned to yard work (a passion). It needed restoring after a long hot summer. It would take a lot of work to bring it back to satisfaction. Nonetheless, it would be enjoyable work for me to undertake and I was eager to begin.

After making a few days of good progress in the yard and around the house, I began turning some attention to editing the bio (again). I had edited it many times before I left, but I knew I could make it better and was sure there were many more typos to catch.

It wasn't long after I arrived home, I received a text from Evelyne stating her desire to fly in for a visit and help me edit and publish the book. A sudden change of heart, we agreed on a date for her arrival. I offered to pay for the airline ticket, but she wanted to fund her own travel and arrangements. She was a head strong woman about most things once she set her mind to something. She got no argument from me. I figured it would take about 2 to 3 weeks to edit and find a publisher. It seemed like a reasonable length of time since I had done so much work on the text prior and felt it needed a final look by a third party to finish. Little did I know at the time the obstacles we would run into publishing the bio.

Within a few days, I was picking Evelyne up at the airport. I was so glad to see her, and think she was glad to see me. We greeted each other as two longtime friends with years of knowledge and respect for each other. It was a relief knowing we yielded to the feelings of discovery about who we were and where this was going. For sure, this road had never before been traveled by either of us. Everything had taken on a new "coat of many colors."

Determined to keep everything superficial in order to maintain my distance from stress, I prepared to hold back all physical pleasantries with respect to my original intentions of inviting her. The main objective of editing took precedence over all else. Maintaining this posture proved to be difficult. To strike a balance and truth to previous conversations, I explored all spiritual related activities to take advantage of growing and sharing spiritually to advance in the direction of Christendom. We incorporated daily prayer in our activities and read together from various books on subjects of interest at night. We attended First Assembly of God in an adjacent town. A Spirit filled church Evelyne and I grew to love. The worship services were particularly vibrant, and she witnessed the moving of the Spirit with the congregation's praising of God at a different level. It resonated within her, and she felt at home. She eagerly drew closer to Christ and the Holy Spirit. Her appetite was insatiable. She converted to Christianity only 3 years previously. She had been brought to the seat of Grace by a couple she adored in Idaho, who exposed her to the faith. This was a new and exciting part of her growth, and she was determined not to fall short.

The conversion not only changed her from within but redirected her life in every way. She realized the significance of the change and desired a deeper understanding.

As she connected the dots bringing her to me and Lafayette, she explained her mission from God to take care of and love me. This was a little radical at first and my impulses wanted to resist the notion ... it was hard to dismiss her sincerity.

The thought kept surfacing in my subconscious mind she was indeed an Angel and spoke the truth! A spiritual truth I might be able to believe. Maybe I wanted to believe. Just a little. God had his own ideas in mind, and he soon provided proof he was in control and not I. He executed his plan for me through witnessing the spiritual outpouring taking place within Evelyne's experience connecting with my own awareness. Eventually, I surrendered, complying with His will, gratefully, even if it wasn't gracefully.

This is where my heart started to take over. I began to see my part as a mentor in her spiritual dimension and growth as far as I could take her. At least, I could share any insights of my spiritual training, understanding, knowledge, or wisdom for what they were worth if only to continue our deep conversations on things requiring the Holy Spirit's guiding presence. We could try to find the answers to her questions in a role of spiritual duality of research together. If I didn't know the exact answers I knew where to look in the Bible. Of course, there would be long discussions in and around most subject matters, and I could see she lacked comprehension of the scriptures. Only enough to accept Jesus Christ as her Lord and Savior. She was a clean slate and would have to consume a lot of material and provoke a lot of understanding in areas where faith is all you have to hold on to. I found myself anxious to be there for her and delighted in her growth. I also knew it would benefit me in mine.

Over the following weeks, she met most of my family and friends, providing numerous opportunities to tell her incredible life story in a variety of settings or in any conversation she found herself. Of course, I didn't miss an opportunity to prompt her to tell her story either. Everyone got to hear the details of her conversion to Christianity and how it enhanced her life. The life story from the beginning and leading up to conversion at 69, was a story deserving of publication. The more times she told it the more I appreciated her as a warm, and sincere woman who made a significant choice in her later years proving it was never too late to turn away from the convenience of years of living in a world without spiritual consciousness and commitment. She could have continued a path without Christ, shriveled up into non-existence and living a retched, loveless, and scared life by the claws of tragedy and misfortune. Yet here she was, standing tall in a sea of evil and darkness all around, taking full account of herself and others only wanting to love and be loved. Such courage, fortitude, stamina, and vulnerability, such selfless courage. It was hard to hold onto my position in the weakness of the empathy I felt for her brought out by listening to her story so many times. It was in the imagination of her strength of character where a fascination grew. I recognized and fully grasped this strength. It was something I could cherish. There is not a great deal to cherish in much of human behavior as I have observed. She would take a place alongside only one or two others in my life I had witnessed with such a deliberate change.

I prided myself (biased as it may seem) in my ability to consume work. I legitimately thought no one could outwork me, but she was a working machine, proving quite capable of matching my enthusiasm and effort in any project or task. Even those uninspiring or difficult. I often saw her work to the point of exhaustion. She proved to me she was the "workingest" woman I ever met, bar none. Her insatiable commitment to walking 1, 2, or even 3 times a day was a priority. Each walk was at least 2 miles, nearly an hour long. She walked in 95 degrees, 90% humidity, rain, or wind. She would also walk in 20 degrees, 50% humidity or higher, with snow and ice on the ground. It was a commitment which was astonishing. We would ultimately power walk together with Cali as exercise we all needed, but also as therapy from the difficulties of life. It proved to be a significant part of each day for both of us. Most times she would walk off and leave me behind no matter how fast I was. Like a bird gliding over a lake in graceful flight. She stayed in great shape at all times.

She was quite capable of meeting me on an intellectual basis. Not that I consider myself an intellectual by any means, but for as much as we strived for understanding, filling our curiosity with knowledge, and soul with wisdom. We tried hard to share concepts in numerous areas. We often found ourselves in deep conversations discovering old and new "points of view" and challenging previously held knowledge providing another nudge toward wisdom. It opened up an opportunity to new and better ways to understand the "unknowable" - evermore trying to find the right piece for a puzzle and clarifying previous understandings or lack thereof.

This gave me every opportunity to explain things and concepts she was unsure about to the best of my knowledge or capabilities. Her ferocious tenacity and appetite to learn and grow in God's grace lit up my intellectual interest, putting it in overdrive. In an attempt to explain a phrase or meaning behind the words, I ultimately reacquainted myself with the scripture and its significance based on understanding from deep in my past. In a sense, I relearned things either forgotten, misinterpreted, or learning for the first time. I cherished those conversations with her and drew in confidence from the discipleship and mentoring. It strengthened my own faith and wisdom, and the desire to draw closer to God and the Holy Spirit. Even though it seemed to be a virtual reality, it was reality for me, because I accepted it as truth and not coincidental. I stood at a crossroad, and I knew it. I chose acceptance and surrendered to His power of transformation within me.

We continued editing the bio and began sourcing a candidate to publish. We settled on a well-known publisher with a good track record for publishing material in the Christian motif. After the prospective publisher reviewed the manuscript, they notified me I would need to make major modifications to the text. The bio could not use real names of companies, people, or other private places which might infringe on privacy laws. The legal restrictions for copyright were boundary under publication law.

After considering the required work to rewrite the bio to accommodate these restrictions, I decided it would change the whole purpose of writing it and distort the essence as fiction rather than a real biography. The intent of the bio was to recount my life for the benefit of my daughters and this purpose would not be complete without the names and places they could relate to in their memories.

I proceeded to self-publish the finished book without copyright or publication assistance except for the formatting and printing by FedEx. Before I decided to self-publish, I accepted being held liable for something and added a disclosure in the preface of the book stating the memoirs were not for public consumption and were for my daughters, never really investigating the legal risks.

I eventually submitted the electronic file to FedEx and ordered 25 copies for family and friends. As it turned out, after I got the finished order and was satisfied with the proof, we ran across several errors and duplicated text. Apparently, somewhere between working with the prospective publishing company and the self-published version, I managed to forward the printing company, what I thought was a final edited file only to find out after printing 25 copies it was not a final. We started over editing the whole bio again since now I couldn't be absolutely sure which file was the final. Truly unfortunate for the time we had already invested. It added another two weeks to the editing process. I can't say how many times I ended up editing, but I suspect it was at least 25 times or more. After we became satisfied with the finished product, we quit and let the cards fall where they may. We printed only 11 copies this time. It was a costly mistake.

By this time, Evelyne had been with me for weeks and had become a comfortable companion and friend. We spent all our time together.

I followed up with doctors' appointments used to monitor my health. In September, my PSA count became elevated which is a primary indicator for prostate cancer. We scheduled blood tests every month so the PSA could be monitored. The next evaluation would be in October. In the meantime, we learned after a cardiovascular work up, there appeared to be some blockage in the carotid arteries in my neck. I felt the man in the dream reaching out to grab me. We scheduled the surgery to place stents in both arteries. Recovery lasted 6 weeks.

After an eye evaluation, we learned I had cataracts in both eyes. Another scheduled surgery, one at a time over the following 4 weeks. It did improve my eyesight to some extent, but mostly it deferred the danger cataract causes.

While all this was going on, the next PSA check showed a spike over 70 and we sent a biopsy to an oncologist. Late October, the biopsy was performed, and the results were not in my favor. 14 out of 15 samples showed malignant tumor growth in the prostate gland. A series of scans were conducted to provide confirmation of the cancer which had spread in the lymph system. The results were positive. At least one lymph node showed up near the aorta in the lower abdomen. It was apparent I had another fight with cancer ahead of me. I could not help but feel the presence of the shark from the dream bearing down on me. This would be the 4th round. The first course of recommended treatment was estrogen hormone therapy to neutralize the male hormone, testosterone, in my body. Not knowing the side effects of this treatment at the time, I agreed to take a one-month duration shot. This would give me time to research on my own the whole prostate disease and be better able to make the decisions required for a quality-of-life agenda.

We took a more progressive approach to the fight and had all the medical records forwarded to MD Anderson in Houston for a second opinion. We scheduled a consultation in January to see their impression of the diagnosis, and treatments available through their facilities. As my research showed, prostate cancer was usually slow growing and manageable in most cases. There were numerous treatments, but it depended on the extent, severity of the cancer, and condition of the patient. While I wasn't in any immediate danger, it certainly didn't signify risk free, cancer-free life ahead.

We had about 2 months before we appeared for our appointment, so Evelyne and I made a trip to Hendersonville for the Christmas Holidays to get away from the evident troubles emerging. We made the drive over a couple days, and I was glad to return to NC. We spent a great Christmas together and got to spend time with friends. I got back to my routine of working out and playing golf. It was a great month and we continued to grow together more and more each day. The spiritual part of our relationship had grown deeper as we read scriptures and held many conversations about meaning, understanding, and application to our lives.

Some of the feelings I faced crept into my thoughts. I knew my throat cancer could reoccur at any time. So far, I had been able to manage it, but the treatments had taken their toll and the damage progressively deteriorated tissues, requiring elevated daily maintenance. Speech and eating habits were becoming more frustrating and time-consuming. Emotional stress would increase. Recent surgeries indicated further deterioration by aging. Now, there was a new life-threatening agent of concern. I would be fighting prostate cancer. I started to realize how this might affect my long term, and Evelyne, if she remained by my side.

After the bio was completed, the original purpose of inviting her to come to Lafayette was satisfied, but she was still by my side and showed no sign of changing course. I hadn't committed to her in any way except as a dear friend who expressed a desire to be with me. By the time I had gone through the surgeries and biopsy and the full impact of the medical issues would become apparent, she seemed to be even more determined to remain by my side and in full support. She discussed it with me often and how she felt she was on a mission from a divine origin to care for me. She would many a time let me know how much love she had for me. It made me a little uncomfortable to a degree because I didn't know if I felt the same way. I had become extremely fond of her and found it comforting to know she felt so strongly. I struggled with the fact I allowed her to come into my innermost sanctum and my heart in such a short time. I sensed the risk I was taking with someone I barely knew. I also apprehended how alone I would be without her demonstrating daily love by attending to my every need. I felt guilty in allowing myself to let it go as far as it had. But I enjoyed everything about her and had grown close to her in many ways. I could not erase my heartfelt concern for her in what was facing us … facing her if I let the relationship continue.

I had been through the agony of being the caretaker for a victim of cancer and the treatments myself, when my first wife was diagnosed with lung cancer. She was 45-year-old at the time and the news was devastating. She passed 9 months later. The second time I made the journey through the valley of the shadow of death, I was the victim, and my second wife was the caretaker. As the victim, or as the caretaker, my experience taught me it wasn't a journey I wanted anyone to have to make. If possible, I would do my best not to put anyone into this situation. Ever!

This was the first and foremost issue on my mind, as I began to think about my options. I found the courage and will within me to break off the relationship. It came abruptly and would be emotionless on my part. It wasn't going to be easy to approach the subject, and I dreaded the inevitable end to the closeness and fondness I felt for her.

After a week of struggling with how to bring myself to discuss it openly, I came to terms with it, once and for all. I may not have wanted her to leave on such an ending, but I was going to have to make the decision. It was for her own good. I would break the news without a lot of discussion and tell her she was going to have to leave. And I did. There is no justification for the pain I caused. I was unprepared for the aftereffects. She didn't take the news well and immediately went into an emotional spiral. I could see and feel the anguish words can cause. It crushed her, completely, to her core. I felt guilt creating such torment and remorse for letting the relationship develop in the first place. But I had to hold my ground on the emotional side of this decision because I knew my ultimate fate could lead to even greater distress and damage later on if left as it was. The hysteria lasted for a number of hours, well into the evening. I took a solemn approach and felt I could not afford to offer any empathy to her, or I might not be able to end it venerably. She ended the evening crying herself to sleep if you could call it sleep.

The next day, she recovered to the degree she requested 3 days to pack, rent a car, and ship some items back to her home in North Carolina. Of course, the least I could do is agree for her to stay. I could not expect her to leave immediately. Three days would be a long time to withdraw to a neutral corner of the house and avoid any indication I might change my mind. Having conversations would also be hard, and questions after questions prodding into my own emotions, always ending in, "Why?" This would be stressful and draining.

After a couple days, she finished packing boxes and suitcases, and rented a car to drive home. She would be leaving the day after next and decided she wanted to have a talk. By this time, the emotions and stresses had diminished to a simmer, so we did. I explained why I felt she needed to leave and discussing it one more time would not change anything because she didn't want to hear it. She finally said to me how much she loved me and how she felt God himself had sent her to care for me. I could see the agony on her face as the tears flowed down relentlessly. She shared her life story so many times with me and others I could quote her stanza by stanza. I felt so much more today than I had at any time in the 5 months I had known her. There was so much commonality and similarities between us. I felt myself drawing closer to her soul and spirit. For the first time, I believed what she was saying and feeling. What came to mind at that exact moment in time was she could be an Angel, a real Angel.

She pleaded one more time to stay with me and care for me in every way, making my life better. By this time, I was exhausted once again with her pursuance and decided to give myself a way out for the rest of the evening. Leaving the answer to her plea until the next day, giving me a chance to decide and reorganize my own emotional priorities. I needed some space, and not let this emotional pressure make the decision for me. There wasn't a lot of sleeping going on at night with all the weight hanging in the balance.

By the time the sun came up and coffee was made, the fog lifted. The answer would come from somewhere, I wasn't sure where. I felt peace in the present. I was sure it came from the heart, and I was happy about it. To be loved so deeply by another human being with such a display of sincerity and sacrifice was not something I could let casually slip away. It was like a load had been lifted from my shoulders. A load I had carried around for many years. It was something I needed to acknowledge and embrace.

And so, I found myself at the ultimate fork in the road. In order to embrace this love in any meaningful way, I had to put all other – all previous – experiences with love and relationships to rest. I had to release all biases which built up within, leading to failures and disillusions in relationships leaving me wanting. Somehow the strength and courage to take the risk overtook my reluctance and victory over these latent emotions won.

The path forward, however, was not to be an easy one and once the decision was made to accept her mission as my own, we got down to the business of carving our way through the jungle of medical appointments and procedures to our destiny ahead.

The appointment with the oncologist at MD Anderson confirmed the cancer and the activity in the lymph system much to my disappointment. I could see I faced another fight if I was going to opt for a quality-of-life path of treatment. In our final discussions, we agreed to take a 3-month hormone shot. We would throw in with the MD Anderson protocol and use them as primary medical care since they were already primary for the head and neck.

Even with all the health issues, surgeries, and obstacles, we found ourselves being carried along by this ever-redeeming wave of spiritual balance and energy. At every decision, every turn, everything worked out for each other's best interest and wellbeing, even when circumstances took difficult turns. The forks in the road became easier to navigate with the Holy Spirit lighting the way. We were able to remain focused and centered on our spiritual ascension back to spirit form.

Tao Te Ching (5th century philosopher):

Watch your thoughts, they become your words,
Watch your words, they become your actions,
Watch your actions, they become your habits,
Watch your habits, they become your character,
Watch your character, IT becomes your destiny.

SUMMATION

(Proverbs 16:9 *NIV*)

In their hearts humans plan their course, but the LORD establishes their steps.

God's grand plan for every human is truly a wonder to behold. An unending work in progress. The unfolding of our individual and collective stories through trials and tests ultimately leads us to the Truth if we have ears to hear and eyes to see.

It took me almost a lifetime to realize I could not lean on my own understanding and strength. To overcome my own self-reliance, I *chose* to humbly surrender and trust the promise(s) God made us.

My biography is, among other things, a depiction of our (Evelyne and Homer) suffering at the physical, mental, and emotional levels. Scripture tells us suffering is part of life in this fallen world. At the heart of the Christian faith is a God Who knows what it is to suffer. Far more than suffering "like us" He suffered "for us" in the person of His Son, Jesus Christ. Transcending suffering is the key to overcoming our human nature and opening our hearts to God and His infinite Grace. It is our way to freedom. How can we know joy if we do not embrace pain?

The other goals are to make my story colorful and uplifting from my experiences and travels.

Furthermore, weaving the details of the mystery behind the synchronicities and guidance of the Holy Spirit enlightened my path.

My conversion to Christianity was just the beginning. Embracing a true and lasting union with Christ is my aspiration. I have learned through this process to recognize the battle of duality within myself and took on the challenge to subdue and conquer it. Instead of "knowing about God," I was moved into "knowing God" and created a relationship with Him.

I wrote my biography for the sole purpose to stand as a witness to God's Glory. Sharing my story is my testimony. God's perfect timing in my awakening, led to receiving Jesus Christ as my Savior, bringing a whole new meaning and purpose. I was given a new heart, a rebirth, and a light within me to shine on my path.

Homer and I were drawn to each other because we were pursuing the same goal. Our common purpose had all the markings of a spiritual ascension.

I hope my biography will bring forth inspiration to anyone who reads it.

Made in the USA
Coppell, TX
03 August 2024

35550430R00154